Devising Theatre with Stan's Cafe

Devising Theatre with Stan's Cafe

Mark Crossley and James Yarker

Bloomsbury Methuen Drama
An imprint of Bloomsbury Publishing Plc

B L O O M S B U R Y
LONDON · OXFORD · NEW YORK · NEW DELHI · SYDNEY

Bloomsbury Methuen Drama

An imprint of Bloomsbury Publishing Plc

Imprint previously known as Methuen Drama

50 Bedford Square	1385 Broadway
London	New York
WC1B 3DP	NY 10018
UK	USA

www.bloomsbury.com

BLOOMSBURY, METHUEN DRAMA and the Diana logo are trademarks of Bloomsbury Publishing Plc

First published 2017

© Mark Crossley and James Yarker, 2017

Mark Crossley and James Yarker have asserted their right under the Copyright, Designs and Patents Act, 1988, to be identified as authors of this work.

British Library Cataloguing-in-Publication Data

A catalogue record for this book is available from the British Library.

ISBN: HB: 978-1-474-26705-2
PB: 978-1-474-26704-5
ePDF: 978-1-474-26707-6
eBook: 978-1-474-26706-9

Library of Congress Cataloging-in-Publication Data

Names: Crossley, Mark author. | Yarker, James author.
Title: Devising theatre with Stan's Cafe / Mark Crossley and James Yarker.
Description: London; New York: Bloomsbury Methuen Drama, 2017. | Includes bibliographical references and index.
Identifiers: LCCN 2017003690 (print) | LCCN 2017022139 (ebook) | ISBN 9781474267069 (Epub) | ISBN 9781474267076 (Epdf) | ISBN 9781474267045 (pbk. : alk. paper) | ISBN 9781474267052 (hardback: alk. paper)
Subjects: LCSH: Stan's Cafe (Birmingham, England) | Theater–England–Birmingham–History–20th century.
Classification: LCC PN2596.B52 (ebook) | LCC PN2596.B52 S73 2017 (print) | DDC 792.09424/96–dc23
LC record available at https://lccn.loc.gov/2017003690

Cover design: Louise Dugdale
Cover image by Graeme Braidwood

Typeset by Deanta Global Publishing Services, Chennai, India
Printed and bound in Great Britain

To find out more about our authors and books visit www.bloomsbury.com. Here you will find extracts, author interviews, details of forthcoming events and the option to sign up for our newsletters.

Contents

List of Illustrations

Acknowledgements

James and Mark would like to express a huge debt of gratitude to the following people who have contributed to the book, giving their generous time in interviews and many informal chats over the past three years. In your absence, we may only have had a pamphlet.

Sarah Archdeacon
Paul Arvidson
Gerard Bell
Amanda Hadingue
Laura Killeen
Rochi Rampal
Graeme Rose
Craig Stephens
Nick Sweeting
Jack Trow
Jon Ward
Nina West

Thank you also to:
Graeme Braidwood
Ed Dimsdale
whose photographs we have used
Mark Dudgeon and Mark Taylor-Batty
for their editorial support

Mark would also like to thank his wife Siân and his children Beth and Joseph for allowing him to have quite an intense and clandestine relationship with someone called 'Stan' for several years. He would also like to thank James for inviting him on this adventure.

James would like to thank his fellow travellers in Stan's Cafe: artists, administrators, producers, promoters, supporters, advisors, board members, family and friends; without you and without the audiences, there would be nothing to write about.

Sarah and Eve have been enthusiastic and encouraging throughout, while Rosemary and Peter helped in ways they'll suspect but never know; thank you all always.

Finally, Mark is a smart and generous collaborator; he did most of the work, so as far as the book is concerned, the most thanks go to him. Thank you, Mark, it's been fun.

Preface: Some Thoughts on Reading the Book

This book is designed as a record of Stan's Cafe's journey as a theatre company over the past quarter of a century or more *and* an insight into their artistic ethos, aesthetic and working methods. It is structured, loosely, around the key elements of a production process, all the way from the genesis of ideas through to performance and audience reception. Every major chapter is prefaced by a short distillation of its contents, entitled **What's in this chapter?** Chapters 6, 7, 8 and 9 begin with a brief context setting, entitled **Setting the Scene**, to establish how the company's practice sits alongside (or contrary to) developments in contemporary theatre, with ideas drawn from key theorists and practitioners who have influenced twentieth- and twenty-first-century performance. Throughout the book you will see reference to **(TW)**, denoting **Things in the Wings**, which is an appendix of really interesting things that add background detail to the topics and people discussed in the chapters. Follow the numbers to the appropriate reference at the back of the book. Similarly, you will notice cross-references such as 'see **Performing**', which denote that a specific topic is returned to in detail within another chapter. At relevant points in the text, James has written **short descriptions of key productions**, highlighted in text boxes. At the end of each main chapter focusing on the company's methodology, you will find a section entitled **Stan in Action**, in which James offers a range of practical ideas relating to that chapter's theme. Many activities are taken directly from their own rehearsals and are designed to give the reader some immediate ideas for making their own unique work, with a little inspiration from Stan's Cafe.

To whet the appetite, the book begins with **The Route to @AE Harris**, which paints a brief portrait of Stan's Cafe as we see them now and an expeditious review of their development since 1991. This initial glimpse into the company's history is then expanded upon in the first main chapter, entitled **Stan in Context**, which aims to place Stan's Cafe within local, national and international contexts, to fill in the details so that you may understand their practice and the ethos behind it. There have been other texts that have contextualized the company and described their development and key productions but this is the first time the company members themselves have reflected at length about what Stan's Cafe means to them and how they perceive it. Following on from this context setting, we consider the methodology, beginning with **Ideas**; why do they deserve to be made into a piece of theatre, where do they generate from and how are they handled in the initial stages of rehearsal? If an idea makes it over these early hurdles, it is then subjected to the rigours of **Rehearsing and Directing**, which is the title of the next chapter. This scrutinizes the progression from the improvisational instincts of early shows through to the more structured processes of recent years, and the impact of location and ethics on how they have made work. The final sections in the chapter consider the significance of editing and James's directorial approach. Two specific aspects of the creative process are then explored in chapters entitled **Text** followed by **Space and Time**. In **Text**, we investigate the range of texts that are both used as an impetus for a production or are developed within rehearsals to capture the devising decisions and provide instruction for the performers. We propose a range of text types that are particularly relevant to the company's practice. **Space and Time** are the inescapable elements of theatre and Stan's Cafe have their own unique way of experimenting with the elasticity of their boundaries. The aesthetic of the company places a particular emphasis on the scenography for each production and this aspect is explored in detail. **Performing** for Stan's Cafe requires a plethora of skills and a confidence to embody the company's style. The performers who contribute to this chapter identify a multitude of strategies that they must be conversant with as there is such a diversity of styles from intense and intricate dialogue to physical theatre through to the curation of installations. However, they also highlight the importance of the underlying 'Stan' aesthetic that has been nurtured over the past twenty-six years. The dynamics of contemporary theatre spectatorship are considered in the last main chapter, entitled **Audience.** Stan's Cafe constantly reframe the audience's experience as the eclectic range of productions means that you can never predict what the next show will ask of you. Some are intimate encounters for one person, complete in under five minutes, while others are collective experiences, witnessed over many hours. All performances, however, are united in their invitation to the audience to co-author the work, reflecting a deep respect for the intelligence of the spectator. In **Finale,** James offers some final thoughts on the journey the company has made so far and the future direction of Stan's Cafe. The book is completed by **Things in the Wings**, which collates all the useful, tangential information from the chapters into a series of 'at a glance' descriptions. This written text is also supported by a section of the Stan's Cafe website that shadows each chapter with additional colour photographs, fragments of video, audio and hyperlinks. This resource can be found at www.stanscafe.co.uk/book.html.

We have endeavoured to write a rigorous but very accessible book that will appeal to theatre-makers, academics, students and a general readership interested in contemporary performance and eager to know more about a theatre company with a rich history that has, until now, been under-investigated. In particular, we hope you enjoy hearing from the company members themselves who have been fundamental in developing the company to its present position and nurturing the Stan's Cafe 'family', as it is so often described. To make recognition of the contributors (listed in the *Acknowledgements*) easier and a degree more personable, we include their first names and surnames on the first occasion that they appear within each chapter, and then just their surnames after that point, unless structural elegance prompts the inclusion of a forename again. Academic convention may suggest something different but we are aware that you may delve into this book in a very random order, depending on your need or time pressures, so a 'first name check' would seem useful in every chapter. Likewise, we offer the date of each production on a similar basis, identifying its first year of performance and thereafter simply using the title. James is always James.

So, enjoy the book in whatever order, timescale or location you wish. Take it on holiday, take it into rehearsal, quote it in an exam. Give it as a gift, buy it as an indulgence for yourself or, even better, purchase fifty copies for a library. Try not to lose it on a train.

Mark

Introduction

James

When I was in my first year studying theatre at Lancaster University, I was both super keen and cynical. A trip was proposed to see People Show, a British theatre company (**TW 1**) in the Brewhouse, Kendal, and I spent the whole journey there sitting in the mini-bus thinking 'Why are we going to see this lot?' The lecturers were full of enthusiasm for the company and the wonder that they had been running for more than twenty years. To my mind, this was a mark against them; there was no way a company that old could be anything other than a bunch of tired, washed up, has-beens struggling for any fresh ideas. Of course, I was wrong and they were good, interesting and different from what I'd seen before.

Being different from what I'd seen before wasn't difficult; I'd seen practically nothing. At that point, I thought theatre was the Royal Shakespeare Company, panto (**TW 2**) and the school play, all evidently more fun to do than to watch. My ambition was to be a film director and a theatre studies degree would merely be a step towards that goal.

Within weeks of enrolling, this story had changed. I was introduced to so much inspirational new theatre that I found myself resenting and being baffled by a society that had kept it secret from me for so long. I was inspired by theatre as a form; the way it could be so slippery, playful and powerful. I came to recognize that the special quality which makes some theatre totally unendurable is the very same quality that makes other theatre so utterly riveting. My gaucheness, my ignorance, arrogance and inquisitiveness led me to ask questions and seek answers that resulted in exciting theatrical adventures. These adventures suggested I had a facility for putting together theatre and, compared with the lumbering nature of film at that time, theatre felt like it could be punk. In contrast to a world where even the most famous film directors were still fighting their studios for artistic control, I saw theatre as a world where every production could be a 'director's cut'.

So, when graduation came and went, there wasn't much question as to what would happen. With Graeme Rose, I set off on our adventure and this book is the story of that adventure, told from a certain perspective, leaving out much of the anguish and frustration and our tedious 'hilarious anecdotes', tales of broken-down vans, misunderstandings and near misses; instead it focuses on how we have tried to make the best theatre we can possibly manage for as many people as we can get to see it.

Our story, like many, starts off slowly and gathers pace but it has been running more than twenty-five years so, no doubt, cynical youths now travel in mini-buses to our shows. Hopefully, they'll think we're good and interesting and different from what they've seen before but, if not, then I hope we make them furious and compel them to go off and make some extraordinary show as an antidote to ours – I would love to see it.

We certainly don't feel in the least tired or washed up. We're full of beans and the ideas are flowing but we know we can't relent because if we do we will die and we're not ready to die just yet. We sent an invitation to our 25th anniversary party to our friends at People Show; 'we're sorry', came the reply 'this date clashes with our 50th Anniversary Party'. Damn them!

2

The Route to @AE Harris

Finding @AE Harris[1] is no easy task, even if you are familiar with this specific corner of Hockley just north-west of Birmingham's city centre. It is a rapidly gentrifying enclave known enigmatically and enticingly as the Jewellery Quarter due to its rich tradition in those artisan trades, yet still well beyond the usual English tourist trails. If you're lucky and can navigate off the inner ring road, you will find your way up Constitution Hill and through the back roads bustling with light industry, Hall St., past The Brown Lion Pub and left down Caroline St. The British Telecom tower will suddenly and briefly appear in the distance, before you take a right up Northwood St. towards what looks like a dead end. Just beyond a sharp turn into James St. sits the factory buildings of A. E. Harris and Co. (Birmingham) Ltd, a metal-pressing firm of over a hundred years standing and the current home of theatre company Stan's Cafe.

Pressing the buzzer next to the imposing meshed gate, you hear it sound in the distance and, eventually, a member of the company lets you into what is essentially a corner of the factory. Traversing a courtyard, you note that it is embellished with a dilapidated pub table and chairs, industrial pallets and old bikes. To the left is the office and to the right the studio theatre. Straight ahead you find yourself in the kitchen, often masquerading as rehearsal room, furnished with two long melamine-topped tables battered by years of scalding hot mugs and microwaved cuisine. Tea cloths dry next to faltering pot plants and cracked tiles. A washing machine, microwave, fridge and tumble dryer contend for space with shelves of toilet rolls and table salt. As a general

---

[1] @AE Harris is the branding for Stan's Cafe's performance/rehearsal space at the A. E. Harris Ltd factory.

rule, three out of four strip lights work. The windows are a multitude of dusty, single panes, frames painted with gusto in thick white gloss. Doors to the outside are bottle green but beneath this, layers of forlorn blue paint from some long-abandoned décor peel in their own good time. Dark brown walls give way to a hopeful shade of buff halfway up to the ceiling. This is the glistening present tense of Stan's Cafe. The long and circuitous journey to this apogee is dealt with in detail in **Stan in Context**, but for now, to sharpen the appetite, let us start with a brief glimpse into where it all began.

In the late 1980s, James Yarker was studying drama at Lancaster University in the north-west of England. The university at the time was a renowned centre of experimental theatre, led by influential practitioners including Pete Brooks, the director of Impact Theatre Cooperative, who James and other key members of Stan's Cafe cite as a major influence on the company. In the same period, Graeme Rose, another Lancaster graduate, had begun his own theatre company named 'glory what glory'. James admired Rose's acting and experimental practice and, once graduated, looked for an opportunity to work with him. Rose had reciprocal respect for James's approach to theatre; he recalls that even while still at university 'James was a force and very serious about his art'. After three shows, 'glory what glory' was, in Rose's words, 'running out of energy', so the stars aligned to make a new collaboration possible. The story goes that the two of them met up in London and, after a long day of ambling about the capital, took refuge in a 'greasy spoon' café off Brick Lane in the East End of the city. For those readers unfamiliar with this type of eatery, it's enough to know that the words greasy and gourmet don't normally adjoin within a sentence. From this conversation, the seeds of Stan's Cafe were sewn, including the name, as it was the eponymous Stan's establishment in which they sat. 'We liked the name,' James clarifies, 'as it wasn't aggressive or punning, as so many other theatre companies seemed to go for at the time, and we liked the fact it was unusual and that it suggesting a fictional world. Strange things might happen in Stan's Cafe and who indeed was Stan?'

Figure 2.1 The original Stan's Cafe in which the theatre company was conceived over an all-day breakfast.

When it came to locating the company in the UK, Graeme and James once again travelled a contrary path to other fledgling theatre companies, who were often setting up in cities with more established contemporary theatre traditions, particularly London or Manchester. They chose Birmingham in the West Midlands as their base in 1991, as James notes:

> Graeme had grown up in Birmingham and it seemed like a good option because it was a big city and a cheap place to live. There was a good energy there in the early Nineties and we didn't know of anybody else there doing what we wanted to do. We fancied trying to be big fish in a big underpopulated pond.

The city itself, as will be evidenced throughout this book, has been a regular source of inspiration for the company. The manufacturing vitality, multicultural diversity and industrial, urbanized landscapes of Birmingham have underscored many performances. Local places and events as disparate as the orbital bus route around the city to the closure of the Longbridge Rover car plant have played their part as stimuli. The geometry of the @AE Harris building itself, with its spartan and elongated factory floors, has influenced several of their later productions, affecting scale, duration and audience spectatorship. Location and space have had a fundamental effect on the company's practice, emancipating ideas and, conversely, acting as creative constraints.

Although Birmingham-based, the company have travelled the UK, Europe and the world extensively, touring large- and small-scale work. As early as 1994, they took *Bingo In The House of Babel* to Theatre 95 in Cergy-Pontoise, Paris, soon followed by many other shows, including *It's Your Film* (1998 onwards), which found its way to Brazil, Canada and Germany among many other places. *Of All The People In All The World* (2003) has been a global phenomenon, seen in cities all across Europe as well as North America, Argentina, Japan and Australia. The importance of their local environment is not lost on Stan's Cafe, though, as they work extensively across the city of Birmingham and the Midlands, leading arts education projects **(TW 1)**, nurturing new artists and collaborating with regional partners including the Royal Shakespeare Company in Stratford-upon-Avon. In the fledgling years, many pieces were previewed in their home city at the Midlands Arts Centre (now MAC Birmingham) **(TW 2)**; more recently, Warwick Arts Centre has supported and commissioned new work from them and is often the first venue selected for premieres including *The Anatomy of Melancholy* (2013) and *A Translation of Shadows* (2015), while Birmingham Repertory Theatre commissioned and co-produced *Made Up* (2016).

However, for a theatre company of such regional, national and international stature as Stan's Cafe, there has been relatively little written about them with only a few significant references, articles or chapters to be found. This is the first book devoted entirely to their practice. There have been some notable if sporadic analyses over the past few years, including a brief reflection on their interpretation of *The Carrier Frequency* (1999) in Hans-Thies Lehmann's Introduction to *Postdramatic Theatre* (2006) and then from Simon Parry (2010),

Nicola Shaughnessy (2012), Adam J. Ledger (2013) and, particularly, Marissia Fragkou, who wrote a chapter on their practice in *British Theatre Companies 1995–2014* (2015).[2] Their collective wisdom will be referenced within this book, principally in **Stan in Context**. James and other core members of Stan's Cafe are undoubtedly the most prolific sources of written reflection to date via a variety of essays and blogs on their own website, but there has never been a comprehensive analysis of their history and methodology, particularly from the company themselves. Fragkou herself states: 'With the exception of Ledger, no other existing publication has yet paid close attention to the company's material contexts of production, and there is no study, prior to this one [Fragkou's], that examines the company's diverse aesthetic approaches, international reach and politics' (2015: 227). Hence, that is why you are thumbing through these pages now, as James and I thought it was time to address this void through the voices of those within the company and hence shed some light upon the goings-on of the last quarter century.

In the twenty-six years since the company began, the collaborators, devisors, actors, participants and critical friends of copious hues (many of whom appear in this book) have multiplied, dissipated and reconvened countless times over. Rose himself stepped back from shared artistic leadership of the company in 1995 but continues to play a major role devising and performing in many current works. James likes to refer to artists and collaborators who have worked with the company as being 'in the orbit of Stan's Cafe', so that one day when the project is right and the stars align, they may return to the creative inner atmosphere. There is a sense of family and long-term commitment governing the ethics of Stan's Cafe so that numerous performers have worked with the company repeatedly. Simultaneously, the projects every year are so diverse that the family is forever expanding, across disciplines, continents and generations.

---

[2] Fragkou's chapter in *British Theatre Companies 1995–2014* (2015), alongside analysing methodology, also contains specific information about the funding behind the company, which is not dealt with in this text but may be of interest to particular readers.

The performances created by Stan's Cafe vault the boundaries of easy categorization as they span experimental, improvised theatre all the way to adaptations of centuries-old texts, from scripted plays to installations on a vast scale. Some performances have lasted no more than a few minutes while others have fought their way through the exhaustion of four, twelve or twenty-four hours. Sometimes the spoken word is the essence of a piece while the very next work may eschew the voice completely. There is no single medium that defines their practice as many projects are interdisciplinary or move away from dramatic forms into experimentations with radio, opera, performance art and beyond.

What may, however, be seen as a constant is an ever-present attention to our humanity and our inherent vulnerability, manifest in the personae on stage as they struggle to fend off the encroaching tide or re-enter the earth's atmosphere or when we are given access to the margins of their lives in which their frailties and corruptions are exposed in cramped corridors, the dark recesses of the stage or the avarice induced by a mere tulip. This fascination with the fragility of humanity has even seen them distil our singular presence on earth down to an individual grain of rice, heaped among a myriad of other grains, at once both precious and yet precarious. Ultimately, the integrity of their work stems from their desire to communicate honestly and clearly, wherein the entire scenography and the roles of the performers are uncluttered in pursuit of theatrical clarity.

Perhaps, as we plunge into the interior of this book, it is this all-embracing term *theatre* that will come to our rescue. Theatre is a wonderful, playful and elastic host that allows many media, disciplines and spectatorial modes under its one capacious roof. Beneath its rafters, drama can fuse with film, radio can be broadcast on a live stage, rice can represent race and religion, while opera can enfold a bouncy castle. Wish us luck, then, as we try to bring some order to this eclecticism.

By the way, it's pronounced *caff*.

3

Stan in Context

What's in this chapter?

The intention of this chapter is to place Stan's Cafe in some sort of context, to fill in the background so that you may understand their practice and the principles behind it more clearly as the book progresses. Perhaps it may be helpful to think of this chapter as starting with a bare stage on which sits the current individuals that constitute Stan's Cafe. Piece by piece, we will wheel on some scenery, fly in some backdrops, arrange some props and switch on a few lanterns to animate the company and illuminate the shadows of past and present. Reference will, of course, be made to the variety of texts that have been written about the company in recent years, but our intention is to emphasize the Stan's Cafe perspective on how they see themselves, their history, influences and ethos as well as how they relate to local, national and international contexts.

What is this *eclectic* thing they do?

Often it is said that something or someone in the arts is difficult to define, they are beyond categorization and so forth. It's debatable if this is always actually true as there are arguably many artistic entities that can, for pragmatic purposes, be easily described and placed in some generic box or other; this includes many theatre companies, by the way. However, there is certainly a case to be made that Stan's Cafe genuinely defies simple identification or brisk mapping onto a matrix of related performance companies or styles. To extend the geographic metaphor, they rarely remain in one artistic 'location' for long and when they do reveal themselves they are often at the opposite end of the compass from where they last appeared and heavily camouflaged by the hybrid art forms intertwined within one piece. Nick Sweeting, an advisor and producer for the company over many years, highlights the implications of this approach: 'The question that exists throughout Stan's Cafe's history is what work do they produce? The conundrum is they don't have a readily identifiable "home". It's a company that has benefitted but also suffered because of that.' Sweeting's comments are echoed by Gerard Bell, one of the long-term collaborators: 'I can't think of any company that is comparable and I think they have very varied artistic traits which makes them hard to pin down and hard to market. It lies in this nexus between doing work that lies outside the mainstream of theatre but at the same time it has this strong theatrical impulse within it.' As noted at the end of **The Route to @AE Harris**, it is this term *theatre* that may come to our aid in threading the disparate strands of their practice together. Jon Ward, a composer for numerable Stan's Cafe productions, unequivocally sees theatre as the defining element: 'I don't think it is hard to pin Stan's Cafe down. It may seem like that but it isn't. Everything is about theatre, that is the thing that all shows have in common, they are designed to meet the criteria of what is theatre.'[1] It may be asserted that it is this litmus test that guides the selection of subject matter, the devising and editing of material and the final performance context, content and form. As James will explain further in **Ideas**, every nascent plan for a show is interrogated for why it should be theatre as opposed to some other artistic expression (novel, film, artwork, speech and so on). It must justify itself as needing to be theatre in order for the ideas to be explored in the theatre; otherwise, it must be taken somewhere else and made into something else.

---

[1]   There is a certain reluctance on our part to define theatre in generic terms as often it is only identifiable ostensibly 'in the moment'. However, readers may find it helpful to refer to Jack Trow's explanation, in the **Performing** chapter, of why *Of All The People In All The World* (2003) is a theatre piece rather than an installation, as this might illuminate the point further.

The elusive nature of Stan's Cafe practice has led James himself to refer to their style as a 'brandless brand', while Fragkou begins her own chapter by highlighting the breadth of the practice: 'Its projects range across theatre, film and live art, and have been presented in a wide range of spaces with inventive and critical uses of scenography and technology' (2015: 207). She also notes, resonating with Sweeting and Bell's sentiments, that their limited profile in academic writing and arts curricula 'can be attributed to the lack of a consistent and recognisable style which resists the academy's and industry's tendency to pigeonhole artistic work according to specific theoretical and stylistic vocabularies' (227). Potentially you may start to see a problem here in the collective vacillation and obfuscation, but the more you talk to James and those closely associated with the company, you begin to sense a note of contentment in this uncertain hinterland and a palpable pleasure in the freedom it brings. Arguably it is even more than that as this resistance to artistic trends, industry expectations or box office pressures signals something fundamental about their core values, a desire to make something meaningful rather than just the imperative to make *something* that looks like the last thing and pays the bills. Back in 2001, James was very clear in his determination to pursue the ideas rather than establish a 'house style':

> Good business sense would be to knock out at frequent, predictable intervals, shows which, though different from each other, are consistent in their form and tone. Instead we pursue whatever ideas interest us in whatever direction they lead us, regardless of what art form they may wander into and whether they are 'the kind of thing we do'. (2001: 28)

With over twenty-five years of company history behind him, James is now able to reflect on the heterogeneous style that has organically developed since 1991. Early on in the conversations for this book, he pinned his colours to the mast by stating: 'I'm not fussed by definitions of what art is', indicating a far greater interest in the efficacy of what is created than an acquiescence to any formal constraints or historical artistic conventions. This was then quickly elaborated upon: 'We just make what we make and let other people argue about what it is. It's in our constitution to be diverse.' For James, theatre is a broad church or, in the words of Freda Chapple and Chiel Kattenbelt, a mutable 'hypermedium' (see **Ideas TW1** and **Space and Time**) that can be a 'home to all' within which all media, genres and forms can reside (2006: 24). This means that, as a theatre company, the palette of ideas and forms of expression open to them are an endless set of permutations, informed by an appetite for intellectual thinking and broad cultural sources which reveal themselves in what Bell refers to as 'un-emphasised erudition', an intelligence that is worn lightly yet distinctly.

For those uninitiated to the company, even the briefest of glances at Stan's Cafe's back catalogue would draw attention to the miscellany that includes devised hour-long performances, either site-specific or theatre based, a four-and-a-half-minute performance for a single audience member who sits in a photo booth, a vast installation piece using the medium of rice, a twenty-four-hour durational piece using Scalextric, a play commissioned from a Serbian playwright, a four-and-a-quarter-hour semi-improvisational work based on a Wagner opera and intermedial performances blending film and live actors, not to mention the plethora of educational projects which will certainly have to wait for another volume. There has rarely been an occasion when the company has followed one work with another based on a similar genre or form. Often the impetus for the next piece is to explore the diametric opposite of what is currently touring. While there may be a sense of contentment about this eclecticism, it is perhaps more accurate to clarify that there are moments of doubt in the transgressions of disciplinary boundaries but, likewise, an acceptance that these are an invigorating necessity, as James indicates:

> I sometimes worry that some people spend their whole life getting good at stuff and then we come along and 'have a go', like forming a band for *Lurid and Insane*. But I was proud that we really went for it with a full set list, properly did it. And the film for *A Translation of Shadows* – it was a proper film. I think it's important to be scared when you're starting a new project.

There is always an air of unpredictability when attending a Stan's Cafe show, a sense that you are present at an experiment; something is being tested out and creative jeopardy is in play. New ground is being broken and no one is quite sure where it will lead. Jack Trow, a collaborator for over a decade, signals these risks and rewards in offering us his own distillation of the company's eclectic approach:

> What makes a Stan show a Stan show? I like that you don't know what you're going to get, whether it be piles of rice in a room or a show you watch for an hour and clap at the end. I like the fact you can't pin that down. I like that there isn't a formula of form or content. What there is, is an identifiable experiment at the heart of it, so if it doesn't work that's fine too.

Where did it all start?

The first port of call would logically seem to be Birmingham, as this is where the company planted its flag, but it's worth taking a moment to rewind to Lancaster University in the late 1980s. Again, for those of you unfamiliar with UK geography and the eccentricities of where university drama and theatre departments reside, you may want to look on a map north of Manchester and keep going up the M6 motorway. Just before you reach the Lake District, you'll find Lancaster, home to one of the most influential UK university theatre departments over the past few decades, led at times by major figures including Baz Kershaw and Geraldine (Gerry) Harris. It was here that the 'family' of Stan's Cafe were born and nurtured in the undergraduate and postgraduate experiences of James, alongside his co-founder Graeme Rose, associate director Craig Stephens and influential early collaborator Amanda Hadingue as well as the lighting designer Paul Arvidson, actor Ray Newe and graphic designer Simon Ford, all of whom studied and met at the university in this period. Lancaster was not only the point of congregation for members of the company, it was also the locus of key influences that would inspire Stan's Cafe to initially form and then evolve in the fashion that we see today.

You can't over-emphasise the importance of Pete.

This affirmation from Amanda Hadingue emphasizes the fact that all of those from the company who studied at Lancaster University cite the arrival of Pete Brooks into the department in 1986, as a fellow in theatre, as hugely significant. Brooks had been a member of the influential contemporary British theatre group Impact Theatre Cooperative, active from the late 1970s to the mid-1980s **(TW 1)**. His radical approach to devising and his emphasis on postdramatic, non-narrative forms had a major effect on those who studied with him. Rose remarked that 'it shook the rules of what we knew as theatre'. Yarker, Rose and Hadingue were directed by Brooks during their time at the university and later Hadingue, Rose and Stephens worked for Brooks' next company, Insomniac Productions, on seminal shows including *L'Ascensore* (1992) and *Clair de Luz* (1993). Looking back, Hadingue now believes that 'his aesthetic is very recognisable in the early shows of Stan'. Brooks introduced James and others to the work of international practitioners including the German choreographer Pina Bausch and the Montreal-based La La La Human Steps as well as Station House Opera and some of the newly formed British avant-garde theatre companies, including Forced Entertainment **(TW 2)**. James recalls seeing them for the first time on a university trip in 1987: 'Pete took us to see *200% and Bloody Thirsty*. I loved the fact that it felt underground; it was a thing I recognised emotionally but had never seen before. I was seduced by the fact that it was simultaneously stupid, clever, poetic, funny and heart-breaking.'

Lancaster University and the city's Storey Institute have been the birthplace and incubator of many other experimental British companies including Ursula Martinez, Third Angel, Metro-Boulot-Dodo, Proto-type and Imitating the Dog. Both James and Rose acknowledge the significance of the fertile atmosphere of theatre-making that was so prevalent at that time, with many undergraduates and graduates seeking to make their own work and create new companies. The particular significance of the university has been reflected upon by a number of artists, including Rachael Walton, the co-founder of Third Angel, who suggested, in an interview with Deirdre Heddon and Jane Milling in 2003, that there was a noticeable 'Lancaster theatrical language' (2015: 249). This has been partially questioned by Heddon and Milling themselves, who wondered if it was more apt to acknowledge a 'university contemporary theatre language' (ibid.). Whatever the case, the impact of the dramatic practice at Lancaster upon company members, and specifically James, cannot be underestimated, as Rose notes: 'James took full advantage of the facilities and freedoms at Lancaster, particularly the Nuffield Theatre and saw it as his space to experiment in.' The resonance of these university years can be found most transparently in a show James created in the second year of his undergraduate studies, a four-and-a-quarter-hour semi-improvised performance, entitled *Infected* (1988), which was held together by tightly planned time-coded tasks for each actor to adhere to. This strategy may sound familiar to any aficionados of the company as this model of practice was used again as the organizing logic for *Twilightofthefreakingods* (2013).

Birmingham: The early years and artistic influences

The adoption of Birmingham as the base for the company was, as mentioned in **The Route to @AE Harris**, influenced by several factors; Rose's familiarity with the city alongside the logistical and economic benefits of locating to a large industrial hub in the middle of the country with no obvious competition in their chosen field. There were, of course, potential dangers attached to such a move, as to be away from recognized centres of performance-making risked marginalization of the company. There was a strong tradition of theatre in education practice in the city and a certain legacy of avant-garde experimentation through the work of Birmingham Arts Lab (1968–82) (**TW 3**), but by the 1990s, the sense of a creative hub had dissipated somewhat. Rose emphasizes this when reflecting that, by the time they came to set up,

'Birmingham was not on the radar for contemporary practice', yet to an extent, it was for this very reason that they were drawn to the city. The Custard Factory Theatre Company (**TW 4**) were arguably the most notable name in Birmingham at that time but their practice was orientated towards innovative adaptations of Shakespeare rather than original devised work, so the ground was clear for Stan's Cafe.

By their own admission they were poor, yet, in Rose's words, 'driven by a sense of naivety and a willingness and appetite to make it work'. In the beginning, there was no specific building that the company called home and the first few shows were envisaged, devised and executed on the lowest of budgets and the most meagre of resources. Persuaded into this cut-price adventure was Richard Chew, as composer and performer, who worked on the very first show, entitled *Perry Como's Christmas Cracker* (1991) (see **Ideas**) through to *Voodoo City* (1995). Performances were assembled from objects 'pulled from skips', as James puts it, and rehearsed in the spare room of Rose and James's rented house in Balsall Heath (a low-rent area of the city that has hosted successive generations of migrants from around the world) or in borrowed spaces. Amanda Hadingue evokes this period with recollections of her first production with the company:

> I went up to do the Moseley Road Baths piece (*Canute the King*, 1993). I don't really remember rehearsing as such, I just remember planning it a lot on the floor of James and Graeme's house, writing little ideas for scenes on cards and shuffling them around on the floor. There wasn't a rehearsal space really, we were loaned a little bit of space at The Custard Factory, which hadn't been fully developed then. We were given a room there, which had broken windows, it was snowing outside and there was no heating. We had to carry what set we had from the house to The Custard Factory. It was all very Dickensian. We then tried to make this very ambitious and slightly over-reaching piece of site-specific performance. It was a bit of a baptism of fire. There are lots of tales about that piece. The lighting rig was banned just before the show so we performed by candlelight, which sounds a trendy thing to do but then was just a bloody nightmare. But it was a young theatre company trying to make outrageous things.

Figure 3.1 Amanda Hadingue and Graeme Rose in the stage adaptation of *Canute the King* (1993), for which a swimming pool full of water was replaced by a few centimetres of water over linoleum.

Hadingue's influence on the company in these early years is important to emphasize, particularly following Rose's departure to form his own new company The Resurrectionists in 1995 **(TW 5)**. Hadingue reflects that

> when we started working on *Canute* I really felt I'd found a kindred spirit in James. We both seemed to be pushing in the same direction in terms of what interested us about theatre. We had different backgrounds, I studied English Literature and had probably been a more enthusiastic consumer of popular culture, all of which fed into how I thought as a deviser. These influences were possibly a useful adjunct to James' skills, background and interests.

For James, she was an intellectual foil, interrogating the ideas alongside him while bringing performance acumen into the rehearsal space which helped refine the stage aesthetic. There was even a moment, in these early years, when Hadingue might have stepped into a joint artistic director role alongside James but her commitments to other companies diffused this possibility and James has remained the sole artistic director ever since. This strong relationship between James and Hadingue was complemented by the improvisational skills of Sarah Archdeacon (then Dawson), whose first production was *Bingo in the House of Babel* (1994). In her own words, she 'brought a sense of play whereas Amanda brought more precise performance skills, matching James's intellect. That particular dynamic between them really informed the look of the shows.' Archdeacon's own influence on the company, both during and after her time with them, is accentuated by the composer Jon Ward: 'She is still there, so much of her aesthetic and values remain in Stan's Cafe. I think a lot of her seeped into James.'

In these initial years, from the early to mid-1990s, the company trod a precarious show-to-show existence, not knowing where money might come from and whether they would survive to make another piece. Hadingue remembers that during this period 'James kept the company going by living off Brussels sprouts and we all lived in the ramshackle house that he'd then bought'. Stephens recalls that

> when I came in for *Simple Maths* in 1997, we didn't get funding for the next show. The company was only just ticking over and it was a pretty bleak time. Then we made *It's Your Film* (1998) in a week, with an upturned bookcase for the platform and a few bits of hardboard nailed together and whatever else was kicking around from previous shows. That show just completely took off with international touring and opened up different doors.

After struggling in temporary makeshift spaces for the first few shows, the nearby Midlands Arts Centre stepped forward in 1994 and helped the aspirant company with access to rehearsal space, in which they developed several of their early shows. James has always recognized the support of MAC as particularly significant, as in 2007, when he wrote:

> When you start a theatre company it's tough getting gigs; no-one has heard of you and, if you're devising your own stuff, no-one has heard of your stuff either. You need someone to step forward and place their trust in you. For us Dorothy Wilson, then Director of Programming at MAC, was one of those people. She believed it was the duty of an Arts Centre to encourage local arts companies. She booked *Memoirs of an Amnesiac*

sight unseen. Having seen that she let *Perry Como's Christmas Cracker* into the intimate/tiny Hexagon Theatre and having proved ourselves not to be total chancers, Dorothy became an advocate for Stan's Cafe and later, when we grew more formally organised, she became the company's first Chair and steered us patiently through our infant years.

Although the space given to them was a welcome advancement on earlier hardships, it was only available on a by-the-hour basis and restricted the company from rehearsing over extended periods and setting up more complicated productions. So, in 2001, they moved to a former lathe factory close to the city centre and away from fixed schedules and noise limits so that they could, in James words, 'work till the inspiration ran out'. Following a compulsory purchase order on the land, the company was forced to move again and what followed was a series of 'grim' temporary bases. Eventually, in 2008, Charlotte Martin, the general manager at the time, found A. E. Harris Ltd as a location for *Of All The People In All The World*, which needed a large-scale floor area to house the 112 tonnes of rice required to represent the world's population. This temporary venue was so popular with both the company and its audience that Stan's Cafe extended their rental of it from six weeks to an open-ended lease (the space was branded @AE Harris). James recalls that 'bringing the office, storage and rehearsal space together was really transformative'. The company are still based on this site but have scaled back the floor space occupied for reasons of fiscal prudence and (human) energy conservation.

The impact of early creative influences on Stan's Cafe is certainly not underestimated by James. He underlines this with a very English analogy: 'Artistic influences are like test cricket batting averages. In the early years they can make more of a difference'. Alongside the presence of Pete Brooks, he cites an abundance of inspirations on the company as they sought to forge their own identity:

Station House Opera (**TW 6**) just wowed me. Their piece *Cuckoo* (1987) was the first non-narrative piece, first piece without words that I'd seen. I've always loved them and their endeavour. Even the shows I didn't like, it was because they were too ambitious which is admirable. I'm also influenced by their use of rules that underpin the form and that way of organising a show was very influential on our company. In the mid 90's I was particularly influenced by their piece *Road Metal Sweetbread* when I learnt they re-filmed for each show to fit the theatre they were performing in. That idea of remaking the same show for a different venue just unlocked a bit of thinking for me. It helped *Of All The People In All the World* which is the same but different everywhere it goes.

This flourishing of media hybrids alongside physical practices that blurred the lines between dramatic and dance forms created fertile ground and receptive audiences for the Stan's Cafe style as it produced a range of cross-disciplinary and visual, physical work. There are also a number of smaller UK-based companies, no longer in existence, that James cites as influential contemporaries, including Glee Club and Index Theatre, and he is sanguine about why Stan's Cafe survived those early years when many did not.

I joke that it's not who's best, it's who hangs on in there the longest. When I started this it could have been a real dead end. Giving it five years seemed like a sensible thing. By that time, we'd done *Ocean of Storms* and we'd just got the Barclays New Stages award performing upstairs at the Royal Court, and that felt like a thing! 'That's enough to be going on with' we thought, 'let's give it another five years.' Then *It's Your Film* came along and we went to Rio de Janeiro which was a thing. Then revenue funding arrived and *Of All The People In All the World* took off. In 2002 Creative Partnerships[2] started kicking in and suddenly that's a new area of interest and excitement. Now you start to think 'I'm not sure what else we'd do apart from this theatre company business.' I'm not sure what the exit strategy is, I don't have one – run off the end of the pier?

---

[2] Creative Partnerships was a UK government creative learning programme, established in 2002 and designed to develop young people's creativity through artists' engagement with schools in nominated areas across England. Following the 2010 election of the UK coalition government, funding was cut by the Department for Culture, Media and Sport and Arts Council England in 2011, with activity in schools ending in summer 2011.

Fortunately, there was enough success at crucial points close enough together for the company to put down roots in the city and build a reputation. However, the initial attraction of Birmingham is also acknowledged as having restricted their ability to cultivate a national identity, particularly within the artistic circles of the capital. 'The very thing that made Birmingham attractive then starts to work against you. If you're not in London you don't get any publicity, there is no vibe around you. We took *Canute the King* to the ICA (Institute of Contemporary Arts) and it didn't go down very well. It was just a love story, not cool in any way.' This view from James echoes his instinct, perhaps even his intention, that Stan's Cafe have never been or wish to be fashionable. Their work is less consciously confrontational or iconoclastic than some of their contemporaries in Britain, hinting at why their work has often been more readily welcomed on a European and international stage rather than within the UK. It's perhaps not surprising that this profile has emerged, as European dance-theatre has been an abiding interest for James, as he admits: 'It's always been the thing I love to see most.' Among many European artists, he cites the Belgian choreographer Vim Vandekeybus and his company Ultima Vez alongside the Austrian choreographer and director Johann Kresnik, known for his work with the Bremen Theatre in the Tanztheater style as pioneered by Pina Bausch (**TW 7**).

> As a student I saw Kresnik and the Bremen Theatre doing their ballet version of *Macbeth* at the Kings Theatre in Edinburgh. Up until then I'd somehow thought that exciting theatre was restricted to these almost underground settings and here was something mind-blowing, strange and terrifying on this main stage, on a grand scale with opulent production values. I found that extraordinarily exciting and encouraging.

From an international perspective, both The Wooster Group and Robert Wilson (**TW 8**), alongside Bausch, have had a lasting impact on James and the company in terms of scale, ambition and visual impact.

> At some point early on I saw The Wooster Group at The Riverside Studios in London. It was incredibly complicated with high

production values but still fiercely avant-garde. I found Robert Wilson's productions beautiful, Pete showed us a recording of an *Arena* documentary from 1984 about Wilson and his work and I fell in love with it from afar. I loved (and still love) the possibilities of authoring it yourself as an audience member. The quality of lighting he used, his collaboration with Christopher Knowles. The notion of very long shows that you could come in and out of. At that time there seemed no possibility of seeing any of his shows live so *Infected* was my attempt to solve that problem by making my own imaginary version of a Robert Wilson show!

As will be evidenced throughout the book, Wilson's minimalist aesthetic and his obsessive attention to visual imagery and temporal precision has informed many of Stan's Cafe's productions.

Ethos and aesthetic

It's full of nice people. That's an under-rated quality in theatre.

Gerard Bell

At its core, Stan's Cafe are indeed a nice group of people and it is this ethos of kindness that fundamentally informs their aesthetic (**TW 9**). With unnerving regularity, everyone you meet from the company returns to the essential affection and mutual care within the collective of artists, collaborators, advisors and administrators which are evident in their work and in the way they conduct everyday life. Often, without any prompting, people refer to themselves as part of the 'Stan's family', into which they find themselves, in Rochi Rampal's words, 'pulled in without realising'. Sweeting commented that

a lot of companies might refer to the idea of a family but there's something different with Stan's Cafe. I don't want to put it in too grand a way but I think it comes down to the central personalities of James and now Craig as well that has led to a feeling of warmth for the company and the breadth of the work. Quite uniquely at Stan's Cafe there is no-one with an ego. Family and friendship come first. Often it's a chat about football with Craig (over a cup of tea) before work is discussed.

The significance of Stephens alongside James must be acknowledged at this stage as his influence on the company has been profound since he joined in 1997. Sweeting suggests that 'Stan's Cafe wouldn't exist without Craig. He has a work ethic that is quite extraordinary. There is a selflessness about them both.' Fealty towards the company and a dedication to working above and beyond what might reasonably be expected is a recurring theme, as emphasized by Bell: 'There is an inner core who are very devoted to the company and very loyal to it, defend it, care for it and without that level of care the company wouldn't survive, because it makes big demands on itself so needs that care beyond the call of duty.' This allegiance is reinforced by Ward: 'My relationship to Stan's Cafe is monogamous. I feel like I work *for* them when other times I feel freelance. I feel like their success is my success.' In talking to Hadingue on the nature of James's character and how this imbues the practice, she reflected that 'James is restrained, he might never give you a hug but there is always an expression of love in the work. There is a strong moral quality to what is made.' This morality is echoed by Ward once again in his perspective on James's role as artistic director: 'James has developed a leadership style without intending to. It's about moral purpose. He's a devoutly moral person.' James himself has, on occasion, identified the significance of friendship as a cornerstone of the company's ethos, as in 2004 when he stated in an interview that 'personal relationships are more important than genius, work at them in all areas' (Hill and Paris 2004: 107). Perhaps, then, the best method of finding a central strand to their artistic aesthetic is by acknowledging this underlying kinship and humanity that informs each production, as the practice is too diverse to define a noticeable company style. Arguably, with Stan's Cafe, it is easier to observe recurring intentions, underpinned by a resilient ethos rather than persistent forms or content, as Rose succinctly expresses: 'It is our fundamental humanity that the company is interested in.'

The exploration of our vulnerability and fallibility runs through the whole of the company's practice and informs the aesthetic. Typically, the personae on stage (as often they are not characters in a conventional sense – see **Performing**) are struggling to cope; they are not in possession of the facts and are often 'all at sea'. Many times, they will fail to complete their tasks and their mistakes will be laid bare, be that the confusion of the cardinals in the eponymously titled show or the unravelling of personal identity and memory in *Be Proud of Me* (2003). Fragkou (2015) relates this quality in their work to the notion of 'the poetics of failure', as proposed by Sara J. Bailes, and Stan's Cafe undoubtedly explore both the elegiac *and* absurdly comedic potential of our misadventures, as Bell reminds us 'humour is seldom absent in Stan's practice' (see **Rehearsing and Directing**). Their style, however, is framed so that we are never asked to either revere or ridicule protagonists; rather we are invited to recognize ourselves and our own predicaments. This engagement with events on stage or in the performance space requires active participation on our part as there is no emotional raft to drag us onto the shore. This aesthetic has confidence in the audience, as partners, to make a concerted engagement with the work, sensorially, emotionally and intellectually, thereby creating connections between fleeting images, sometimes sparse and sometimes intensely layered. Rose highlights this point when he says: 'The audience is given control of the narrative. Prescriptive readings are avoided so there is always an openness in the narrative to draw your own conclusions and sympathies. There are certain ciphers though through which you are encouraged to view the work, particularly as an innocent.' Shaughnessy, referring to *Of All The People In All the World* (2003), construes this role for the audience as 'a level of participation which moves well beyond the associative' (2012: 128). Fragkou (2015: 213–14), citing James again, notes that 'spectatorial engagement is facilitated by offering "provocative material to work with and space to do that work", and inviting "the creation of personal poetic links between passages, motifs and ideas"' (Yarker 2001a) (see **Audience**).

Figure 3.2 Stan's Cafe performing *Of All The People In All The World* in Hamburg (2008).

Of All The People In All The World is a performance installation in which human population statistics are weighed out in grains of rice, one grain per person. The weighing is done by performers in dun-brown house coats, shirts and ties using old-fashioned balance scales. The rice is presented on labelled sheets of white paper. The statistics represented are carefully chosen to relate to the venue, current affairs, historical events and occasionally themes chosen by the promoter. Audience members are free to explore the installation in their own time and talk to the performers about their response.

The relationship between the personal and the political, the localized and global, are recurring themes for Stan's Cafe. Shaughnessy attends to this in regard to *Of All The People In All The World*, as she refers to the company's intention 'to explore the relations between microcosm and macrocosm' (2012: 118), concluding that 'whilst Yarker's recipe is simple, the piece is profound, working on a number of levels. It explores the relations between the individual and their environment and the situation of the individual in relation to "all the people of all the world". Among other things, it is a project exploring place; the place of the individual in the world and their relationship and situation (represented visually) to others' (ibid.). This examination of our place in the world, both in our immediate environment and on a wider global or spiritual level, can be seen in many productions from the plight of the stranded 'astronaut' in *Ocean of Storms* back in 1996 right through to the testing of faith played out in *The Cardinals* from 2011, as Hadingue puts it: 'The people on stage are often lost, disconnected from where they are and looking for meaning.'

On a more pragmatic level, the working methodology of the company is rooted in collaborative devising, which builds on the trust between artists who have often known each other for many years. Performers including Sarah Archdeacon, Richard Chew, Amanda Hadingue and Graeme Rose and, in later years, Gerard Bell, Jake Oldershaw, Rochi Rampal, Bernadette Russell, Craig Stephens, Jack Trow and Andy Watson have worked on many projects, spanning decades of commitment to the company. Adam J. Ledger, writing about the company in 2013, underlined the significance of this 'ensemble trust' when he observed how their work 'often relies on the availability of a mutually aware collective and an experienced Stan's Cafe "family"' (166). Despite the importance of the ensemble, he also highlights the absence of a fixed set of strategies: 'Stan's Cafe is not an ensemble company which shares a fundamental training or who train together. There may be shared cultural touchstones … but in terms of making the work, ensemble skill or technique appears in rehearsal as a set of creative strategies teased out by collaborators' (164–5). This collective effort is reflected in the fact that, for all shows, the performers are also credited with devising the work. Stephens phrases this disposition eloquently: 'You can see a bit of everyone in everything that we do.'

There is undoubtedly a democratic ethos present in the rehearsal space in which James, to use the words of the lighting designer Paul

Arvidson, 'presides like a chair person'. He is the key figure from which most of the initial ideas are generated and through whom all major ideas and final decisions are filtered. As James himself has said: 'As artistic director I tend to bring the core ideas to the table for each new project. These may well have been influenced by discussions with other company members, they may arise out of previous shows we have worked on or common lines of thought, but I tend to set the agenda first off.' However, once into the rehearsal period (disparately referred to as 'fuzzy', 'fluid' and 'intense' by contributors), the key driving force is a desire to 'serve the idea'. This is what leads to the diversity of performance strategies and forms of presentation as the company seeks out *what is necessary* (see **Rehearsing and Directing**) rather than what they are currently comfortable doing. If the piece requires complex, verbally dexterous acting rooted in a written script (*The Anatomy of Melancholy* 2013 or *Finger Trigger Bullet Gun* 2014, for example) then time is given over to the dramaturgical reflection for this, while *Of All The People In All The World*, for example, demands a completely different curatorial approach as Simon Parry noted, regarding this show: 'The performers inhabit their roles with a certain lightness more akin to live art or some street theatre' (2010: 329). This eclectic approach is reflected in the range of media forms and genre influences on their practice. Specific examples of this will be teased out within the chapters that follow but there is undoubtedly a strong filmic influence on the work, from the overtly titled *It's Your Film* to the jump-cut editing style of the short scenes in *The Cleansing of Constance Brown* (2007) or the vivid, pictorial aesthetic of *The Cardinals*, inspired by the films of Sergei Parajanov (**TW 10**). In recent years, the overt attention on film as a subject matter and metaphor can be seen in *A Translation of Shadows* (2015), which used Japanese silent film as inspiration, and *Made Up* (2016), which centred on the characters of a young film star and her make-up artist.

These influences are a reminder that the creation of, and interrelationship between, images on stage or on-site is often at the core of their practice. Ledger frames the rich visual style of Stan's Cafe within Lehmann's conception of a 'visual dramaturgy', which is 'suffused with sequences and correspondences, nodal, and condensation points of perception and the constitution of meaning ... defined by optical data' (2013: 164). It is also worth noting though that, even while film has a significant influence on this visual aesthetic, digital technology is not utilized as a matter of course as James is wary of using new media 'simply for the sake of its novelty', as he stated in 2004, again reminding us that fashion or trend is not the deciding factor. Music and sound, however, are central to their aesthetic, as Bell is keen to underline: 'Melodrama is a major element, literally melodrama – music and drama- there is always music to it.' Their sound signature, developed over many years with composers from Richard Chew to Jon Ward, Brian Duffy and Nina West, is distinct in its brooding and unresolved tones. West underscores this point when she remarks that 'I have "Stan sounds" and I wouldn't use them anywhere else' (see **Rehearsing and Directing**). In parallel to this, the significance of spoken text and language must not be forgotten as it is prevalent in a range of recent productions including *The Anatomy of Melancholy*, *The Just Price of Flowers* (2009) and *Finger, Trigger, Bullet, Gun* as well as earlier work such as *Good and True* (2000) or *Be Proud of Me*. The choice to utilize a visual or verbal form (or both) is the consequence of the interrogation of the idea and how it needs to manifest itself as theatre (see **Ideas**).

In the first few years of the company, there was a certain focus on physical, improvisational practice (see **Rehearsing and Directing**), often regulated by rules-based activities, and this was utilized both in rehearsal and, at times, in performance. Hadingue recalls how often they would 'try to improvise the whole show on the first day of rehearsal just to give it a go'. Stephens reflects that

> the early work I did with Stan was very much improvisation based. *Good and True* and *Simple Maths* were certainly created that way and that playful approach carried on into performance. It's about trusting and having fun with the people you're with. James gave us tasks to do, we just went for it, recorded what we'd made and chose from that.

This process was first adopted in *Memoirs of an Amnesiac* (1992), then *Canute the King* (1993), *Voodoo City* (1995) and *Ocean of Storms* (1996). These early shows epitomized the low-tech approach of the company, adopted partly out of economic necessity and partly driven by the intention to make immediate and accessible theatre.

Over the years, the significance of improvisation as a devising tool has diminished in favour of more preformed ideas leading from the start (see **Rehearsing and Directing**). James correlates this with later shows 'becoming tightly bound up in the relation between form and content. The further you go back, the broader our themes were and the looser our sense of form.' While the devising strategies may have evolved, there has been a clear and long-term intention to adopt a consciously performed style, embracing the theatricality of the event in preference to naturalistic or psychologically accurate characterizations (see **Performing**). Fragkou, citing James, writes: 'A common denominator in Stan Cafe's artistic portfolio is the choice to eschew mimetic representation, and its attempt to "convince someone about something which is blatantly untrue" (Yarker 1996). ... Performers often embody a range of different characters within the same piece, commenting on the failure to "represent" or to "perform" by trying 'to get the story right' (2015: 210). The framing of the events within the performance is therefore crucial and many performers, including Archdeacon, Hadingue and Rampal, comment on the amount of rehearsal discussion given over to considering how the action was framed – who were these people, what world did they inhabit, to what extent were they performing for the real or an imaginary audience? (See **Rehearsing and Directing** and **Performing**.) Allied to this is a fascination with what an audience is able to witness. The rooms in *The Cleansing of Constance Brown*, in which so many clandestine or unnerving events occur, are hidden to us and all we see is the corridor. In *The Cardinals*, we are privy to the backstage mechanics that reveal the frailties of the protagonists and their naïve relationship with the Muslim stage manager. Rampal, who played this latter role, comments: 'This was the key thing in this show. The audience was party to something that they wouldn't normally see. What you see and what you don't see is central to Stan's work.' As will be discussed later in **Ideas**, the worlds that are constructed by Stan's Cafe seem parallel to our own, strangely familiar and yet detached, operating with their own dystopian or heterotopian rules of behaviour, relationships, time and space.

From a political perspective, James and Stan's Cafe are not overtly led by any agenda and it would be more accurate to emphasize the ethical dimension of their practice. Politics is a term worn lightly by the company and if it is ever invoked by those interviewed it is always referred to in the personal, relational or community context or as an interest in the exploration of ideas and viewpoints outside of the mainstream. In 2001, James encapsulated the ethos when he stated: 'Our art is trying to promote the possibility of an alternative worldview not a specific ideology; the possibility of something that is outside of the market, outside sporting competition, outside conventional consumerism, an alternative way of thinking, a glimpse into some other world' (2001: 28). This pursuit of the alternative realizes itself not only in the content of their performances but in their choice of company location, their application of an accessible DIY aesthetic and their continued resistance to a homogenized style that is easily marketable.

Local, national and international profile

When Stan's Cafe formed in Birmingham the theatre community was very small and disparate, if not desperate. It feels as if changes in focus in regional higher education institutions have helped that, more people have started theatre companies and more have stuck around or moved to the city. It is in all our interests that theatre thrives in the city, we need everyone to be making great work and inspiring audiences to come to the theatre. As Stan's Cafe has gained resources we have been able to play our part in helping to build this community.

For Stan's Cafe, as evidenced by these comments from James, being based in Birmingham carries with it a certain responsibility to foster creativity within the city and the West Midlands region, championing the area as a centre of innovative, contemporary practice. The company played a central role in nurturing the city's fledgling BE Festival of theatre and performance, hosting it at @AE Harris in its early years and continuing to support it to the present day. Laura Killeen, a production assistant at Birmingham Repertory Theatre and independent researcher on the company's local impact, remarks that 'BE Festival wouldn't have got off the ground if it wasn't for Stan's Cafe. For years the festival was held at Stan's Cafe's venue before moving to Birmingham Repertory Theatre, but it needed James's foresight in the beginning.' She notes how many local companies, including Kiln Theatre and Little Earthquake cite James and Stan's Cafe as a significant supporter and mentor of their practice, recalling how Olivia Winteringham, the artistic director of Kiln, was 'encouraged by Stan's Cafe to remain in the city. They used their resources and rehearsal space for free and performed one of their first shows, *Eat Your Heart Out*, at @AE Harris.' The ethos of kindness and collaboration undoubtedly extends well beyond the boundaries of their own practice, as Killeen reflects: 'They not only think about themselves, they think about the wider cultural offer of Birmingham and having that diverse cultural ecology. They always look beyond themselves and have a generous spirit towards other independent theatre makers in the city and region.'

Stan's Cafe was established as a touring theatre company and continues to view itself in this way despite cultural conditions that make this very challenging at times, as James explains:

> It is important to us that we share our art with as many people as possible and we don't want just be parochial about this, we want to take it all over the country to be as widely available as possible. The market for small scale touring theatre in this country feels like it has been on the decline ever since we started, so this touring experience can be hit or miss. In this context international touring has become crucial to us. Taking our work abroad gives us a strong sense of being wanted and valued, it generates valuable income, provides an exciting diversion from domestic work and allows us to reach and meet new

audiences and new artists, to learn and experience new things, see shows we would never see in the UK and generally refresh ourselves.

Since Stan's Cafe began, they have steadily built a reputation in the UK and abroad for unpredictable, experimental work that is often beyond the bounds of standard theatrical practice. There have been times when their profile has suddenly spiked, such as with the global success of *Of All The People In All the World*, and there have been times when the company has been embraced on the global stage yet left relatively ignored within the British context. Lyn Gardner of *The Guardian* newspaper most notably stated in 2009 that the company was 'the most interesting company working in the UK today' and she has consistently been one of Stan's Cafe's most ardent supporters. Fragkou writes that 'a common note of praise encountered in reviews by critics and industry professionals concerns innovation' (2015: 226). She then cites David Tushingham, curator and dramaturg for the Salzburg Festival and Duesseldorfer Schauspielhaus, who commented that 'in a world where all artists have to claim they are innovative, Stan's Cafe are the real thing' (ibid.). However, work including *The Cardinals* and *The Anatomy of Melancholy* has met with mixed reviews, including from Gardner, often with comments focusing on the austerity of the form, which has tested the patience of some reviewers. Therefore, at times, UK journalists or the British artistic establishment have not always followed her championing of the company. Sweeting attributes this partly to James's decision not to make easily packaged shows that can tour medium-scale UK venues and build a reputation, including in London, but he believes there are other factors at work:

> If I look back on my time with the company one of my regrets is that we weren't able to put the company into a more prominent place in the independent theatre scene. For me it's better to view the company as we would view artists such as Anthony Gormley, Richard Long or Andy Goldsworthy. Nobody questions why they make one room installations, land art or vast metal figures. They just back the vision. James is one of those artists that we've let fall through the cracks. The

combination of being based in Birmingham, mixed critical reaction, the eccentricities of funding and diversity of work have mitigated against his emergence to the level of national profile that he deserves. If I could get on my soapbox and make a speech to the theatre funders, makes and viewers of this country I'd say you missed a trick there, you missed out. It upsets me when I say that because he makes some of the best work I've ever seen.

While the UK may not have embraced the company to quite the extent that is merited or expected, they have certainly made an impact on the international scene, touring extensively across Europe and North and South America as well as Asia and Australasia. *It's Your Film* (1998), ironically, as we have already noted, a very small-scale, low-budget creation, was the first show to gain international interest and, after touring the UK, travelled across Europe as well as Canada and Brazil. *Of All The People In All The World* has played a particularly significant role in placing the company on the world stage, appearing at festivals in, among other cities, Adelaide, Hamburg, Melbourne, New York, Stuttgart and Toronto. The epic scale and memorable iconography of the event have been noted in effusive reviews for the show that have helped to build its reputation and global profile. The Swiss-German newspaper *Neue Zürcher Zeitung*, for example, wrote of the show in 2010: 'Part amused, part amazed, one looks, marvels and understands.' *The Cleansing of Constance Brown* and, more recently, *The Cardinals* have both found significant success overseas, and for the latter, this was particularly the case in United States and Australia.

It has been suggested by many people that the eclectic nature of their work suits the international festival circuit far more than the constraints of British theatre touring. Their work is often better placed in the context of diverse, festival practice (what Sweeting refers to as 'their ideal world') rather than within a programme of standard theatre events in which their show may be difficult to market or erect on a conventional proscenium arch or thrust stage. A festival audience is also perhaps more open-minded to divergent forms from one venue to the next or one day to the next. James, in his self-effacing manner, conjectures that the success of work at festivals may be due to the fact that 'in festivals you tend to be something a bit exotic from overseas and therefore people approach you expecting something a bit different'. Whatever the reason or the result, James and Craig seem at ease with their profile both in the UK and abroad although there is arguably a slight anxiety when considering the overt promotion of the company or themselves. Stephens, for example, once commented that he found it strange and rather awkward when tweets went out from the company marketing a show with his name specifically mentioned. This degree of reluctance to be in the limelight has perhaps impeded Stan's Cafe, when other contemporary companies have knowingly sought or otherwise found cult status bestowed upon their artistic directors and their practice. Some may say that a greater degree of recognition should be conferred on Stan's Cafe but sometimes even critics seem to tune into the company's air of restraint, as can be seen in this translation of Helmut Ploebst's review in Vienna's *Der Standard* (2007): 'It is an understatement to say *The Cleansing of Constance Brown* is a great performance, but understatement suits the British, so let's leave it at that'.

Conclusion

So there you go. We've wheeled things on and flown things in as we told you we would; we've cast some light into the shadows and given voice to how the company perceive themselves. Perhaps what is revealed by this stage is that Stan's Cafe are somewhat stubborn when it comes to context, or indeed the spotlight, but this is not something they pay much heed to, as Rose remarks: 'I'm past worrying what people think. There is an enormous amount of respect for the company and people trust that Stan can deliver on things and can provide a fascinating alternative solution'. This pursuit of 'alternative solutions' leads them down manifold and tangential paths, as you hope to squeeze them into one box they dissolve into another, and so on and so forth. They are reminiscent of Rubik's Cubes (more of which later on), as you are always able to solve one side, possibly two, but the other four (for most of us anyway) will always continue to confound. Hopefully what we have achieved is a sense of the company not merely as a producer of theatre but also a caring community of people who place as much importance on relationships as on creative output. In this regard, their methodology is as much ethical as it is theatrical. The eclecticism, therefore, is not a conscious plan; it is a consequence of being who Stan's Cafe are and what they represent.

4

Ideas

*My favourite metaphor at the moment is that all the ideas that need
to come together to make a show exist as stars in the sky but it's only
when you recognise that some of them form a constellation and
belong together that a show appears. The connections are easy to spot
when they are pointed out to you, but before that, they're just random
points of light in the blackness.*

James

What's in this chapter?

In this first chapter, on the devising process, we start at the beginning
by attempting to tackle the amorphous and murky world of ideas. We
focus on where Stan's Cafe ideas generate from and how they are treated
and potentially manhandled in the very early stages of development.
We draw upon a range of performance examples but with a particular
attention to *Home of the Wriggler* (2006), *The Cleansing of Constance
Brown* (2007) and *The Cardinals* (2011). The chapter begins by
briefly considering who has the ideas for the company followed by an
exploration of certain recurring features that appear at the inception of
Stan's Cafe's projects, starting with the theatrical interrogation of the
idea: Why does it deserve to be a piece of theatre? Having wrestled with
this question, we then reflect on the eclecticism of source material, the
'making-sense' process, the coalescence of idea 'constellations' across
time and the use of dramatic constraints to test and mould the ideas,
allied to the significance of location in grounding the often ambiguous
and fragile protagonists and narratives.

Who has the ideas?

If James had suggested that we all do a show as ice skating elephants
we'd have given it a bash.

Paul Arvidson

Arvidson's elegant turn of phrase emphasizes both the significance of
James as the predominant instigator of initial ideas and the trust that
the company have in his creative visions. It is also crucial, however, to
underscore that this strong authorial presence has always been married
to an egalitarian ethos in which the company members' perspectives are
of central significance. This balance between James's individual thought
processes and his attentiveness to the collective voice is reflected in
Amanda Hadingue's recollections of the nascent stages in each production:

> There is no question that as we approached a show in those early days
> it would have been James that would have done the thinking, come
> up with the title, come up with a little box of ideas to put on the table,
> possibly designed the set, maybe got a bit of text to put in there, and
> then everything else was up for grabs. Certainly, when you turned up
> in the rehearsal room it was a shared process.

This ethos within the company is indicative of their intention to
nurture productive relationships built upon respect for personal as
well as artistic sensibilities. This echoes Hadingue's reference to James,
in **Stan in Context**, as being a 'kindred spirit', a friend as much as a
theatrical collaborator. James is predictably self-effacing when asked to
what degree the initial ideas come solely from him:

> Yeah they generally do. But the others never say: '*Ooh* that's a great
> idea James! More often they say "O … K, erm … we'll give it a go"'.
> It's mainly my impetus, but whilst some of the ideas end up on stage
> close to how I had imagined them, most go off on a journey and with
> the input of the rest of the devising team end up far better than that
> initial idea.

As far as this chapter is concerned, we will focus on James's particular approach to the generation of ideas, while always mindful that many hands are at work in the Stan's Cafe methodology.

Why are 'you' theatre?

On an almost continual basis, James engages in an exacting process of theatrical interrogation and justification for any given idea. In other words, it must have a reason to manifest itself as a piece of theatre rather than anything else: an essay, a rant, an exhibition and so forth. The key question that guides his thinking is: *Why should this be theatre as opposed to any other form of expression?* This is how James describes his relationship with ideas:

> It's tough being a theatre maker, you have to go everywhere in disguise. If you don't they accost you. They approach you shamelessly on every street corner, in queues, at gallery openings and movie screenings; they bug you while you're reading the newspaper or trying to catch some reflective time alone by the canal. Unless you're careful, wherever you go, wannabe theatre shows are continually throwing themselves at you. You can't get into a lift without them pitching to you and they won't even shut up when you're watching OTHER theatre shows.
>
> Most of the wannabe shows are pathetic, too flimsy, they've got the germ of something but not enough. They're usually solos and don't carry enough weight. These wimps are easily dealt with; you tell them to come back when they've found some mates. Then, if they are properly tenacious, they'll come back with a bit of a gang or a band of other previously rejected wannabes. Sometimes hiding in the crowd there will be a bit of a show you recognise from long ago who was under deployed. They still may not be up to it, but now maybe you can advise them on an element they're missing, maybe you can call up another idea to fix the problem, but on other occasions you'll have

to send them off again. Ultimately, if you're lucky, they'll come back looking tight and muscular like a bunch of super-heroes in spandex with complimentary interlocking superpowers. Now you can audition them and the audition is simple. 'Why do you want to be a piece of theatre – are you sure you're not a piece of dance, a novel, radio play, sculpture or academic lecture in disguise? Do you excite me? Do you scare me?' If the answer to the first question is convincing and the other two are 'yes' then they may just be ready to go into rehearsals ... when their time comes, maybe next month, maybe next year, maybe five years down the line.

This constant receptivity to what's 'round the corner' nurtures the eclectic style synonymous with the company's practice. One of the main reasons why there is no definitive Stan's Cafe performance mode is that the nascent material guides the process and performance methodology rather than an imposition of a 'house' style or the reliance on the idiosyncrasies or ideologies of an auteur. Neither is theatre nor, more specifically, drama, its genres, themes or forms, the dominant source of stimuli (**TW 1**). Ideas are consistently drawn, appropriated and nurtured from vastly divergent origins spanning family lives, childhood memories, the city of Birmingham, obscure literature, popular culture, the Bible, European history or global politics, let alone the demands of specific commissions, to name but a few. Content and form of artistic media beyond drama are often the initial source for many shows, somewhat unexpected when you consider how vigorously the theatrical test is applied by James. *A Translation of Shadows* (2015) was inspired by early Japanese film, *The Black* Maze (2000) was a response to a fairground House of Fun, *Lurid and Insane* (2001 and 2003) was set up as a rock gig, several performances including *Pieces for the Radio* (2001) and *Tuning out with Radio Z* (2010) are rooted in radio broadcasting and *Twilightofthefreakingods* (2013) has a narrative and timing structure based on Richard Wagner's epic opera *Götterdämmerung*. This list could go on and on.

Making sense

In working towards a theatrical justification of ideas, there is a process of *making sense* by looking for logical, rational steps that move ideas on from a to b to c. James often discusses the development of ideas in terms of: if we start *here*, then *this* becomes the next obvious or plausible event, and if we then establish *that* element then we are naturally led towards x, y and z, creating ideas in progression. This approach must be distinguished from a singular, linear development, however, as often several tangents will be interrogated at once, yet a rationale for the progression of each is identifiable. Note James's logical process of decision making, married to a theatrical justification, for *24 Hour Scalextric* (2009):

> Once you have unfettered use of a large industrial space (@AE Harris), thoughts naturally turn to what fun you can have in the space that no one else would allow you to have. The obvious answer was that you could build a massive Scalextric track. With a very long track it made sense to have a very long race, which in turn suggests 24 hours and a shadowing of Le Mans. Thus far very good, but the nagging question remains: where's the art in that? The answer was to provide a live commentary on the race, unbroken and webcast.

This making-sense process can often be informed by the pragmatic conditions that the company has to operate within in terms of finance, timescales or restrictions of venues. The artistic vision of many practitioners, including Stan's Cafe, is often in creative tension with the practical constraints of production and presentation. Regularly asked questions within the company that restrain or at least reframe the ideas stage for Stan's Cafe include: How many people can the company afford to cast in the show? How long can we afford to rehearse? Can we afford live music? What size and complexity can the set be and still be squeezed in a van, carried into a venue and put together in the time available? Are the touring venues all end on? Do they have wings? What are the technical facilities available at host venues? Do the laws of physics allow

Figure 4.1 Fatigued, James Yarker and Craig Stephens enter the last few hours of their marathon sporting commentary in *24 Hour Scalextric* (2009).

a particular effect? The influence of immediate practical considerations can be noted in James's explanation of how *The Cleansing of Constance Brown* emerged as an idea:

> It most immediately rose out of *It's Your Film* (1998). That show was massively successful for us. By 2000 we were performing it hundreds of times each year, but it was never going to get us very far as it could only ever be seen by one person at a time. Unusually, I performed in that show and that meant working six hours a day doing these very simple actions, so I had a lot of processing time to think about other things, principally, 'How do we scale this show up so more people can see it?' I started by speculating what the largest *Pepper's Ghost*[1] was that you could reasonably tour with. *Pepper's Ghost* is the device that generates the visual effect that drives *It's Your Film*. Essentially it's just a carefully

---

[1]   *Pepper's Ghost* is a Victorian stage illusion created by John Henry Pepper. It involves the use of an angled piece of glass to superimpose images from one hidden space into another seen space, hence creating a ghostly sensation, as through the use of changing light levels, the objects can appear and disappear.

placed piece of glass, so I thought (ludicrously) that we could tour with a sheet of glass that would give us a proscenium 2m wide, allowing us an audience of five per row and maybe six rows back, so thirty people, not massive but a big step up from one. So what show do you make where the proscenium is two metres wide? I thought, if it's going to be very narrow then it should probably be very deep. So what's the deepest stage you could realistically expect a venue to accommodate? Maybe fourteen metres? So, if it's narrow and deep, then it's probably a corridor.

If the show is set in corridors, then they're going to be 'corridors of power'. Then I started thinking about Greek tragedy and how all the really dramatic stuff happens off stage and is reported about on stage. That seemed like an interesting challenge, especially if we denied ourselves the use of words as the immediately preceding show *Home of the Wriggler* was very caught up in language so this show would have none. How can we tell the audience what's happened off stage if you're not allowed to speak to them?

In this progression of ideas, on several fronts and from one step to another, it could be suspected that the content of each show becomes ever more expansive and divergent but, actually, the pre-eminent intention for James and the company, particularly in recent years, has been to find the central, singular idea, the lodestone that draws the elements together. James cites one of his key influences in regard to this aspiration:

We were looking, more and more, for simplicity and I remembered that Robert Wilson said 'On an empty stage, if you put just one thing, it becomes very important. Put a hundred things, and the effect will be weaker. My work must be about one thing first. Then, it can be about a million things, but it has to be about one thing first'.[2] That idea really appeals because if you can boil it down, you can *then* fly off and explore other things.

---

[2] Source: Robert Wilson interview with Jonathan Vickery for *Art and Architecture* journal. May 2007.

This pursuit of a pivotal, clarifying idea manifests itself across the full spectrum of performance modes that Stan's Cafe adopts. Thematically, the concept may be hung on a keyword or phrase such as 'cleansing', while space and time are often reduced to their minimal requirements with figures often remaining within a single location and uninterrupted temporal span until the end. There may also be a key central task set for the participants to achieve, such as the curation of the rice or the commentating on a single event.

Constellations across time

To borrow James's initial metaphor, ideas are, from a temporal perspective, very much like stars. As we look at the night sky in any given moment, the emanating stellar light is from the past and, simultaneously, if astrologists are to be believed, they augur what is to come; in a single present moment, they are also past and future. In temporal terms, the accumulation of ideas is, likewise, a fluid concurrent combination of past, present and future stimuli. It may be helpful at this point to jettison any misconception that ideas are singular entities, created and existing in isolation from other ideas or from other moments in time, or indeed other people. You'll have noticed earlier that James imagines ideas as a 'gang or a band', pestering his consciousness, resonating with Stephen Johnson, the renowned American science author, who refers to ideas as 'networks' rather than singular 'eurekas' or 'epiphanies' (2010). To borrow James's conception of the constellation once more, ideas are out there in their infinite billions and the art for Stan's Cafe is in identifying them and recognizing the constellations they may create (**TW 2**).

> It's rare that a show will come from a single source idea. It's more likely that an idea for an interesting staging question might be seen to line up with an interesting subject matter. Or perhaps 'That's a brilliant title! I wonder what the show is that has that title?'

In light of this perspective from James, any assumption that we 'get' an idea is a slightly misleading notion, in the sense that 'getting' an idea gives the impression that an idea is a discreet, singular, clinical 'thing' outside of us, found in a discreet future time and space beyond where we are now, as if the only option is to adventure into an imaginative realm *in front of us* to discover it. Experimentation with time and the potential for layering and fracturing temporalities is a central trait of the company's practice (see **Space and Time**), and this spirit of adventure should equally be applied when grasping their formation of ideas, embracing a more imaginative and flexible vision of time and moving past the notion that ideas only come to us over some future horizon. They may do, but equally we may turn around to find that they have been following us all along. David Wiles, in *Theatre and Time*, encapsulates this conflation of past and future within the present when citing Aristotle's perspective on time: 'According to Aristotle, the now is what holds time together, making past and future time into a continuous whole' (2014: 15). In the maelstrom of ideas that swirl around every Stan's Cafe project, there are layers of time involved, a complex map of temporal locations that the company draws upon to direct them towards a performance. An instinctive idea, ignited by the present excitement or pragmatic requirements of 'now', often fuses with a future *could we risk?* while being informed by a past *remember when?*

The antecedence of performance ideas for the company is a particularly intricate profusion of threads stretching back into James's and the company's collective memories. Sometimes threads are noted but left hanging, often picked up and stitched into a project years later. There is certainly an attentiveness given to memories, voices or texts from the past as well as decades of experiences accumulated by the company. These contributions may be as diverse as the stories of ex-workers at the Rover car plant used in *Home of the Wriggler* or the 'urgent and profound' (as James described it) 400-year-old text of Robert Burton used in *The Anatomy of Melancholy* (2013). These examples are also an illustration of the company's willingness to adopt ideas from a range of cultural sources and to work across media and forms, adapting a variety of texts and narratives into live theatre (see **Text**).

The three examples below highlight the eclectic, yet unerringly logical, fusion of threads nourished by *past* personal memories, company experiences of previous projects and *current* social, industrial and political upheaval alongside a confident sense of how James envisages the alignment of ideas into the *future*.

Home of the Wriggler (2006)

I'd seen a Russian film – *Letters from a Dead Man*[3] – back in Sixth Form which was set in a nuclear winter (the kind of cheery thing I was into at the time), It's all sepia coloured and for scene after scene I'm thinking 'This film's lighting is really dodgy, it's flickering and pulsing up and down.' Then finally there's a scene set in 'the generator room'. You see they're all living underground in the cellar of this museum and generating power by pedalling these bikes to drive dynamos. The flickering of the lights in all the scenes up to that point was suddenly explained in the narrative. That made a real impact on me and years later it came back to me and I thought it could be interesting for the performers to power the show themselves, live on stage. So you've got that idea that just sits there. It sits there and sits there and nothing comes of it. And then many years after, in Birmingham, there is a threat to close the Rover car plant. I was moved by the way people in the city responded to this, there was a real community uprising. It got me interested in how engines work and the supply chain (for a while the working title was 'The Engine Show'). The factory is an engine at the heart of the community. Former workers described it as a miniature city. The car has all these components coming together to make it work; maybe this is a good metaphor for the community

---

[3] *Letters from a Dead Man* is a 1986 Soviet science fiction film directed by Konstantin Lopushansky, in which a town is destroyed by a nuclear missile launch that was triggered in error. Healthy citizens are admitted to underground bunkers while those remaining above ground are left to die. The central character of the Professor writes letters to his son from whom he has been separated, eventually leaving the safety of the bunker to return to the surface to comfort those who are dying, giving the film a sense of hope at its finale.

or a society. So that came into the equation as well. And then around this time we found out that my wife Sarah was pregnant with our daughter Eve. Suddenly there's this freaking idea of bringing a new person into the world and what are the implications of that? What world are we bequeathing this child? And at the twelve-week scan the nurse says something along the lines of 'It's a wriggler', so there we go: Birmingham/The Earth, Eve/Humanity – Home of the Wriggler. So, those three ideas essentially became a show. A bunch of workers in a post-oil world tell the story of a car plant and its community in order to understand how the world once was.

Home of the Wriggler

Using a range of pedalled and hand-cranked dynamos, a cast of four generate the power needed to light their own show. The show is a fast and slippery form of tag-team storytelling where a large cast of fictional characters are described or embodied by a team of shift-working performers some time in an ambiguous future. Written as fiction but closely based on interviews with factory employees and their families, this fragmented and many-layered narrative describes the community in and around Longbridge, Birmingham's large car plant, from its foundation in 1905 to its closure in 2005.

The Cleansing of Constance Brown (2007)

Sometimes you're not even aware of how much you are tapping into your own past experiences. It was in a post-show discussion, after a performance of *Constance Brown* in 2007, that Graeme reminded me that we had once played with a real corridor as a stage way back in 1996 as part of a free weekly workshop series we ran called *The Gift Sessions*. One evening we ignored the hall we'd hired and used the corridor outside, asking what would happen if you made one end of the corridor the past and the other the future? I remember enjoying the feel

Figure 4.2 Bernadette Russell and Amanda Hadingue share a dim light in *Home of the Wriggler* (2006), while Craig Stephens holds up an old car headlight to provide backlighting and, out of shot, Heather Burton is peddling like mad on a bicycle hooked up to a dynamo.

of that exercise but being frustrated we couldn't do *Scooby Doo* chases (unfeasible re-appearances on the opposite side to where you've just exited) because it was a real corridor. We ended up cutting the *Scooby Doo* chase from *The Cleansing of Constance Brown* but we had a lot of fun playing with time slippage in the corridor (see **Space and Time**).

I also remember seeing an exhibition at the Serpentine Gallery in London, in which there were dioramas of anonymous, white corridors with junctions off them and skylights. I found these empty spaces very evocative – like stage sets waiting to be populated. By this point 'The Wriggler' had been born and turned out to be a girl, so I found myself looking at the world from an *even* more feminist perspective. So if it's corridors of power then perhaps we need to look at the place of women in those corridors of power.

Somewhere in the mix was the fact that we had previously made a show called *The Hearing of Susan Tuesday* with a bunch of university students. I had loved the title of that show and felt it was a shame we couldn't use it again. So I just recycled the format of *The Something of Somebody Something*. The challenge was to identify a good first 'something'. I found

'Cleansing' very appealing as it has so many contrasting readings and so many of those are extreme. Constance was alliterative and I liked the fact it was both a name and a concept. Brown is both a name and a quality; it's simple and familiar and delivers a satisfying rhythmic end to the title. The title became a key reference point in devising the show, and it helped provide a couple of the show's rules.

So before we even started devising, I'd establish this notion that we'd be looking down a corridor that changes its format as it jumps around in time and space. I knew there should be no words, a cast playing multiple roles and that every scene had to include some form of cleansing, the brokering of power and a figure who could be identified as Constance Brown.

The Cleansing of Constance Brown

Performing on a stage 2 metres wide and 14 metres deep with seven doors on each side, a cast of seven actors take on multiple roles and use only visual imagery to interweave nine narrative strands. These narratives, which occasionally dissolve into each other, are set in a range of locations at different times, and the themes uniting them all are ones of power-broking, cleaning and the presence of a figure who could be Constance Brown. Due to limited sightlines down the corridor set, audience numbers are limited to fifty who sit close to the action, surrounded by a powerful soundtrack, and at the show's conclusion are invited to exit through the set.

The Cardinals (2011)

I've always loved the vision of the human figure in a toy landscape. I don't know why, but that's a visual picture that I've always loved. My grandparents used to live in Rye,[4] and there used to be a model of the town with a recorded narration and sound effects and at the appropriate moment sections of the model would light up and you'd

---

[4] Rye, for those of you unfamiliar with the English landscape, is a small town near the coast in East Sussex, a county in southern England.

be told about the smugglers and so on. I really loved it and desperately wanted to see a giant human figure in that landscape. The same with model railways where the operators stand in the centre of the loops of track. So that idea had been around for a really long time, since I was eight or nine or something.

Around the time of devising, certain people were doing a fairly slack analysis on the Gulf War, suggesting it was a modern-day crusade. Was there an imperialist dimension akin to the Crusades? I didn't believe this but was interested that the Crusades had some contemporary currency. Maybe you could weave an anachronistic story into it. Again, when we got into it, reading more books, we didn't find the Crusades very riveting, but we were already committed to the show. It became apparent that in order to tell the story of the Crusades properly, you needed to explain why Jerusalem was important and if you're going to explain why Jerusalem's important to Christianity then you need to explain Jesus and to explain that you need to talk about the Jews and once you're there you may as well go back to the beginning of creation. At the other end, if you go from the beginning of creation to the Gulf War, you may as well continue to the end of history. So the show becomes a quasi-Biblical history of the world and not just the Crusades. In fact, the Crusades section has dwindled to a two- or three-minute blip in the show. You have to be flexible in this way, you have to know when sticking to your original idea is the thing to do and when to slacken your grip on that idea and let the show slide into something different but better.

The Cardinals

Three Cardinals perform a biblical history of the world from Creation to the Apocalypse using a small puppet theatre in which, for the most part, they take the place of any puppets. This miniature theatre allows them to perform simple stage tricks such as having God's hand descend from the sky, but the tremendous complexity of their visual world creates chaos backstage. As the Cardinals' proscenium arch is imaginary, the audience are party to the backstage chaos and a young female Muslim stage manager's attempts to help the Cardinals through their performance.

Though occasional whispers are heard from the Cardinals, negotiating events backstage, this semi-improvised text carries little or no significant content and the Cardinals' own show is performed entirely without words. In the place of text, the stage manager plays a soundtrack of beautiful religious music through a terrible sound system, using audio cassettes that are crashed on and off. Despite the Cardinals apparent theatrical naïveté and occasional moments of conflict, with their stage manager they manage to steer their show to its conclusion via the Crusades and contemporary Middle Eastern politics. When, ultimately, their fictional world is unmade and the gates of hell opened, the Cardinals' poise, gazing down on the startled audience, unruffled from on high, suggests maybe they always were more in control of the spectacle than we had hitherto imagined.

Figure 4.3 In *The Cardinals* (2013), the audience are privy to the 'offstage' action; here, Craig Stephens as King David is about to be replaced by Gerard Bell as the Virgin Mary.

Constraints

In testing the theatrical resilience of ideas, the company regularly places overt constraints as a frame for the fictional events. This can immediately be seen from their first full show, *Perry Como's Christmas Cracker* (1991), in which they imposed a specific genre style on top of a contrasting narrative. In the performance, a couple of inept theatrical impresarios attempt to shoehorn the nativity story into the pantomime form. The couple's sacrilegious and theatrically inept attempt to combine two of Britain's most popular theatre forms is shaken apart by its own flawed concept and the intervention of a member of the audience, whose extremely weak memory of the original nativity story nevertheless carries sufficient conviction to steer the show to a more classical rendering of the Christmas story. Here we also see, right at the beginning of the company's history, the presence of the 'innocent', as identified by Graeme Rose in **Stan in Context**, acting as both the constraint *and* a cypher for us to project our own empathies and uncertainties upon.

Constraint has been an ever-present and defining feature of dramatic and literary construction,[5] working to hold *tension* (what is at stake for the characters) in place and release it as and when the writer wishes (**TW 3**). John O'Toole succinctly states: "The dramatic tension lies in the constraints faced by the characters in their pursuit of the resolution of their purposes. "Drama is the art of constraint"' (1992: 27). Dramatic constraints, including those in the work of Stan's Cafe, may often materialize in the form of emotional, psychological or fiscal restraints, keeping the characters' actions and desires in check. Protagonist-based constraints can be noted in a variety of their shows, most notably the restriction or absence of information and the fragmentation or loss of memory, as illustrated in *Perry Como's Christmas Cracker*. Likewise, in *Good and True* (2000), the four interrogators struggle to construct

---

[5] It is also worth noting that James cites Brian Eno's *Oblique Strategies* in the **Stan in Action** section of this chapter, which were created to 'unblock' creativity through the use of constraints written on a set of cards (see **TW 6 – Brian Eno**).

Figure 4.4 Graeme Rose as Bob playing Auntie Gabriel, Mark Reynolds as Bill playing The Prince and Sarah Liney playing audience member Mary playing a dog called Hamlet disguised as a reindeer in *Perry Como's Christmas Cracker* (1991).

the 'facts' surrounding the case of Joanne Watt, while in *Be Proud of Me* (2003), the central male protagonist attempts in vain to remember who he is, who he can trust or what his mission is meant to be. There are correlations here with the many writers or playwrights who have sought to constrain their characters with degrees of bewilderment, from Franz Kafka's *The Trial* (1925), in which Joseph K was accused of an unspecified crime by an unspecified agency, to Harold Pinter, who built dramatic tension upon the fatal ignorance of Ben and Gus in *The Dumb Waiter* (1957), or Stanley's fractured memory in *The Birthday Party* (1957). However, James often seeks a much more demonstrable barrier to coerce protagonists into action and in these instances, utilizes form or scenography (see **Rehearsing and Directing**) rather than narrative content or character trait. Figures on stage may be subjected to a textual restriction, a non-verbal rule or a physical limitation and this can be seen, among many examples, in the use of tourist phrase books as initial dialogue in *Be Proud of Me*, the narrow corridor and omission of verbal text in *The Cleansing of Constance Brown* or the restricted confines of the puppet stage in *The Cardinals*. Not only may these constraints eventually function as structural elements of final performances, they are fundamental to scrutinizing the idea in the early stages of development. It is interesting to note James's phraseology when he refers earlier to 'denying themselves' the use of words right from the outset in *The Cleansing of Constance Brown* in order to discover how best to tell the story of what is hidden behind the doors: creativity through self-imposed adversity. It may be suggested that, on a regular basis, the constraint *is* the idea, at least *one* of the principle ideas, generating the tension for the action on stage and also acting as the creative jeopardy to energize the team within Stan's Cafe. These formal constraints are often a necessary strategy to give coherence and security to the inherent and intentional ambiguity of Stan's Cafe narratives as the sparse characterizations and fleeting vignettes of action that are typical of their work demand some form of explicit anchorage to cling to.

'Locating' the idea

Correlating with the attention on constraints, ideas often seem to have an emphasis on site or location, be that an engine, corridor or stage within a stage, to act as a metaphorical 'grounding' for pieces (**TW 4**). Location, in this sense, does not necessarily mean the need for an actual geographical point, fixed in space and chronological time, although in some instances conceptual and physical locations intertwine. The events in Stan's Cafe's work are often suspended in extraspatial and extratemporal situs (see **Space and Time**), resembling and reflecting but never quite matching the real world; akin to the heterotopic spaces envisaged by the French philosopher Michel Foucault (**TW 5**). Stan's Cafe's 'locations' can be viewed as heterotopic spaces; they are never simply fantastical, even in such epic work as *Twilightofthefreakingods*, as they always seek to ground us in the limitations and fragilities of humanity yet they are not fixed in a time and place, wholly in correlation with the world around us either. These twilight spaces create fissures and permissions for characters and situations to appear from the margins, stable enough to be inhabited but precarious enough to create insecurity and therein a need to *do something*, to understand, to survive, to escape, to act. As Samuel Beckett understood when locating *Waiting for Godot* (1952), the description: 'A *country road. A tree. Evening.*' is enough to be familiar and yet, in equal measure, disconcerting, when nothing else is proffered beyond the bounds of that setting.

The vulnerability of humanity in an uncertain, if at times hopeful, world is a central motif for the company as witnessed in the manipulation of women by men within corridors of power or the exhausted, fractious and palpably mortal cardinals. This fragility is notably distilled in *Of All The People In All The World*, in which a grain of rice, symbolizing a single human being, is powerfully used individually and en masse to 'translate' the statistics of global power, population, birth, death, obesity and *X Factor* wannabes (among numerous other figures) into carefully curated mounds. Lyn Gardner, the theatre critic of *The Guardian* newspaper, referred to the rice, in 2008, as 'grains of truth'. In Stan's Cafe's work, the personae and the theatrical frame they find themselves in are often initially alighted upon as a locus of uncertainty and change. Our Sisyphean predicament is regularly set against overwhelming elemental or social forces; be that a rising tide in *Canute the King* (1993), where the original production was performed in Moseley Swimming Baths in Birmingham, or the grip of the Cold War in *Any Fool Can Start A War* (2014). In relation to this notion of vulnerability there is, at times, an inclination to construct arduous physical tasks which place the body under a degree of stress or challenge – the pedalling of bikes to power the lights on set in *Home of the Wriggler* (see **Performing**) or the non-stop, day-and-night commentary by Craig Stephens and James during *24 Hour Scalextric*.

Conclusion

As the book progresses, you may wish to note how these initial instincts of James and the company resonate throughout the rehearsal phases and impact upon the final performances. It is, however, important not to over-fixate upon them as the eclectic nature of Stan's Cafe practice will always make a fool of anyone who tries to precisely define the origins of their work. They are at least worth noting as key tenets of James's methodology for pulling the stars into line in the nascent stages of each new project. These features can also be seen across the practices of other contemporary UK and international practitioners including Pina Bausch and Robert Wilson, both already identified as major influences on the company, although Stan's Cafe have a particularly unique and understated way of combining their ideas.

What can safely be said is that Stan's Cafe are not short of ideas. Ideas grab James on the street corner, at the cinema or on the canal bank. Ones from the past never seem to know when they are beaten and rise again to be hopefully reborn in the next project. What is also clear is that constellations of ideas are drawn together for every piece of work and that ideas flow exponentially from other ideas. As the writer John Steinbeck neatly put it: 'Ideas are like rabbits. You get a couple and learn how to handle them, and pretty soon you have a dozen' (1988: 124). Be that as it may, ideas on their own don't win prizes. They are starting points, constellations in the making, which require a controlled ignition through exposure to the rigour of experimentation and reflection. For now, that would seem enough of an excuse to read the rest of the book.

Stan in action: Ideas

We're regularly asked to help university students to devise shows and in this curious setting 'having an idea' is perhaps the most challenging element of the process. Having ideas in the wild is an organic process; you can spend months doing a terrible kitchen porter job, incubating an idea you desperately want to pursue. Having ideas on demand in captivity with people you may not even like is like asking pandas to mate in a zoo. For people who need to have an idea *now* without it welling up from an ardent desire, maybe these (what Brian Eno **(TW 6)** would probably call *Oblique Strategies*) may help.

They are all in their way formal constraints, but don't let this deceive you; there is no reason that building a show from this starting point will make the show a sterile exercise. You can work backwards from these cues to shows that are 'about something', that 'say something', that give people an emotional kicking.

Things

1. Go and look at the contents of your fridge; what you find there is the sum total of everything you can use to make your show with.
2. Do a ten-mile walk, pick up stuff off the street and make a show out of this stuff.
3. Make a show you have to tour for a week in a suitcase that also contains everything else you need for that week, including your spare pants – you can use your spare pants in the show.
4. Go to a charity shop with £20, buy all your props in one go, then make the show from the props. Go with £30 and get the soundtrack as well. Go with £50 and chuck in the lighting as well.

Adaptations

5. Your show must be a nativity story told in pantomime format (like our very first show, *Perry Como's Christmas Cracker* 1991).
6. Restage Britain's *Prime Minister's Question Time*. Restage *Prime Minister's Question Time* but without words. Restage *Prime Minister's Question Time* but substitute in another text entirely (in *Come Together* (2008), we restaged Primal Scream's song of the same name – minus the music).
7. Use a TV listings magazine to find the short description of a television programme none of you have ever seen. Recreate this programme for the stage, just from this description (this idea is nicked from our friends' *New Guide To Opera*).
8. Choose one of Roger Hargreaves' *Mr. Men* books and make your adaptation so sophisticated, heart-wrenching and unrecognizable that you can give it a different name and owe the Hargreaves estate nothing (are our lawyers okay with me suggesting that?).

9. Choose an unstageable text and stage it. You can try *The Anatomy of Melancholy*, but I wouldn't recommend it unless you have plenty of time to spare.

Cart before horse

10. Choose one of these titles and make the show that matches the title: *The Freedom of Snake Jones, Freak Time Charlie's Big Downer, Last Second of Paradise* (Station House Opera made *A Split Second of Paradise* in 1985, so if it's good enough for them …) or *Blip Bloop Blagh*.

Make the show you'd like to see

11. What makes you most frustrated, angry, passionate? Make a show about that but be careful; if you can just rant on about the subject and theatre just gets in the way then it shouldn't be a theatre show, it should just be a rant.
12. Sit and discuss the best things you've ever seen in theatre and why they were good. Make something that delivers that feeling in a different way.
13. Sit and discuss the worst things you've ever seen in theatre and why they were so terrible. Make something that twists these things in such a way that bad becomes good or make something that is the opposite of these things, or re-do the show and fix the problems.

Philosophical shows

14. Make the biggest show about the smallest thing.
15. Make the smallest show about the biggest thing.

Autobiographical shows

16. Don't make a show about your lives, unless you've had really amazing lives, in which case … MAKE A SHOW ABOUT YOUR LIVES.

5

Rehearsing and Directing

What's in this chapter?

This chapter is about what happens in rehearsals between the gestation of initial ideas and the performances themselves. Stan's Cafe, as can be surmised from the book so far, never rehearse the same way twice, as each new production raises its own original challenges so a new approach to tackling the ideas and realizing them as theatre has to be developed afresh. So, in some respects, this chapter is about recognizing and celebrating the eclecticism of Stan's Cafe rehearsal methods as they have evolved over the years while acknowledging that there are certain consistencies of approach in terms of the interrogation of the ideas, attentiveness to the theatrical *frame* (**TW 1**), a commitment to collaborative decision making and an ever-present balance between the aesthetic and technical challenges each show presents. Over the course of twenty-six years, the rehearsal strategies of the company have shifted in emphasis from a predominantly improvisational mode to a more methodical process of scenographic construction (see **Space and Time**) and textual editing. To this end, the chapter looks back at the methodologies of the early years, then charts the development of the devising process into the forms that are prevalent now. The significance of collaboration within the rehearsal process is considered in terms of creating the shared authorial voice, then attention turns to editing and how it is deployed to resolve the tension between the generation of extensive devising material and the realities of distilling a show down to a theatrical form, ready for performance. Directing suffuses the whole chapter as decisions are made at a macro and micro level at all points within rehearsals and the collaborative process necessitates and encourages devolved directorial choices, particularly in terms of acting and design. However, in the spirit of demystification to which the book aspires, the chapter concludes with some specific reflection on the directorial methods within the company. To begin, though, James wastes no time in invoking military metaphors to capture the skirmishes, collateral damage and unadorned attrition of going into battle in the rehearsal room.

Rehearsals as war: An introduction from the commander in chief

It would be lovely to say that our rehearsals follow Michelangelo's example, deftly and sensitively chipping away at our block of theatrical marble until we have released the show trapped inside, unfortunately we can't. Once we have had the idea for the show and raised enough money to make it happen, then it is time to go to war.

The war is always unpredictable and your tactics must be flexible, if you encounter tough resistance on one aspect of the show you may choose to move troops to another position and attack a different aspect. A wild plan may lead to an effective guerrilla raid that unlocks a whole front, but sometimes there is no alternative but to slog it out in the trenches wearing the show's resistance down until it capitulates. Sometimes retreat is a smart strategy; freshen up, clear your heads and seek new inspiration before returning to the fray.

We may be in a position to bring in heavy set artillery or soundtrack support – let lose some shock and awe to help the infantry. A skilled sniper can decapitate the show leaving just a mopping up operation. There are many ways to win the war but few of them are easy. As commander it's important for me to stay safe, away from the front line, on some high ground, ideally behind a desk. The actors intermittently return to share the intelligence they have gathered and we combine this with what the situation looks like from my vantage point and then we go again. Eventually, like Michelangelo by different means we achieve our liberation and what's left is to parade the streets to wild cheering and the waving of flags.

Tools for the job

As initially highlighted in the **Stan in Context** chapter, there is a noticeable absence of a fixed methodology that can be badged as indicative of Stan's Cafe and, when asked, the associate director Craig Stephens is clear on why this is and what guides their approach:

> We don't really have one way of doing things, not really. It changes from project to project and what the demands of each might be, rather than a consistent methodology. The starting point is: How do we make this show? What then will our rehearsal process be? A lot depends on the actors in the room. New people bring in new ideas.

James, in keeping with the industrial environment of the company, relates the notion of methodology to a manufacturing process: 'You have to think about the tools you need to perform this particular job. You have to look at the job then choose your tools.' For many of the early productions, the principle tool was *task-based improvisation* (**TW 2**) within short, intense blocks of rehearsal as a means of bringing shape and order to a loose set of ideas. As the years progressed and the company developed a team of long-term collaborators and a certain confidence in their own modus operandi, the toolbox has been replenished with apparatus to respond to the more clearly defined initial concepts conceived of by James. Graeme Rose suggests that this method is now the most successful model of devising for the company: 'Stan works best when there is an external structure that James has conceived of. He thinks of the broad brushstrokes and then with the rest of the team we are able to fill in the detail.' Stephens echoes this when he says that 'the bravery and risk are in James's ideas. He has the capacity to see an idea through and take people, including the audience, along with it.' What both James and Craig Stephens acknowledge is that it is impossible and unproductive to rely upon a fixed methodological formula as a means of creating successful shows, as many of their most popular and well-received productions have come out of their bolder and more experimental processes. As James puts it: 'Our most successful work has been stuff that's felt more "out there" so there's an encouragement to be quite bold.' With this in mind, then, a predictable or repetitive methodology is never realistically going to reveal itself and, as with all things related to Stan's Cafe, the recurring qualities are as likely to be identifiable in the ethos as in the demonstrable methods.

Is tea a warm up?

We'd drink a lot of tea then improvise, improvise, improvise.

Sarah Archdeacon

As may be recalled from **The Route to @AE Harris**, the kitchen at @AE Harris is more often than not the starting point for much of the initial discussion among the cast and the director. Sometimes this choice of location is for pragmatic reasons of bodily warmth (as will be considered shortly) but, more significantly, it reflects the importance of collective discussion, 'working towards sharing a vision' in the words of James. At the heart of the rehearsal process is an interrogation of ideas, so it is unsurprising to find an initial emphasis on conversation and a corresponding willingness from the team to begin at this point; as James puts it: 'We've always worked with people who like ideas and are happy to engage with ideas and want to make shows about ideas.' Rose adds: 'If you come into the rehearsal room you'll find us drinking tea, lots of tea and wrestling with ideas.' The recourse to tea is therefore apt for a company named after a cafe and indicative of the intention to 'wrestle' with the concepts within the show so as to find the best theatrical means of expressing them and establishing what James and Craig refer to as the 'vocabulary' for the rehearsal room. 'There's a lot of talking, backwards and forwards' says Stephens. 'It shakes down when we get into the physical rehearsal. It's like sieving for gold. All that talk isn't wasted as you've got all that ammunition in your head to use when you need it. It gives you the confidence to try something out as you know you've already discussed it.'

The acceptance of a polyphony of voices in the kitchen and beyond is born out of the company's collaborative ethos and also from the range of backgrounds that the collaborators bring with them into each new project. Actors, new to the company, tend to join individually and are absorbed into an existing team, refreshing a shared understanding and a continuity of approach between rehearsals. All of the main performers are practitioners in their own right, often establishing their own theatre companies or collaborating with others across the UK and overseas (**TW 3**). This brings a wide breadth of knowledge and skills to the company beyond acting talent. Everyone, therefore, is seen as a contributor to the making process as well as the performance of the final show.

The instinct to make tea and conversation the nexus of initial rehearsals is also understandable when you consider the challenging conditions endured by the company throughout their history. An abiding memory for many actors has been the austerity of the rehearsal spaces used throughout the years and the impact this has had upon the shows. Amanda Hadingue has vivid memories of these testing times with the company:

> It was just a battle to keep warm most of the time. We made a lot of work in frozen old factories. *Canute the King* was made in The Custard Factory when it was still a building site, before there was heating and when we rehearsed *Home of the Wriggler* I recall that we had to go next door to a café if we needed the toilet or just to get warm. Working like this led to us inventing elaborate ball games just to get warm. *Tuning Out with Radio Z* was made @AE Harris and I'm sure the glow from the Red Rad heaters influenced the look of the show.

Gerard Bell, who has performed in many shows including *The Cleansing of Constance Brown* (2007), *The Cardinals* (2011) and *The Anatomy of Melancholy* (2013), has similar memories of the gruelling nature of the rehearsal spaces that shows were created in: 'At the end of those rehearsal periods I'm always unhealthier. It's just so bad for you. You're working in such cold, damp and dusty places. It's not a sane thing to do! It might have been easier in summer, but shows always seemed to be rehearsed in the depths of winter.' The company often appear to find themselves locked in rehearsals during the coldest months of the year so there is an understandable attraction to an intimate space for conversation, a case of conceptual warmth resisting physical exposure. James and Craig reflect on the pragmatic symbiosis between working conditions, methodology and their artistic aesthetic:

> **James**   Sometimes it's just about not wanting to be cold. Having to transition between this womb like space *(the kitchen)* and the cold practical space is difficult.

> **Craig**   *Home Of The Wriggler* (2006) was a good example of that. We had one room that could be heated and the rest of the space didn't even have electricity. We were rehearsing in December.

> **James**   It's no accident that the costumes for that were parker coats!

> **Craig**   It's a two-way thing. It's partly a necessity and it's also partly our world. This industrial, slightly messy space that we've chosen. If we were inclined to make work rolling around in our pants, then this wouldn't be suitable but that's less our inclination so it suits us. Sometimes though, when you're sweating in an Australian church in an oversized coat you wonder why! I'm not sure we'd pick a place like this now as we've got older.

This tolerance of difficult conditions over many years indicates the company's commitment to rigorous theatre-making in challenging financial circumstances, emphasizing its physical manufacture and made overt in the stark industrial sets and task-based activities rather than cosy artifice. It also reflects the 'pull' of the Stan's Cafe orbit, as many actors berate the conditions but seem to find themselves returning to work for the company time and time again, as Bell reflected: 'I kept saying to myself that I wouldn't make another piece under those physical conditions, and I keep saying that to myself but once you've been involved, you always seem to return.' The arduous experiences of Stan's Cafe are replicated in contemporary practice across the world, as companies seek non-theatre spaces, often industrial, to enable experimentation with form and content away from the conventions of traditional auditoria. Ariane Mnouchkine, for example, established the avant-garde Le Théâtre du Soleil at La Cartoucherie, an old munitions factory on the outskirts of Paris, and the Builders Association staged their first performances in derelict New York warehouses. Marianne Weems, the artistic director of the Builders Association, highlights the challenge of such conditions and why they are so often endured:

> The bottom line is that the work is done well when every collaborator commits to being in the room and in the conversation for as long as it takes to make the show. Sometimes this means years. Often it means breakdowns (people and equipment), usually in an industrial space (sub-zero or sweltering), while attempting to keep the train on the track. (2015: xii)

In the end, this is exactly what matters for Stan's Cafe, that people are in the room together with a common purpose to make something that is likely to be difficult, requiring fortitude, endurance and a coat.

Evolving methods

In the early years, when clusters of ideas were looser, the company's initial instinct was to begin with physical improvisation to get ideas on their feet, followed by development and editing of those ideas, often spurred on by limited time constraints. James recollects the basic schedule of these early rehearsals:

> The very first Stan's Cafe shows tended to only have four weeks for rehearsal. The first week would be improvisational with everything up for grabs. So we'd say – 'Here are a load of themes, let's freestyle around those.' The second week you'd have identified promising lines of enquiry and pursue those, trying to keep a spirit of free enquiry but knowing that material needs to be identified that could be in the finished show. Third week was about detailed development stuff you'd already made, plus structuring material and the final week was,

polishing, plugging gaps, resolving problems, sorting tech and getting
ready to go on stage.

Hadingue similarly recalls how,

> at the start of rehearsals, James would arrive with the main themes of
> the show (which might sometimes change during the making), usually
> a design idea, and often some writing. From *Bingo In The House of
> Babel* (1994) onwards, rehearsals took the form of round-the-table
> talking, followed by some improvising. In those early shows we'd do
> a lot of improvising. On one of the first days we'd improvise the whole
> show and just get up and get going with lots of props hanging about.
> James would often set us a set of rules for us to play with. You'd then
> discuss how these could be developed – what to keep and what to
> jettison and those ideas could come from anybody.

The significance of task within the improvisational structure was a key
feature as this eliminated any individual introspection on character and
psychological motivation. Tasks, as set by James, kept everyone focused
on the overall performance concept. Sarah Archdeacon recalls the
relationship between task-based improvisation and the development of
text in the first shows she was involved in:

> The tasks were very specific. This meant that it removed it from self,
> you could immerse yourself in doing the task. In *Voodoo City* (1995)
> we improvised around objects having voodoo powers, being taken over
> by the objects. Lots of questions about who were these people? Why
> are they on this rooftop? We called it *Terry and June*[1] *Do Voodoo* as it
> was a domestic scene where objects run amok. Improvisations would
> often run on longer than you thought they should but then something
> interesting would occur in those last few moments. If it worked it was
> lifted and became more or less set as you don't want to risk improvising
> it on the night, some bits were taken away and scripted and then you'd

---

[1] *Terry and June* is a reference to a British TV situation comedy of the same name, which
    ran from 1979 to 1987, starring Terry Scott and June Whitfield. It was about a middle-
    aged, middle-class couple – the Medfords – in a quintessentially suburban setting; hence
    the contrast when Stan's Cafe appropriated it for voodoo improvisation.

learn it. Dialogue would start in improvisation but then come back scripted by James.

Archdeacon's reflection also indicates the ongoing conversation about framing (see **Space and Time**); in what context are these people performing, and are they consciously co-present with the audience or disconnected in a separate world? Hadingue recollects how often this came up in rehearsal conversations:

> You're very aware that you're making work that is like our reality but it's sidestepped it in some way to a slightly different parallel world and we always came to a point where we had to pin that down and agree upon it. It could take days and days of wrangling to decide things like: Do they know people are watching? What are they performing and why? Is it a ritual?

For certain shows, such as *Lurid and Insane* (2001), the frame was more obvious as in that instance it was built into the concept of the show masquerading as music gig, recognizing and exploiting the presence of the audience. In *Home of the Wriggler*, the notion of the performance as a working shift for the performers simply emerged through the devising process; the 'workers' have to turn up for their allotted time and retell the stories while powering the stage (and their parallel world) by riding the exercise bicycles. As Stephens recalls: 'It was performed like a job, as if in to a void so it didn't matter that no-one was watching. They clock on, tell a bit of the story then clock off.' For other shows, however, particularly in the first decade or so of the company when the starting points were more nebulous, the issue of framing was a constant challenge to resolve. For James, framing is an ever-present issue in the rehearsal room: 'We come back to framing as a conversation time and time again. Sometimes we think we've resolved it and then someone pokes a hole in the solution and we're back to square one.' Bell notes how many of the more recent shows are also built around physical framing constraints:

> A lot of the shows seem to be about limited frames – *It's Your Film, The Cardinals, The Cleansing of Constance Brown, The Just Price of*

Flowers. It's very significant across a range of pieces. For *The Cardinals*, the ideas that it would be framed within a small puppet theatre and observed through the lens of the Muslim stage manager were right there from the beginning.

Rose, who also devised and performed *The Cardinals*, reinforces the significance of frames within the production: 'Once the frame was created that gave us a lot more structure whilst at the same time it proved quite limiting, but in this instance the limiting of the options and the vocabulary liberated the material.'

The emphasis on task-orientated activities as the basis for the devising has remained as a thread throughout the company's history, enabling the performers in the rehearsal room to engage with the more ambitious conceptual ideas that frame the production. The functionality of the tasks, focusing on the unpretentious 'doing' of something, often set within restrictive parameters such as the dialogue being limited to tourist phrase books in the case of *Be Proud of Me* (2003), grounds the activities. It guards against affectation or the need for any individual actor or any single moment to attempt to signify a grand narrative or metaphor. As Archdeacon puts it: 'It might be about big ideas but because it's performer led that's not what enters the rehearsal space. You're being inspired by the big ideas but finding a task that relates to them and you can play with it. We'd open up intellectual ideas through improvisation.'

As the company moved from relatively short rehearsal periods in the warm comfort of MAC Birmingham (1994–2000) to slightly longer processes in less hospitable settings (2001 onwards), there has been a noticeable shift away from improvisation as the central tool for devising. Stephens notes the change in rehearsal methods over the years when commenting that 'our default position now is to sit and chat for a bit before getting on our feet. Maybe before we would have tried getting on our feet quicker but that's not our instinct these days.' The more spontaneous, physical approach of the 1990s and very early 2000s may have been tempered in recent years by physical conditions but also ideas now tend to have a greater gestation time, with James bringing more fully formed concepts to the table. Discussion is therefore a crucial phase as a means of 'sharing the vision', understanding the performance tasks demanded by the idea and solving the logistical, scenographic and editorial challenges that are presented. Crucially, James is mindful of it not being too cerebral and detached from the practice in these early rehearsal discussions:

> You guard against it being too theoretical at this stage as you know that a staging element has to come in. The shows are not intellectual theses, they need to be embodied, emotive, surprising and seductive. Talking gets us a certain way but it is in the 'doing' that we learn most, where we find ourselves surprised and excited. I think as I've grown older I've grown more scared of just 'doing', it is a problem I'm looking to address.

Over the years, timescales for rehearsals have, for the most part, expanded and now the company will often use a two-part process in which the team meet for a week well before the main rehearsal phase to discuss the concepts, consider areas for research, try out performance ideas and share initial ideas with the design team. This allows time to develop material or consider potential staging solutions in the interim before the main devising period begins a few months later. Bell notes that at this early stage: 'James has always done a lot of research with Craig ahead of the rest of us. If you think of us on a track, James is out front, Craig is just behind and the rest of us have just left the starting line trying to catch up.' On many occasions, if you walk into the kitchen during this first stage, you'll find what many refer to as the 'post-it' phase, in which ideas are dissected and edited by the whole group with a plethora of coloured post-it notes[2] denoting themes, scene titles, events and so forth, stuck all over the table or on a wall. Through the course of rehearsing, post-its with rejected ideas will be moved to the periphery, and others may be collected and replaced by a single 'umbrella' note. Eventually, the post-its will have resolved into a series of scenes or events that represent a running order, the equivalent of

---

[2] Other brands of semi-adhesive paper rectangles are available.

a rock band's 'set list'. As the shows tend to resist simple chronology, the post-its prove ideal for exploring hypothetical, fluid relationships. It may be close to opening night before this set list is committed to a single sheet of A4 and stuck up on the set. Here, James outlines a few examples of the split rehearsal process and the rationale behind it:

> To go from nothing to an audience sitting in front of a show in a four-week rehearsal process was always galvanising but never ideal. Adding two extra weeks to the process helped but the sense of sharing a first draft remained until we learnt to detach at least one of those weeks from the main bulk of rehearsals and use it as an exploratory 'pre-rehearsal' time. This early exploration allowed us to try out ideas and focus the main rehearsals more efficiently, it gave us the opportunity to link publicity images or text more closely to the final production, it gave us time to prepare set or more ambitious technical ideas, perhaps most importantly it gave us time to reflect away from the rehearsal room informed by practical experience.
>
> *Good and True* (2000) demonstrated a clear advantage of this approach. Initially the intention was for this show to be in two halves with an interval (such were the 'locked in' tropes of the 'experimental scene' back then that having an interval felt like a radical groundbreaking idea!), the first half was to be set in an interrogation cell and the second half was to be a courtroom drama. In our 'pre-rehearsal' rehearsals we found the interrogation room so compelling and so rich that we refused to leave it and abandoned the idea of an interval. In this same process a contractual obligation forced us into two public *Work in Progress* presentations, this prospect felt so intimidating and exposing that we turned to comedy as a defence mechanism and, against our expectations, found that we enjoyed the show being funny. When main rehearsals started they were focused on a comedy set entirely in an interrogation room and our line of enquiry was well set.
>
> The pre-rehearsal period doesn't need to be long. For *The Cleansing of Constance Brown* we pulled people together for two days. One day was spent around a table working on ideas for possible material, the other day was spent on our feet trying ideas out physically and

establishing dimensions for the set. The pre-rehearsal period doesn't have to be a long time in advance of the main rehearsals either, it may just be the two weeks of a Christmas – New Year holiday period but this is enough to get measurements for a set, a shopping list for materials and a list of props to start making.

A Translation of Shadows (2015) necessarily had a significant pre-rehearsal element as an hour-long film had to be shot in Tokyo and edited before main rehearsals could start. As part of this process Craig and I each wrote a Benshi (live narration) script for a different film by Yasujiro Ozu **(TW 4)**. We performed these to each other and what we learnt through this process informed us of elements we wanted to include in the film we were shooting. The logistics of filming in Tokyo on a tight budget helped us shape our screenplay, a process we were mentored through by our Associate Artist Oliver Clark. Filming took place in November with editing through January. Main rehearsals for *A Translation of Shadows* were scattered from February through to the opening in April. Touring and rehearsal commitments for other projects prevented us maintaining an extended period of focused rehearsals for this project. This arrangement wasn't ideal and we are looking to avoid similar distractions in the future.

The experimental nature of Stan's Cafe is forged out of their confidence to be led by ideas, however un-theatrical they may seem at first, and to pursue these in discussion and then test out their validity through practice. The physical and vocal work must be rooted in the pursuit of the vision rather than any previous methods or tropes that may have worked before. So while there may be pressures to 'get it on its feet', the ideas must also be tested, evidence from practical exploration feeding back into the conceptual ideas, as James is keen to emphasize: 'The physical stuff always feels more exciting than the paper stuff, but you have to make sure both work tightly together.' To adopt James's analogy, the organization of the rehearsals is given shape by the problems in front of the General at the time, the morale of the troops, the lie of the land and the state of the enemy's defences. There is no rehearsal schedule as such, so that on any given day, the work may follow new tangents, pick up threads from the day before or deal with additional text written overnight by James.

Stan's Cafe regularly speak of being playful, and James admits to having a strong inclination for actors to have 'stuff to play with' in rehearsals. This may be a pile of task-based improvisations or props, as in *The Cardinals* (2011), where cardboard versions of all the key props were crafted to enable the cast to get to grips with the show's performance style; learning by doing was key in this instance, as Graeme Rose's observations on the process reveal:

> When we were piecing together the material it was quite a tricksy process of evolution, manipulating these primitive puppets which were basically cardboard cut-outs. We wrestled with identifying a visual language by coming up with key scenes which helped us understand how the objects might work. It felt very exciting to have the vocabulary of religious art provide the central means of communication, but explored in this primitive way – very mundane, even naive, but communicating big ideas.

Here, in Rose's comments, we see a reflection of Archdeacon's view that the greater thematic concepts are best accessed through 'mundane' practical processes.

This playful approach to rehearsal also allows the humour within Stan's Cafe practice to reveal itself, as noted above with *Good and True* (see **Performing**). Throughout their history there has always been a strong undercurrent of wry, understated comedy which infiltrates the performances, even productions which initially seem more austere. *Of All The People In All The World* (2003), for instance, finds moment of amusement with the juxtaposition of statistics that expose the sublime and ridiculous qualities of life. Jack Trow also revealed that a decision was made during rehearsals that the performers for that show would refer to each other by their title and surname (Mr Trow, Mr Rose and so forth) as an incidental faux formality, harking back perhaps to an era of balance scales and dun-coloured housecoats, lightly done so as not to undermine the integrity of the performance. Although *The Cardinals* had a knowingly absurdist, comic dimension built into its premise (a team of cardinals performing a puppet show), there was no active pursuit of humour within rehearsals, as James explains:

> We just concentrated on making the most beautiful puppet show we could, given our means. We kept adding elements to enhance the beauty and as a result we ended up with a puppet show so complex it was almost impossible to perform. Early attempts at running sections of the show always threw up great comic gaffs, so notes would run 'this went wrong fix it, this went wrong fix it, this went wrong – it was hilarious keep it', we set lots of the mistakes as material for the finished show and in the process performers made the transition into actors.

Bell, who devised and performed *The Cardinals*, also recalls his surprise at the emergence of the comedy within the production: 'A film crew came over from Montpellier before we took *The Cardinals* out and they were interviewing me and they said – "Where did this typical British humour come from?" And you thought "Oh, I didn't know we were doing a comedy" but of course we were. It was intrinsic in the whole set up.' The company have never sought a reputation for comedy, but it is their capacity for self-deprecation, perhaps built upon a British Midlands modesty, that has always enabled them to balance the exploration of complex, serious ideas within often-comical frames, as Hadingue encapsulates in another recollection of *Canute the King* (1993):

> Within the structure we hoped it was possible to touch on themes such as power, love, ambition, failure, even national identity. This is, of course, a lofty claim for a piece in which Graeme talked to his socks in a changing cubicle and we shared an underwater tea of foam sandwiches, but Stan's work has always enjoyed investigating serious issues via the ridiculous.

A central feature of experimentation is problem-solving, and many hours within rehearsals are taken up with tackling logistical challenges. Blocking, as such, is not seen as an issue that they specifically decide to resolve as the negotiation of the space and the creation of the mise en scène are always priorities.

Craig   We never really think about blocking a show as we just find our way through it.

James   It's just continuous.

Craig   As a performer you're finding your way through that show and your relationship to other performers so you find the best place to be on stage. There is no point where we say 'Now we need to have a blocking rehearsal.'

This pragmatic approach to creating work is often required due to the physical demands of shows, which require performers to move with agility and speed from one location to another. This is epitomized in *The Cleansing of Constance Brown*, which had very precise images on view to the audience but, in order to achieve this, demanded exact timing and rapid changes behind the doors in the corridor. Stephens recalls: 'With *The Cleansing of Constance Brown* you could make the images on stage look very beautiful but the off-stage world was very chaotic.' As a result, artistic decisions were fundamentally affected by practical logistics. Gerard Bell remembers how feedback to each other for this show regularly focused on practicalities: 'I might say "You couldn't possibly do this because of timing", or "These can't be played by the same person", so there were many occasions when roles were swapped.'

In recent years, many of the rehearsal phases for productions have involved the development of 'training strategies' (to use James's phrase) as much, if not more, than the conventional structuring of scenes or learning of lines and action. James finds an analogy here with sport: 'You know that the match will last "so long" and what the goal is but you don't know how the events will pan out so you have to prepare strategies and set pieces.' Several shows, from the beginning of this century, have been built upon such *instructional* frames, necessitating the practice of specific techniques or linguistic and physical tropes so that in performance these can be applied, bringing some order and tautness to relatively loose structures that require extemporization within the performance itself. This approach can be seen in *Of All The People In All The World* (2003), which involves slow and methodical curation of the event; *The Commentators* (2009) and *Tuning Out with Radio Z* (2010), in which both necessitated an intimate radio commentary style in reaction to unpredictable live events; and *Twilightofthefreakingods* (2013) that, while improvised, was guided by a slow Wilson-esque aesthetic (see **Directing** sub-heading and **Performing**).

Collaboration

Yeah I'll give it a go. I'll do the jump off the cliff thing.

Rochi Rampal

Once the initial ideas are in place, collaboration is fundamental in the rehearsal processes of Stan's Cafe. In practice, it means recognizing the actors and designers as devisors with a central authorial voice throughout the devising, offering them time and space to digest ideas, reflect and contribute their own original material, even though they are always following a very strong conceptual lead from James. For those who work with the company, it requires a generosity of spirit, a significant degree of trust and an acceptance of risk, as epitomized by Rampal's attitude, and similarly highlighted by Hadingue: 'Devising is exciting when you can build on each other's thinking, and I believe we pushed each other to think quite hard. It's what a real collaborative process is – you have to be able to take risks with your thoughts and ideas, and trust the responses from your collaborators.' There also needs to be a capacity and willingness to bridge disciplines, all of which are encouraged by the familial working environment. Jack Trow encapsulates this ethos:

> You would think, as we are all working around James's ideas, that it would lead to a reduction in collaboration, but there is such a strong sense of family that this doesn't happen. The people I work most often

with in the company are the people I also socialise with. We all get on so well. James has this orbit of artists of various disciplines and styles and yet people aren't restricted by those disciplines. *Of All The People In All The World* is a good example. I was employed as an actor but very quickly I realised that it was a writing job, you're writing new material for each new location, thinking how one statistic goes next to another. So that's what you get on and do.

Bell similarly captures the liminal state of devisor/performer that actors who work with the company need to embrace:

Officially my profession is 'actor' but that doesn't seem accurate to me when working with Stan's Cafe. In this context, I'm a person who works in performance. At a certain stage both devising and performing become the same thing. You devise as you perform and vice versa. That was certainly the case with *The Cardinals* and *Constance Brown*. You are partly your own material.

The agency and input of the devisor/performers are counterbalanced by the direction of James, who is unequivocally seen as curating and leading the conceptual vision (see **Directing**). Archdeacon, reflecting on her years with the company, firmly believed there was a productive unspoken balance between the two elements as she thought that Stan's Cafe was 'as much performer led as director led'. Her perspective is again echoed by Bell:

The basic process with Stan is that James starts off with a nexus of ideas. He brings these and they are given to the collaborators and the show develops out of that. The collaborative process is very open, there aren't any restrictions on anybody at all but it's within James's conceptual framework. You don't throw in every idea you have because it's a collaboration within those limits. In *The Cleansing of Constance Brown* for example James had the two strong ideas, the corridor and the cleansing. These are what opened up the possibilities for when we were making it, as every scene had to have some type of 'cleansing' in it and every scene had to refer to 'Constance Brown' in some respect.

Within this frame, sections were given over to people to make. The one that's clearest in my mind was the one we called *Jewish Departure*. Bernadette [Russell], Craig and myself took the Jewish story and developed the scenario and these were then interlocked with scenes created for another narrative by another group of actors.

Another facet of the collaboration is the shared approach to research and contextual underpinning for each show. There is a hesitancy here to use the term dramaturgy **(TW 6)**, as although Ledger has referred to their 'visual dramaturgy' (2013) and some of the Stan's Cafe performers allude to it, James is less inclined to think of their discussions in such formal terms, as he outlines: 'There's never been a sense of a dramaturg coming in to help as there's already a load of voices in there. So it's not so much dramaturgy as a looser, more poetic connection with ideas. There is a "bibliography" you could produce behind every show but this is worn very lightly.' At times, external advice has been sought

Figure 5.1 Bernadette Russell and Craig Stephens rehearse the Jewish Departure scene from *The Cleansing of Constance Brown* (2007). Right of frame, Harry Trow and Robin Stephens are visible backstage as masking has yet to be put up.

for productions, notably in the case of *The Anatomy of Melancholy*, for which Erin Sullivan, from the Shakespeare Institute at the University of Birmingham, was asked to advise on the Robert Burton text, but this is a rare occurrence and usually the 'load of voices' find their own organic route to understanding the context in which the work sits. Graeme Rose suggests that 'this isn't perhaps the most efficient way of working and a lot of companies would choose to have a script advisor or dramaturg central to that process and for that work to be done prior to rehearsals'. Specifically, in relation to *The Anatomy of Melancholy*, he recalls that 'it felt like James and Craig wanted to put together a team of minds to wrangle the source text and to generate a multi-perspectival view of the material'.

This in-house approach gives rise to the eclectic range of influences and research strands. There is never a particular steer from James to scrutinize certain texts or become immersed in specific genres and it is much more likely that there will be a collective enthusiasm to engage in background or tangential reading or viewing. The company avoid homage, always treading lightly on their influences so that they infuse but never announce themselves overtly in the final performance; as James puts it: 'You'd have to be pretty erudite to spot them.' The eclecticism is evident in the spectrum of influences from contemporary novels, televisual culture, world cinema, fine art, popular music and theology. For *Lurid and Insane* (2001), for example, the inspiration came from a combination of evangelical, politicized Christianity epitomized by the likes of Billy Graham, combined with the stage showmanship of James Brown. Often, in rehearsals, the rationale for the next staging decision would be framed by those particular references: 'What would happen in a political rally now?' or 'What would James Brown do at this point in his act?' For *The Cardinals*, James and the cast were strongly influenced by the rich tableaux and poetic symbolism of the cinema of Sergei Parajanov and films of his such as *The Colour of Pomegranates* (1968), while for *The Cleansing of Constance Brown*, the presidential scenes were influenced by the American TV series *The West Wing*.

Figure 5.2 Andy Watson plays the President in the finale of *Lurid and Insane* (2001). Graeme Rose is on bass, Heather Burton is just visible to the right of frame and Amanda Hadingue to the left.

The collaborative ethos is continually sustained by the focus on the overall structure of the piece rather than individuals retreating into their own character development. Hadingue noted how 'problems were always focused on the piece, not on individual characters, so we'd all think about different solutions to solve the problem collectively. For example, "What if we all think this or do this at this point". James recollects this quality of holistic problem-solving when they were working on *The Anatomy of Melancholy*:

> There were no names attached to the lines in the script so it was a kind of an auction of who should have them. 'If you have this one then you should have that.' The characters were based around the four humours[3] so when those topics came up it made sense to allocate lines accordingly.

This mindset of collective endeavour is further supported by the regular collaborators having an innate sense, learnt from working on

---

[3] The *four humours* were a medical 'system' devised in antiquity, notably by Hippocrates of Kos. He proposed that human health was a balance of these humours which he listed as *blood, yellow bile, black bile* and *phlegm*. This theory persisted in medical practice until as recently as the eighteenth century.

many productions, of how a Stan's Cafe production should look and feel. Trow suggests that 'rehearsals now can circumvent some of the stages that other companies would go through as there are people in the Stan family who understand how to turn James's curiosity into a show'.

Collaboration is equally important with non-acting artists who occasionally contribute to the conceptual thinking process and are regularly present in the rehearsal room. These artists working on set design, lighting or music have often had an extended relationship with the company. Photographer Ed Dimsdale, for example, had been taking promotional and production photographs for the company for five years when he was invited to collaborate on *Be Proud of Me*, as the show was to be performed in front of a screen of dissolving photographic slides. The relationship between the slides and the live action and also their contribution to the narrative and aesthetic of the show were all part of the collaborative discussion. Dimsdale raided his own archives for photographic material as well as undertaking a series of photographic shoots to create material specifically for the show. This process went backwards and forwards with the photographer fully integrated into decision making, his slides forming part of the show's text. More recently, for *Made Up* (2016), the company recruited make-up artist Andrew Whiteoak who, for the first time in his career, found himself around a table devising a show. His professional experiences were valued, as he taught the actor Alexis Tuttle how to apply the make-up in performance, but likewise he contributed to plot and structuring wherein his suggestions for make-up looks and transitions became central to the form of the show.

Mark Anderson and Helen Ingham collaborated with the company in 2006, designing and building the set for *Home of the Wriggler*. The electricity-generating machines and lights they designed and built for the show came from discussions with the company and dictated not just the look of the show but the physicality of the actors, their movement, their breathing and hence how they delivered their lines. Collaboration is demonstrably a two-way process for Stan's Cafe and designers often have to remain open to input from the company. Late in the process for this show, for example, James conceived of a solution for the production's backdrop which consisted of an exploded diagram of an engine with the parts labels replaced by character names. This late change of direction was then accommodated within the design concept.

Historically, set design has been undertaken by the company in the rehearsal room and collaboration in this aspect of production has not always been productive, as James and Craig illustrate:

> **James** Because set design is often so bound up with the concept of for the show it has felt difficult to get a designer in to help us on this. We have tried in the past; for *The Cleansing of Constance Brown* (2007) we went to a well-respected designer and found ourselves saying 'We want the set to be two metres wide, fourteen metres deep, with seven doors on each side and they need to be hinged in this particular way so it doesn't look like a door and it needs to have a roof on it but *you* can decide if you want it black or grey.'
>
> **Craig** She was very polite and said 'Here is an address of a set maker.'

So even when a set designer is employed (predominantly Harry Trow in recent years), they don't get a free rein, as James clarifies: 'We are always pretty prescriptive, defining the parameters within which he has to operate.' Ideas for set design can come from all quarters, so more often than not the designer's challenge is

> to make sense of our ambitious but vague scribbles. For *The Anatomy of Melancholy*, I told Harry that I wanted a set full of 400-year-old flip charts but he was the one who went away and made the concept work. Craig had the idea for rope lights to denote the trailer for *Made Up* but Harry had to figure out exactly what that meant and how the projection and green screens would be integrated.

Paul Arvidson, another Lancaster University graduate, designed lighting for all the main shows between 1994 and 2011. Arvidson relished the opportunities presented by working with Stan's Cafe as his lighting responsibilities meshed closely with scenographic decisions. The non-realist (**TW 5**) frames within the productions offered room for experimentation: 'It was a dream job for a designer as anything was possible. I saw it as a play-space. The space between what was real and not real gave me creative freedom. It was a very hands-on experience, with something of a punk aesthetic.' He unequivocally saw his main role as a creative devisor rather than as a technician: 'Tech-devising can work in much the same way as devising the "acting" bit of the show and it shares many of the same challenges and beauty. Sometimes, the odd birdie [very small theatre lantern] you stick in at the last minute, makes a beautiful "interstitial scene" all by itself.' The significance of lighting to the overall aesthetic reflects the influence of Robert Wilson, and Arvidson recalls how the Stefan Brecht book, *Theatre of Visions* (1982), about Wilson's practice, had a

> massive impact as it gave us permission in our heads to spend time devising tech stuff as well as performer stuff. In a pre-rehearsal week on *Ocean of Storms* we devoted a significant amount of time to *tech* devising and learned as much about what we didn't want to do, as what we did. Wilson's practice also influenced the way we placed significance on what *not* to light as well as what to illuminate, so it's as much about what is not seen.

Often the lighting designs were very precise, requiring performers to know precisely where to be on stage. 'It was like being on a film set at times' he recalls, 'telling performers to move half a step in this direction or cheat themselves into the light.' However, while the level of technical detail is often complex, the decisions are always brought back to 'serving the idea', as Arvidson puts it. In the case of *The Cleansing of Constance Brown*, for example, the original intricate lighting design involving scrolling colour changers to help distinguish different fictional locations from each other was pared back in the latter stages of rehearsal, partly to deal with the rigours of touring but also, as he outlines, 'to let the intensity of the performances and direction do the talking. It made for a much cleaner looking show and allowed more space for the scenes and costume changes to breathe.'

From a musical perspective, first Richard Chew and more recently Nina West and Jon Ward (working on separate productions) have always been given licence to freely interpret the vision of each production and experiment with unconventional ideas, rather than provide a prescribed type of score, particularly one that does nothing more than emotionally underpin the narrative. Nina West, who has worked on many productions including *Ocean of Storms* (a section of which was re-appropriated for *It's Your Film*), *Be Proud of Me, The Cleansing of Constance Brown, Twilightofthefreakingods, A Translation of Shadows* and *Made Up*, reflects on her own working methods with the company, including the time given to take in the concepts and how processes must adapt to each new challenge:

> They don't press me for ideas or press me to describe them. I'm given space. I come in for a couple of days to absorb it, it starts to tingle and click. What's my place in it? I need to walk inside the landscape of the piece and live in it. From that I create what I call a 'mesh'. It's all the things known and all the things unknown. I try to evoke the environment. It's important not to be literal, otherwise it's redundant. At some point, I just go up to my studio, take a deep breath and begin. I like to work on textures and harmonic sounds, layers of individual sounds that create new sounds. But I never use samples. I need to make an original sound otherwise it feels like I'm cheating people. When I have something I go to James and the crucial thing for him is to know that everything is substantial, everything is there for a reason. There are times when I ignore him though and ignore the usual ways that I'd work, and he tells me I'm usually right. In *Twilightofthefreakingods* the brief was for some electronica and he didn't want melodies but I felt it needed these to sustain over four hours. The music needed to be a performer in its own right on this occasion. I sympathised with the female characters so wrote for them and their relationships which is the opposite of what I might normally do.

Likewise, Jon Ward, a composer for shows including *Simple Maths* (1997), *Of All The People In All The World* and *Tuning Out with Radio Z*, reflects on a similarly open-ended working environment and his own methods and criteria for creating soundtracks:

> James has never given me a brief for anything. He never really tells me anything. Which is great but scary. He once said I should be braver and that's the most illuminating thing he's ever said. I've always assumed this is because he trusts my judgement. The process often consisted of them devising something, then I'd go away, write something, then come down and play it whilst they were devising and see if it worked, perhaps changing it immediately. It was really a parallel devising of the soundtrack alongside the show. I think that's the perfect way to write a soundtrack if you can. Being in the space is the best way. I've always been interested in natural sounds, but deteriorating them in some way, making them seem intentional, looping them for example. Working with the company sowed the seed in me that you shouldn't write music that sounds nice. If you find yourself thinking 'That sounds nice', then you've really gone wrong somewhere.

Editing

There is normally a sense of brinkmanship in every rehearsal process, it's a question of when do you stop making something new.

James

This remark by James reflects the creative tension between the rehearsal process and the realities of bringing a show together, ready for performance. Editing is critical to Stan's Cafe, perhaps more so than for many contemporary companies due to the emphasis on a minimalist stage aesthetic, only keeping the essential elements required, and due at times to the scale of the challenges they set themselves and the density of the initial set of ideas and texts from which they work. Under these circumstances productions require ongoing editing, even after they have begun to be performed, as James identifies:

> Editing is a continual process, it is present in the moment you choose to follow one line of enquiry and not another or choosing to record one piece of improvised material for later reference and not another. Eventually however you feel you have made all the raw material you need, that the show must now lie in what you have and at this point the editing must grow more active and constructive. It is important to be unsentimental about material, you may have great affection for a particular sequence or section but if it doesn't serve the best interests of the show it has to be cut out. In this circumstance I tend to console myself with the thought that 'if this is the quality of material we've binned then the show must be great'.

Instinctively, editing would appear to be a process of reduction, but as James also reveals, it sometimes necessitates addition, with the creation of new material to link existing but disconnected scenes. He identifies 'the missing section' as a familiar but occasional problem, most often associated with the company's older shows:

> When we were making shows built from blocks of discreet theatrical sections we would sometimes get all the material in a line and realise 'we can't go from there to there' so we would shuffle the order and eventually come back to the same running order and the same problem 'we can't go from there to there – we need something in between' we would find we were missing a section and have to make something that filled the gap. My memory is that the gap would usually be before the final section – beginnings tend to be easy, ends tend to be easy, middles are trickier but the thing that allows you to move from the middle on to the end would often be fiendishly difficult to find.

When asked how the missing elements were found in such circumstances, James is suitably vague in identifying any particular method but recalls the typically poetic solution created for *Ocean of Storms*:

> I really don't know how it's done. It wasn't as if this was a narrative challenge 'how do we get the hero to meet the heroine for the kiss at the

end?' It was usually something more akin to a challenge a composer might face trying to establish the chord progression that allows the music to resolve itself. Experience taught us that the solution was always going to be something simple rather than creating more complication. For example, (except of course this is a narrative solution undermining what I've just said) in *Ocean of Storms* we needed some way of our on stage protagonists changing something that would allow the offstage protagonists they had been voicing to resolve all their individual stories. It occurred to me that as stars are used for navigation and are looked to by some for shaping their future then maybe these routes and futures could be altered by moving the stars in the sky. Our set was just metal mesh floor with a chain of blue festoon lights under it, so it was a simple – if physically taxing – procedure to flip the flooring units up and move the bulbs into a circle before replacing the floor. The missing scene had been found. The fact that late in the show it broke the staging convention felt helpful. It felt like the middle eight in a pop song, the audience hears that and they know the end won't be far behind.

Notice how James once again reaches for the musical analogy to express the compositional rationale, yet while the logic for the solution may initially be narrative in this instance, it is also fundamentally structural, tapping into our innate sense of artistic tempo. More recently, removing the interval in *The Cardinals* generated a 'missing scene' as he explains:

The idea of an interval in *The Cardinals* was very attractive as it would give the cast time to regroup and reset it would also give the audience a break halfway through a show whose running time was about 105 minutes. Theologically ending the first half with the death of Christ seemed spot on so all was set fair. However, audiences really didn't like the interval, listening carefully it became clear that they didn't want the spell or the momentum of the show to be broken or interrupted. After a period of vacillation in which the interval went and came and went again we finally excised it permanently and as a result were left with a hole in the show plus a logistical prop wrangling headache. It took a series of rehearsals whilst on tour to resolve all these issues and generate material to fill the hole. Eventually the scars healed over this section of the show and it now no longer feels like a 'fix' but like a valuable scene in its own right.

The notion that editing is a continual process is confirmed by the fact that it extends beyond opening night, as noted above with *The Cardinals*. Audiences change shows, so it is natural that there should be an ongoing process of reflection and refining, contributing significantly to the development of the show after its premiere. Rochi Rampal identifies this in her own experience of working on tour with the company: 'The show is the extension of the rehearsal. It's about making that thing right for the next one and the next one. It's not a video – its impacted upon by us as human beings.' James gives a dramatic example of this post-premiere editing as well as the ruthlessness that is required sometimes:

> *The Cleansing of Constance Brown* was very popular right from the off, but a few people suggested it was 'ten minutes too long', in my opinion there is no such thing as 'too long', what this means is 'not good enough'. Something in the show wasn't working. Alan Rivett, who as Director of Warwick Arts Centre was one of the show's commissioners, spotted the problem. He identified 'The Spa Scene' as the issue, saying it didn't belong in the show. It was a really popular scene with us and with audiences but on reflection Alan was right, just at the point the show needed to be accelerating to a conclusion this slapstick comedy scene came in from left-field and destroyed the momentum. We cut the scene and replaced it by a brief visual moment, the combined effect was to reduce the running time by perhaps two minutes but it solved our problem, the show hadn't been too long, it just had a section in it that needed editing out, it wasn't good enough.

Similarly, *The Cardinals* has been subject to editing post-premiere, with the removal of the interval, as already outlined, as well as a steady editing-down of a section representing the Crusades. James recalls that

> the cast were great with this, they kept lobbying for the Crusades section to be cut and I was quite resistant, perhaps because an interest in the

Crusades had been one of the originating ideas for the production, even though the production's focus had moved on I was struggling to let go. Eventually the cast won the argument, presenting their own solution, they were right, the show is a lot more balanced now.

From these examples, we can see how editing is a multiple set of methods adopted at various stages rather than a defined section of the rehearsal process. While there may be a point in the latter stages of rehearsal where editing becomes a conscious process, often instigated by the brinkmanship of time pressures, there are ongoing strategies to cut, connect, expand and reorder material within the ideas phase, the devising process and beyond into the tour of the show and any future iterations it may have.

Directing

James is a man of few words. He thinks he says things to people out-loud which aren't said out loud but his inner monologue is very chatty.

Jack Trow

Extricating directing as a discreet set of strategies from other aspects of rehearsal is particularly fiendish due to the usual suspects that have already been encountered, collaboration and self-effacement, as Hadingue reminds us: 'Narcissism would be a cardinal sin for James.' These qualities are emphasized by James himself:

Trying to keep ego out of directing is key, the best solution needs to go on stage whether it's yours or not, you have to have the humility to listen to other people, consider what they're saying and admit when you are wrong. As a director it's better to admit you're temporarily lost rather than marching on pretending you know where you're going just to save face. If there are five brains it the room it would be stupid to only use one of them to craft the show.

Alongside the role of artistic director, James has been the principal director of productions throughout the history of the company. In the early years, Hadingue played a significant role as a collaborative decision maker and now Stephens is acknowledged as associate director in parallel to his own performance credits. However, while these roles might be initially delineated, they belie the complex symbiosis between the protagonists during rehearsals and so this section of the chapter seeks to synthesize James's own perspective of his directing alongside the directorial experience for the devisor/performers and designers.

Trow's initial contemplation of James's directorial style is indicative of the views of the devisor/performers and designers who perceive James as a quiet but strikingly cogent presence in rehearsals, who selects his comments carefully and nurtures the space for multiple perspectives. Rampal reflects how 'James gives a lot of space for thought, both his own and other peoples. He's a very thoughtful man, creator and director with very clear ideas. But at the same time very open to how that might shift and change.' Trow correspondingly comments that 'he may not seem very approachable but he is. He's in control of his own ideas so feels confident handing them on.' James's own unassuming view echoes this mindset: 'My favourite processes are those in which I feel I am chairing a discussion and bringing people to consensus rather than telling people what to do. Sometimes I feel that the only decision I am making is when to have a break.'

Through their experience, the collaborators have learnt to tune in to the brief but significant insights that James offers rather than expect a continuous commentary or feedback loop on progress. Inherent in this is a shared confidence from all sides that performers within the Stan's Cafe family have the experience and skills to develop the personae (see **Performing**) in the requisite style for each production and, likewise, that long-standing designers inherently understand the aesthetic of the company. Stephens notes that James 'doesn't create a through line for the actors as some directors do and you are encouraged to find your own way'. Ward commented that 'I never knew if he liked anything I did. You just have to think – do I like it?' West has a similarly spartan experience to Ward when creating compositional work: 'James is usually happy – he might say: Can we have that there? but that's all I get from him. He doesn't say – we need strings here or piano as some would.'

The detailed tasks of performance, composition or design are generally left to those who James sees as having those abilities, as Trow points out: 'If you need specific guidance you would have to ask him.' Often the cast are trusted to supervise their own rehearsal work on a show once the key ideas are in place and the theatrical frames have been established. Hadingue reflected that 'there would always come a point near the completion of a piece when James would assume a more conventional director's role, while we concentrated on performing', as emphasized by James himself:

> It is useful to have actors in the company who have worked with other directors as they bring other perspectives with them and help me, I'm just making it up as I go along. I don't really understand the technique of acting and so suspect I am very little help to actors as they try and solve problems on stage. Acting is their job and it would be wrong for me to interfere with that. I admire people who are able to perform in shows they are directing – having distance and outside perspective on the show as it develops feels vital to me, so being in the show as well would feel very difficult, fortunately being a terrible actor I am very rarely tempted onto the stage except in rehearsals, when I love to get up there.

At times, the rehearsal dynamics are so unique that the normal rules of engagement between performers and director shift a few degrees on their axis, as again Hadingue recalls when working with Craig Stephens and James on *Tuning Out with Radio Z* (see **Performing**): 'The three of us spent a lot of time in rehearsals working out the "rules" of the show, and in performance James's role almost became that of a coach rather than a conventional director, as nothing but the rules were fixed.'

The company recognize that James's focus is primarily upon the realization of the idea or concept, as Trow suggests: 'The detail he's interested in is rarely about the acting. It's the concept that matters', a sentiment reinforced with self-deprecation by James himself: 'I think I'm good at big concept stuff and fine detail tinkering. I suspect my only weakness is everything in-between.' Bell conjectures that there is a constant directorial watch over the political ideas within the work, although as noted in **Stan in Context**, politics for Stan's Cafe are more aligned to viewpoints outside of the mainstream, the 'alternative world view' as James phrased it. Bell comments that 'a political eye is kept on the work in the making of it, it's not the aim but its monitored by a political eye. Making sure the message is the right one is important.' To once more appropriate the military analogy, James's is often best situated on a vantage point overlooking the battle, considering strategy and trusting the infantry to carry the fight. However, as he points out, this vantage point is not always a comfortable one to inhabit: 'It can be quite lonely being the director, the actors have their own gang and you necessarily end up a bit separate. They may be in the firing line during shows but at least they can defend themselves, I'm behind enemy lines in the audience, that usually makes me very anxious.'

Although this section has focused on the role of James as director, the multiple layers of directorial decision making must also be emphasized. As noted previously, the performers are always credited as devisors, inherent in which is a constant vigilance to their role in context and their scenographic significance; there is always a sense of looking back upon their own presence on stage. At times, this can induce moments of creative anxiety as devisors invest so much time and energy on the development of the overall piece that individual roles may sometimes be briefly neglected, as Hadingue recalls when working on *Lurid and Insane*: 'I'd been so caught up in trying to create and shape the narrative that I realized, after the first couple of shows, that I'd completely neglected to attend to my own performance as a discreet thing. I just hadn't got around to creating an individual character, and the piece actually needed it.' While the collaborative ethos creates the occasional additional pressure, its overriding effect is to enable those working on a production to have agency over their creation of role and an input to the development of others, framed within the directorial parameters established by James.

A final thought on the future of rehearsal

Throughout the history of the company, the rehearsal methods have evolved organically to respond to the changing interests and strategies of James, as director and instigator of ideas, and the collaborators he has worked with. In this spirit, the methods continue to adapt and mature, and James is suitably iconoclastic when envisaging the future:

> I'm proud of our recent shows, they have been ambitious, but in a calculated kind of way, it feels time for a change, to shake things up a bit, to re-introduce the galvanizing terror of entering the rehearsal room with less. We should lock up the kitchen and ban paper from the rehearsal room, open ourselves up more fully to surprises discovered on our feet in the rehearsal room we should smash up all the chairs we own. The current discomfort has become too comfortable, it's time to rip up the rule book, this book, rip up this book now!

Stan in action: Rehearsing and directing

Now that you're developing your idea, you need to think of approaches to rehearsal that suit that idea. How you choose to shape your rehearsals will in turn shape your show. Here are some approaches we have taken in the past. I can't imagine you using them, but they may prompt you towards developing your own bespoke rehearsals.

1. Have a musician (or DJ) come in to improvise musically while you're doing your acting 'thing'. See what happens; you probably need to agree roughly what you're going to do together but don't plan too much.

We tried this with *Memoirs of an Amnesiac* (1992) and it proved both fun and useful, so we used ideas from this in the show and kept an improvisation sequence in the final piece.

2. Gather a pile of junk objects together for actors to use as props in the show. How the actors use these objects doesn't have to conform to their actual utility; they can be given a fictional history but we're not looking for 'improv' comedy gags here.

   We have used this device with lots of different spins for a number of shows between 1991 and 2001 so it must have some mileage.

3. This is an improvisation prompt we used when making *Ocean of Storms* in 1996 once we knew the idea had some connection with telephones.

   Tear a few sheets of A4-sized paper into wide, narrow bands. On either side of each band write the names/titles/positions of two people who may be talking to each other on the telephone. Remember, this is part of the process of authoring your new play, so use some flair when writing the pairings.

Lottery company phoning a winner	Person who's just been divorced
Boy phoning girl he's shy about asking out	Mother
TV repair engineer	Disgruntled TV viewer
Prisoner	Girlfriend who's been unfaithful
Utilities sales person	Miser
Submariner	Naval commander
Airline pilot	Cabin crew
Car crash victim	Emergency service control room

When you have completed your pairings, tear all the bands in half to separate the two speakers and place one pile in front of each of two performers. The performers now improvise conversations between the two speakers. They are not allowed to tell each other who they are. They should discover this through their conversation. The challenge is not to race to an answer as to who is who as quickly as possible but to enjoy playing with the ambiguity, uncertainty and confusion surrounding these identities. You can take the top scrap of paper from the top of the pile and put it at the bottom whenever you like.

Having gotten good at this form of improvising, now allow the scraps of paper to get out of sequence so the 'wrong' people are speaking to each other. Write down the bits of improvisation you liked or the match-ups you found useful. Build a piece of script from these; at some point you may choose to sit and write it – almost like a playwright.

We came to enjoy this slipping of dialogue and identity so much we have returned to it regularly since then.

4. Try to work out how to perform your whole show without using words.

Dumping words will make you concentrate on non-verbal communication and what the audience can read from what you are doing. Later you can replace the original words with actors saying what the characters are thinking or what their subconscious is saying, what the author is intending or even the mechanical 'housekeeping' stuff the brain never needs to vocalize ('close your fingers on the glass, bring it towards your mouth, open your lips, tilt the glass, swallow').

We regularly see actors saying one thing with their voices while 'saying' the same thing with their bodies. I know this is often thought of as good acting, but for me it is a waste; there is so much redundancy built into this approach. If you've told the audience something, you don't need to show them it as well; why not show them something different? That's a more efficient use of everyone's time.

6

Text

Our shows may have their origins in maths or improvisation, they may never have any words, but they all end up in a written form, a 'script' if you like, it's just sometimes difficult to recognise these scripts as scripts.

James

What's in this chapter?

The purpose of this chapter is to consider what the word *text* means in the context of Stan's Cafe's practice, the multitude of ways in which they use text and the different kinds of text that can be identified in their rehearsal processes and performances. As we have seen in **Ideas**, Stan's Cafe create work from a variety of sources and employ diverse methods so, in this environment, text is a flexible and debatable term. Therefore, the chapter starts with some brief consideration of what the word text has meant historically and how it now locates itself within contemporary performance. This is followed by a reflection on Stan's Cafe's approach to text in this context and an outline of five principle types of text that the company engage with.

Setting the scene

Throughout theatrical history, the written text, usually created by a playwright, has held a dominant position as the perceived genesis for dramatic performance. Even into the early twentieth century, a certain deference persisted for the written text as the source of the

creative process in theatre. Vsevolod Meyerhold (**TW 1**), one of the
most provocative non-realist directors of this period, still advocated the
primacy of the playwright's work in what he referred to as the 'Theatre
of the Straight Line', a process in which the initial written text was
responded to with a vision from the director who then communicated
this to the actors before, finally, they were given the creative freedom to
perform. However, with the emergence of more radical and experimental
movements, including Dada and surrealism, performance-makers
began to explore the potential of creating work from a variety of
artistic stimuli, often far removed from the written play text. With the
development of post-war, avant-garde practices, epitomized by Allan
Kaprow's Happenings (**TW 2**) and Live Art, there was a re-evaluation of
what text could be conceived of. In 1954, Raymond Williams identified
a range of categories to describe the interactions between performance
and text in contemporary practice at that time. For example, he referred
to *Acted Speech*, in which the text significantly prescribes the action on
stage through dialogue and stage directions as opposed to *Activity* or
Behaviour, wherein the text will be subject to significant variations in
interpretation (1991: 162–3). Richard Schechner (**TW 3**) notably made
a distinction between a *dramatic text*, which he defined as 'the play,
script, music score or dance notation that exists prior to being staged'
(2003: 193) and a *performance text*, which is 'everything that takes place
on stage that a spectator experiences, from the movements and speech
of the dancers and/or actors to the lighting, sets, and other technical
or multimedia effects' (ibid.). This latter term highlights the dynamic,
three-dimensional nature of text and how it is constructed, not just on
the page in the form of *dramatic text* but in the live environment of
theatre itself. In this sense, text is not only something to be read through
the written word but is also interpreted through dialogue, physical
practice and the creation of mise en scène[1] (**TW 4**). Likewise, it may be

---

[1] In the **Space and Time** chapter, we propose that the contemporary term – scenography –
    may be a more comprehensive term than mise en scène to describe the staging of devised
    practice such as Stan's Cafe as mise en scène has historically been connected to an
    interpretation of written, dramatic text.

formed and reformed before, during or after the performance has taken place as artists experiment and change their work in rehearsal and in response to director, performer and audience feedback.

Fluidity between the various stages of theatrical production has become the norm as we progress into the twenty-first century and textual forms and the sequencing of the 'writing' process have therefore adapted and multiplied. Duška Radosavljević strongly argues for the dismantling of the binaries that have existed between the page and the stage *and* between written and embodied text. She notes the growing significance of the term 'theatre-maker', which blurs the boundaries between 'late nineteenth and early twentieth century models of division of labour in theatre, namely those of actor, director, playwright, designer etcetera' (2013: 194), and how these shifts prompt an abandonment of 'loyalty' to authorial text. She proposes that the late twentieth century ushered in 'multi-skilled artists capable of an integrated authorial practice which combines writing, acting, composing, directing and design' (ibid.). It is in this context that Stan's Cafe construct their texts as part of a multitextured and often simultaneous set of practices rather than a linear progression from written script through to performance. Even when a script is prepared in advance of rehearsals, as in the case of *The Just Price of Flowers* (2009), it is subject to the critical rigour and continuous modification inherent in the process and performance model adopted by the company.

Stan's Cafe's approach to text

For *me* text is words. I know in our book we need to say it means more than words but for me Text equals Words. 'I'm going to sit down and write some text.' 'We need some text in here to do that job.' 'There's too much text in here, let's strip some out.'

Initially, it may seem that James's definition of text gravitates towards Schechner's notion of *dramatic text*, and certainly the written word is central to his conception. However, unlike the 'straight line' model, James simultaneously embraces a fluid and organic process of text creation that also reflects the spirit of Schechner's *performance text* and Radosavljević's wariness of textual 'loyalty'.

> We are suspicious of the idea of a definitive version of a text, that the author has encoded 'the truth' in the script and that it is the acting company's job to decode that 'truth' for its audience. Playwrights may have opinions about their work but it only springs to life once they've finished and handed it over. We are more likely to use text as a stimulus or raw material, often to move rehearsals on. We may reference a number of existing texts in making a show but as a rule only our original text reaches the stage. We use words to solve problems and when we don't like them we can change them. We can be mean to words. For every show sprinkled with poetry, another will feature words placed under incredible stress or banished entirely.

It was the availability of a comprehensive *performance text* for Impact Theatre Cooperative's production *The Carrier Frequency* (1984) which enabled Stan's Cafe to restage this seminal piece of devised physical theatre as part of Birmingham's *Towards the Millennium* festival in 1999. Although novelist Russell Hoban made the production's spoken text available to the company, unlike a conventional script this text gave no clue as to what was happening on stage during the performance. This information came from a grainy VHS documentation video which allowed the show's physical choreography and mise en scène to be reproduced. The video recording also captured, in very low resolution, the show's powerful and all-enveloping soundtrack; this key element of *performance text* was re-mastered and loaned to Stan's Cafe by one of its original composers, Graeme Miller.

For now, it may be useful to think of a Stan's Cafe text as the ongoing written articulation of a specific production, a distillation of ideas and process into prose, poetry, dialogue and instruction yet interwoven with, and respondent to, the mutability of their artistic practice. Sometimes this may manifest itself as a pre-existing text

Figure 6.1 Jake Oldershaw centre stage with Charlotte Vincent and Graeme Rose in a large pool of water, performing *The Carrier Frequency* (1999). Atop the scaffolding platforms, Heather Burton, Cait Davies and Mike Kirchner moan.

waiting to be adapted; at times it may be generated at speed for the rehearsal room or develop as a carefully written record of the emergent performance, a means of documentation and recollection in the future. To an extent, then, this answers what the word text means in relation to how it manifests itself, but that is only part of the picture. To really understand the texts of Stan's Cafe also requires recognition of how the company's ethos informs their creation. While, later in this chapter, we will outline specific text types that they utilize, it is the underlying collaborative principles of the rehearsal process and the artists within it that determine how and why these texts disclose themselves in particular forms. Sarah Archdeacon, recalling the first few years of the company, highlights the supportive climate that was intrinsic to the working methodology: 'A strength of the practice, in retrospect, is how, even though James may have taken himself away to construct and write things, he welcomed us into that process. We felt valued and empowered by that and all our roles were respected.' A common thread to all the conversations for this book has been the significance of the open dialogue within the rehearsal process and the ongoing discourse of revision and refinement that is encouraged even after a show has started to tour.

A central feature of this collaboration is the openness to collective role development rather than a focus on individual creativity, and there has always been an emphasis on sharing material generated by any given person in discussion or practical rehearsal. Performers, in the rehearsal stage, see their foremost role as devisors, whereby all decisions as to who should perform any specific line or action are made on the basis of what best serves the production. In this environment, text and its distribution are a group responsibility. Craig Stephens encapsulates this egalitarianism:

> You have an emotional investment in the content of the show as much as you have in your personal performance. In relation to *Good and True* for example we would record the improvisations and watching them back you'd see that you'd come up with some 'hilarious' bit and then it would just be carved up. 'You have that bit; you have that bit.' You might get somebody else's 'bit' and try to make that work.

This interchangeability of text from one performer to another is often facilitated by the significance of non-narrative dialogue and the exploration of physical and visual practice. Their methodology has almost always centred on the presentation of roles or personae (see **Performing**) rather than characters and as a result, there is far less emphasis on the personal, individuated construction of identities on stage. Comparing this approach to the traditional loyalty to authorial text, James wryly notes: 'Identities are often slippery so text is also slippery. I couldn't imagine actors in *A View from a Bridge* saying "I think it would work better if I said your line here and you said my line there."'

This fluency is underscored by the appropriation of various, and at times tangential, texts to create dialogue, such as tourist phrase books mined for *Be Proud of Me*, to articulate the tension between language and expression. Allied to this are many shows where the visual narrative either partially or entirely replaces dialogue and hence the strategy of sharing or transferring who embodies an image, performs a movement sequence, follows a task or speaks the text has greater credence when it is the overall mise en scène and the communication of the theatrical idea that are the overriding objectives.

Text types

In reference to the specific texts of Stan's Cafe, it is possible to identify a few prominent types that reoccur throughout their history. The names we have given to these text types seem the most germane to describe what these texts do and/or where they originate. This is not intended as a definitive list and there are fluid boundaries between each, so that in any given show there may be more than one text type 'in play' and one type may modify itself into another type at any given point. However, it is possible and worthwhile to find some delineation between them as it accentuates and affirms the diversity and complexity of the texts Stan's Cafe develop. The first to be considered is *organic text*, which correlates closely with Schechner's notion of a *performance text*. It is not reliant on an initial written script and is predominantly created through improvisation, trial and error and the dialogue within the ensemble. This 'writing of text' may be done by James or the cast to serve particular needs in a devising process. *Organic text* has been pivotal to many shows including *Ocean of Storms* (1996), *Good and True* (2000), *Be Proud of Me* (2003) and *Home of the Wriggler* (2006). **Notational text** is often generated in response to *organic text* as there is a requirement in the latter stages of rehearsal to fix and document the process as a reference for the director and performers on tour or in subsequent restagings. In these instances, a final draft of the blocking and dialogue will be compiled and notated. **Instructional text** refers to the detailed, possibly time-coded performances that are written in a spreadsheet or task list format. These will indicate activities and timings that performers need to adhere to. This was a format that James experimented with at university and revisited on a large scale for *Twilightofthefreakingods* (2013). **Pure, written texts** correspond with Schechner's concept of a *dramatic text* as they are written prior to the start of a project and form the basis of the rehearsals. This method has been adopted occasionally throughout Stan's Cafe's history, from their first full production *Perry Como's Christmas Cracker* (1991) to *The Just Price of Flowers* (2009) and, more recently, in *The Anatomy of Melancholy* (2013). Finally, throughout the chapter, we offer the idea of **source texts** as a means of highlighting the multitude of usually non-dramatic texts that are written, adapted or appropriated as source material or inspiration for shows. These can be found sources, such as the phrase books referred to above, or PAYE tax codes used as astronaut 'speak' in *Ocean of Storms* or specifically written to provoke or inform shows but never directly used in performance, such as with *Voodoo City* (1995).

All these types of text will be looked at in detail in this chapter but for now here is a brief summary:

- **Organic text** – a performance text, generated through improvisation, trial and error and the dialogues of the ensemble.
- **Notational text** – a written record, in 'script form' made in the latter stages of rehearsal that documents the **organic text** in its final or most advanced stage.
- **Instructional text** – a written text, sometimes in a spreadsheet format or a set of rules, indicating tasks and timings for the performers to undertake.
- **Pure, written text** – texts written prior to the start of rehearsals.
- **Source texts** – these are the texts that inspire the final productions, either by providing material to be directly adapted or appropriated, or as original material written during the process intended to inform but not be directly referenced in the performance.

Organic text

In the rehearsal process, both *performance* and *dramatic texts* have often been generated in tandem to develop the work. In these conditions, text is an organic structure that is not just the end product but is also a creative tool in its own right, acting as a feedback loop to inform the development of a production. This type of text development was particularly in evidence in the earlier years of the company, when improvisation was the primary rehearsal technique, but is still applied to this day in their practice if it is the best 'tool' for a particular theatrical idea, as James identifies:

> As an example of how text may develop, I might give the actors improvisation tasks, listen to them making stuff up, absorb that, maybe jot down some phrases and then in the evening start writing. The next morning the actors would start working with the text I've written, drawing on their words and then we all suggest changes, new words, phrases, things to cut out, swap around or re-distribute. I might then polish this up again, feeding it back a second time and then that draft gets worked over again.

Amanda Hadingue echoes this organic approach in her recollections of early shows, including *Ocean of Storms* and *Home of the Wriggler*.

> Improvisation has been completely central to Stan's Cafe. In *Home of the Wriggler* we were improvising for a while but we weren't really getting anything from it so James went away and wrote parts of it, which was fine. You just need to find the right vehicle, the right language for each show. Those early shows, *Bingo [in the House of Babel]*, *Voodoo City*, *Ocean of Storms and Good and True* that was all material generated from improvisation pretty much. James sometimes had lumps of poetic text (we were all avoiding script writing!) or he would write up a script afterwards, such as with *Ocean of Storms*, based on the improvisations and the rules he had set us. Then we'd go back and improvise again, layering like filo pastry, then he'd re-write and so on.

Ocean of Storms is a productive example to focus on as it employed a range of *source texts* interwoven with *organic text* which, layer by layer, became cemented as the *notational text*. The piece, exploring ideas of home, proximity and intimacy, was inspired by the rich metaphoric

Figure 6.2 Amanda Hadingue as one of the two quasi-angels who scan the airwaves for voices in *Ocean of Storms* (1996).

potential of space travel and used a loose narrative of two quasi-angels searching for a small girl, in a silver puffer jacket, lost in a city. This narrative is interlaced with the parallel story of an astronaut who is attempting to make a perilous journey back to earth. 'By moving the stars in the heavens that people navigate by, these angels can nudge the course of events enough to bring both the astronaut and young girl safely back home,' as James expressed it at the time.

One of the original *source texts* for the production was a fictional diary written by James on the 11C orbital bus route around Birmingham, which he had taken as an initial analogy for orbital space flight. He recalls how he 'bought a ticket and sat upstairs on the front port side seat and imagined I was an astronaut in a space ship orbiting the earth. I wrote an astronaut's diary, filtering everything I saw through this lens. I locked into a poetic mode, did two loops (four hours) on the bus and filled a small book with scribble.' This was then edited down and used as either inspiration for the show or polished and quoted within it. For example, the central figure of the girl in a silver puffer jacket was one of the actual observations James made en-route.

Other *source texts* that James authored for Hadingue and Archdeacon to improvise with were merely slips of paper with eclectic job roles or character descriptions written on them – Pope, mechanic, astronaut, TV repair engineer, lost child and so forth. Initially these scraps of text were used to create telephone dialogue between creditable pairings – Pope/Cardinal, etc. – but failed to elicit anything of note until, as James recalls:

> We weren't generating any material worthy of going in the show until one day, coming back from a lunch break, something went wrong with our system. The stacks of paper got out of sequence and now The Pope is talking to a Garage Mechanic assuming he's a Cardinal. The mechanic in turn thinks the Pope is ready to pick up his VW Polo. Then The Pope ends up talking to an Astronaut, who in turn talks to a School Child whose mother is seriously ill, who talks to a Late Night DJ and so on. Suddenly these conversations were riveting. They were surreal and hilarious but more excitingly they were occasionally very moving. We had stumbled on something we very much liked, something worthy of building a show around. We recorded the improvisations and I remembered bits and we spliced bits together, wrote fresh bits and linking bits.

One of the central writing challenges for *Ocean of Storms* was generating convincing 'astronaut speak'. At that time, James remembers that he was embroiled in Stan's Cafe's administration and navigating his way through the PAYE tax system. It occurred to him that the instructions for filling in all the tax codes bore a close relationship to the typed spiral bound books of instructions followed in the Apollo astronaut's conversation with mission control. He remembers how the phraseologies seemed to overlap:

> Check this reading, switch that on, move to this next step – and my tax code books were saying: *'In the case of this being more than that use Emergency Code B – sub section 4, put this value in that box, multiply it by this constant from that table and detach section C'.* I cannibalised

that text, changed a few words and added a bit of 'OK – will do' and it was ready to be used.

In examples such as this, it is evident how eclectic *source texts* become absorbed into the *organic* rehearsal text.

Now, with intermeshing phone conversations, Birmingham orbital poetry and tax code space speak, they were able to experiment with blending the three text strands across each other. They started with pure phone conversations, then fed in the astronauts followed by references to the child and finally removed the initial phone calls. These were interspersed with blocks of poetry from the orbital diaries. As the crisis developed, these strands weaved much more closely together. This sample of the text is from the latter stages of the performance:

A   We daren't bring you back Jo

S   I want a chance to hold my girl again

A   she sees a bus coming

S   Low slung sky line, industrial spaces, a helicopter hovers

A   It's too risky Jo

S   she's searching in her pockets for the fare

A   Jo, just sit tight

S   I'm going with Brown 6a (19 96) customised

A   She wears a silver jacket pockets and paper shred tissues

S   Reading down with K codes, 53, 57, 11, 48 and 352L

A   OK Jo, I don't want you going crazy out there, let me get some
     figures together

S   I'm reading them off now Al

A Hold on Jo that's 53, 57, 11

S 48 and 352L, I'm skipping to P11

A P11 let's see, that's readings on tables LR + B to D

S check
check
check

A mascara

S check

A silver coin in a dirty hand

S check

A splashes in a puddle

S That's all systems bar SSP, DA and NIC one hundred PC
That's set, looks like we're all set

Notational text

There comes a point in each production when the creative work of the devising process needs to be documented as a means of capturing an agreed version of the performance to be studied and referenced by the actors and, if need be, returned to as the text to be edited during production tours. These are also then available for future iterations of the show if it is required to tour again in the future, and particularly if new actors are brought into the cast and have no knowledge of the original devising process. For these reasons, it is necessary to distil the original organic text into a notated version. However, these may take many forms, from a relatively traditional play script through to instructions for actors or a spreadsheet, which will be looked at specifically as an *instructional text* later.

The Cleansing of Constance Brown (2007) required just such a conversion from a physical set of devised sequences into a coherent written format. The production's central design concept was a 14-metre-long, 2-metre-wide corridor with seven doors on either side, within which a variety of brief narratives were created, each exploring the notion of cleansing. These stories spanned several centuries, from a corporate collapse in which bank records were expunged to a Jewish family fleeing persecution in Nazi Germany, and a climactic image of Elizabeth Tudor being transformed from prisoner to Queen Elizabeth I via a symbolic washing of face and hands. Barring a few words, the piece was non-verbal, which accentuated the challenge of creating a lucid and logical scripted version, as James highlights:

> There was a need to document what we had already created in the rehearsal space. We had used video to capture improvisations in the early days and worked up our favourite bits from this. For a while the whole show merely existed in our collective memories, but the aural tradition only gets you so far. If you want a precise replication, then writing it down starts to help. Our challenge was how to most elegantly notate what is essentially a massive list of stage directions. The world of dance must have this challenge all the time. I've no idea how they do it. We labelled the doors A – G downstage left to upstage left and numbers 1–7 downstage right to upstage right. Each move was then numbered so we could refer to Scene 3 Move 5 for an adjustment to the lighting and so on.

03: The President's arrival

Door 1 is fire exit

Door B is lift

Door 6 president's room.

1. Gerard vacuums out of 6 and down corridor.
2. Bernadette & Craig with sheets from 1 to 6 then leave.

3. Jake with bottles of water and glasses from 1 to 6 then leave.
4. Bernadette with wrapped painting from 1 to 6.
5. Graeme with 2 × aluminium suitcases from B to 6.
6. Jan & Craig as security from B to 6.
7. Craig is posted outside 6, Jan goes in.

This extract highlights the fact that Stan's Cafe texts are often notations of action, as much as records of dialogue, and numeric formats are used on a regular basis for precise codification. However, while there is a need to format the work in writing, this does not preclude the capacity to make ongoing changes. James emphasizes the point that, although there is a need for the script to solidify near to performance, 'if we see a better way of doing something we're not afraid to change it close to the opening night and of course once the show has opened we understand it in a whole new way and this may provoke significant changes as well'. In this context, the term 'loyalty', as employed earlier by Radosavljević, can be reframed in reference to the allegiance Stan's Cafe have to the integrity of the work and their vigilance in returning to the *organic* and *notational texts*, even when the initial devising period has concluded.

Instructional text

Exceptionally, a few Stan's Cafe performances prove so extreme in their ambition or constrained in their production that their performance texts are pre-written, but with instructions for physical performance replacing words to be spoken.

The most ambitious text of this type to date has been *Twilightof-thefreakingods* (2013), which required a vast spreadsheet of instructions and timings in order to communicate the four-and-a-quarter hours of Wagner-inspired action for a cast of eleven to perform without rehearsal. The structuring of this text took its inspiration from the production entitled *Infected* that James had created while at Lancaster

University in 1988 which, partly due to his fascination with the practice of Robert Wilson and partly due to a lack of access to rehearsal space, was created using instructions for actors that could be followed and presented to an audience without any need to rehearse. The performance was written out as a series of timelines and stage maps outlining tasks rather than narrative arcs. Again, as with transferability of text, the potential to adopt such a format was facilitated by a non-realist style which emphasized presentation rather than character portrayal, as James clarifies: 'The show was about the sculptural movement of bodies in space, so the actors didn't have to emote, interact or even act in a classical way, they could just follow instructions. No actor even knew what any other actor was doing before they did it.'

In 2013, Stan's Cafe were in the process of relinquishing the majority of their performance space @AE Harris and were looking to bid it farewell with a dramatic new production. An obvious candidate for this show was an idea, previously rejected by a major German theatre festival, which would collide Wagner's *Götterdämmerung* with the lurid televisual *source* text of *Jeux Sans Frontières* (1965–99), a bizarre pan-European game show with a penchant for dressing contestants in giant foam puppet costumes. James saw this as

> a perfect collision of low and high culture. Having human actors struggling under the weight of these outsize heroes Siegfried and Brunhilde, seemed like a metaphor ripe for exploitation. The opera has a brilliant title both in the original German and in translation and the cataclysmic way The Ring Cycle ends felt like a suitably playful way to say goodbye to our big venue.

The extremely limited budget available for this almost impromptu production forced the company to substitute a bouncy castle for the giant inflatable costumes originally envisaged and also necessitated a highly radical approach to staging what should be a vast opera.

Twilightofthefreakingods stripped all the music and singing from *Götterdämmerung*, replacing them with a new soundtrack mixed live by regular collaborator Nina West. Character and plot were retained from Wagner's story and the timings of George Solti's famous 1966 recording of the opera defined how long each scene should be and when key plot points should take place. Intriguingly, his recording runs very close to four-and-a-quarter hours, the same duration as *Infected* twenty-five years earlier. James entered these timings directly onto a spreadsheet.

Every minute of the show was entered down the Y-axis and all thirteen characters (Wagner's ten principle characters plus three Machinists[2]) run across the top of the X-axis. With plot and incident already defined, the writing process became straightforward, setting out in each cell where each character needed to be on stage at any given time and what they needed to be doing there. From this master spreadsheet, I prepared thirteen individual instruction sheets, one for each performer (in the same way a conductor's score is divided up into the parts for each musician). Key to the performer's job was memorizing their instructions in order to be able to perform without referring to them on stage. All performers met each other for the first time an hour before the premiere performance.

An extract from Brunhilde's script *Twilightofthefreakingods*:

21:38 Reach out for ring.

21:39 Beat chest.

21:40 Turn around and crouch down.

21:41 When the fabric has covered you exit orange mass and into the courtyard.

21:43 Enter Asia from Australia.

21:44 Rest on sofa #2

21:53 Leave via Australia at America/Courtyard door get into the boat.

21:54 Look majestic.

22:12 Step off boat, helped by Gunther.

22:13 Look around mystified.

---

[2] Dressed in the trademark housecoats of *Of All The People In All The World* (2003), these Machinists were originally conceived as performing stage managers but their roles evolved to carry a more sinister edge as they became the industrial future that awaited the artistic world once Valhalla had gone up in flames (A. E. Harris Ltd has now got the space back from Stan's Cafe).

22:14 Start to tremble.
22:15 Point at Siegfried and Gutrune.
22:16 Point to yourself (I am your wife).

Looking at this sample of the script on the page, it might appear at first glance to be a prescriptive text, denuded of performer autonomy, and a reduction of theatre to a set of constituent, mechanical parts. However, what it facilitates and promotes is a structured environment and controlled scenographic framework within which the performers are forced to improvise solutions to basic instructions and the audience are given extended time, reflecting the influence of Robert Wilson and the cinema of Andrei Tarkovsky **(TW 5)**, to interpret an elusive visual narrative. This confidence in mathematical structures as a schema for complex, artistic works reflects James's wider influences, including the musical compositions of Steve Reich and the geometric and linear pop art of Bridget Riley. He succinctly refers to this *instructional* style of text as 'complexity out of simplicity'.

Although *Twilightofthefreakingods* has been the most ambitious example of *instructional text*, there have been several other productions that have made use of this style, including *Simple Maths* (1997) and, to an extent, *The Cardinals* (2011). *Simple Maths* was performed by five people seated in different configurations on six chairs while rotating through five emotional states. Archdeacon, one of the original performers of the show, referred to it as 'an enfolding of situations and circumstances'. There were no words so the text was just stage directions, and the most expedient way to record these was to draw up a table. There is a 'move number' in the left-hand column, then six columns for the chairs (where there is a record of who is sat in each chair and what their emotional state is); a seventh column carries notes of other dramatic moments (like 'Sarah blows her nose', etc.). The 'mathematical' pattern of performers changing seats overlaid with a second, simple pattern of changing emotional states created a third, more complex pattern that, unbidden, generated narrative readings from its audience. Another production in which verbal text remained absent for almost the entirety

Figure 6.3 Sarah Archdeacon, Craig Stephens, Jake Oldershaw, Nick Walker and Amanda Hadingue standing and sitting in the minimalist performance *Simple Maths* (1997).

was *The Cardinals* and, in this case (although the text was developed through devising as *notational*) for Rochi Rampal, who arrived as a late replacement performer, the script was more akin to *instructional*. She recalls receiving her copy of the text: 'The script I got was a spreadsheet. *This is the cue for this, this piece of scenery drops here, this backdrop is for this scene*, all along like that. I'd never had a spreadsheet as a script before! It's a very clear and efficient way of outlining how things work.'

Aside from mathematical spreadsheets, other shows have been run using *instructional texts* to guide performers through tasks. *Of All The People In All The World* has a specific set of Performer Notes which outline the context of the show, followed by guidance on costume, performance mode, weighing and displaying the rice and finding the statistics. This is the section entitled *Performance Mode*:

> Perhaps the best way to describe the performance style is that we are ourselves but with purpose and concentration. So when weighing out or tidying or walking around the space we are focused on the task. It's a bit like working in a museum or art gallery but there will always be tasks to perform beyond simply standing guard. We're not pretending

to be other people though so you don't have to put on a funny voice if visitors ask questions.

Be prepared to answer questions and if you can't answer ask someone who might be able to. Audience members might ask for their personal statistics to be included so record the details in a notebook ready to prepare the statistic.

In total, the Performer Notes are only four pages long, for a show that can last eight hours a day and might be staged for three weeks at festivals. Audiences encountered their own *instructional text* when experiencing the various *Step Series* (2009 onwards), which had a set of maps and instructions of where to go in a location and what may be observed. When arriving at specific locations along the way, they would have to interpret the symbols on the ground to decipher how to embody a certain scene, such as with *Shakespeare's Steps* (2016), set in Stratford-upon-Avon, which involved 'imagined moments from Shakespeare's life in the town'. This diversity of *instructional* text underlines the Stan's Cafe approach to finding the pertinent 'fit' for each show by locating what would be the most effective means of evoking specific theatrical action in a text.

Pure, written texts

As James reminded us, when considering devising methods you have to 'look at the job and choose the tools'. Sometimes the best tool is a text written in advance (in the case of *The Anatomy of Melancholy*, four hundred years in advance) of the rehearsal process. There have been various reasons why the company have opted for this approach but it always comes down to what the theatrical idea requires, as Graeme Rose simply puts it: 'Choosing the right form for the right content.' So methodology that may have driven the last production may be immediately put to one side if it does not meet the demands of the next project. This can be seen in the creation of *The Just Price of*

Flowers, which followed on from some of the most successful devised shows of that decade, including *The Cleansing of Constance Brown*. The piece was a response to the banking crisis of 2008, reframing that hysteria through the historical lens of Dutch 'tulip mania' during the early seventeenth century in which merchants wildly speculated on the price of tulip bulbs until the market collapsed. Rose considers it to be 'one of the most beautifully articulated shows, by displacing that issue and logic to a different time and place it expressed complex issues to which the public are, by and large, blinded. I see it as one of Stan's most successful shows.' The articulation of this idea required the careful structuring of a narrative that explains the development of complex financial devices through a tulip metaphor, which in turn required historical detail and a carefully deployed Brechtian aesthetic; arriving at such a text through devising promised to be both unlikely and inefficient. James recalls that 'about a week before we were due to start our two week devising process for *The Just Price of Flowers* I realised it was going to be way too complicated to devise, so I sat down and started writing it, then we worked as an ensemble on how to stage my writing'.

Serbian playwright and festival director Nenad Prokić **(TW 6)** set Stan's Cafe a radically different challenge when, in 2002, he suggested the company stage *The Anatomy of Melancholy* by Robert Burton, originally published in 1621. James sets out the problem they finally faced up to ten years later:

> This three volume, 1500 page, 400-year-old book is essentially an encyclopaedic self-help manual. So although we did start the process with a written text it wasn't a performance text and wasn't even a story, as a result we had to do a lot of work in the rehearsal room editing this monster into a script. This process was unlike anything we had previously engaged in.

Rose, one of the original devisors and performers for the show, recalls that the book 'resisted being dramatized'. Although early plans had

Figure 6.4 Valerie Cutko as Floristien and Jack Trow as Husband in *The Just Price of Flowers* (2009).

been to add contemporary dialogue to set the book in context, James soon realized that this would be a mistake as

> the key to this project was the challenge of 'staging the book'. I had thought we would need to add contemporary references to keep the audience hooked but I quickly realised (on actually sitting down and reading the thing) that much of it already feels very contemporary already, added our own contemporary words would have spoilt the purity of the project and undermined extraordinary brilliance of the original book.

This decision led to an exhaustive period of textual editing to condense the 1,500 pages into a three-hour show which is framed as Burton adapting and editing his own book for the stage, aided by three fellow academics. In 2014, Stan's Cafe turned the tables on Prokić, commissioning him to write *Finger Trigger Bullet Gun,* his first play in fifteen years and the first *pure written text* written for the company by someone other than James.

Figure 6.5 Gerard Bell as Robert Burton, with his assistants 'vegetal' Graeme Rose, 'sensitive' Rochi Rampal and 'rational' Craig Stephens in *The Anatomy of Melancholy* (2013).

Conclusion

The approach to text for *The Anatomy of Melancholy* illuminates an important distinction to be made between respect and deference in Stan's Cafe's practice. The company pay great respect to existing *written texts,* be they scripts written by playwrights or historic *source texts* from which they adapt material. Unlike more traditional modes of theatre creation, though, there is no particular deference towards preexisting texts or to any sense of their pre-eminence ahead of devised material or non-conventional text such as *organic* or *instructional.* The development of their texts is rooted in the necessities of the performance and what each new show demands in terms of its production process.

A final word in this chapter must go to two types of text which as yet have gone unmentioned, but reflect the close, collaborative nature of Stan's Cafe practice. When talking to actors about their performance experience, they would often refer to what might be called **secret text** and **survival text** created for many of the visual and physically demanding shows, such as *The Cleansing of Constance Brown*. *Secret texts* are often created when actors meet on stage and exchange whispered conversations, inaudible to the audience. Performers say that it helps them create their own private context for the narrative and they never feel the need to tell James, who only discovered the practice one day when standing in for an absent actor during a technical rehearsal. *Secret Texts* are also created privately by individual actors seeking a path through a poetic, non-narrative show to give their personal performance an internal coherence as the coherence for the audience comes from that actor's placement within the wider scenography (see **Performance**). *Survival text* refers to the additional notes added to the *notational text* by the performers to assist themselves and new cast members in navigating their way through a complex routine of tasks. James calls this 'private, backstage choreography', and has often noticed additions to scripts that read along the lines of 'put tights on here, open that door then, put skirt on now, take so and so's bag then, find suitcase under that table then and enter door B'. These adaptations, born of camaraderie and necessity, are a reminder that texts, in the hands of Stan's Cafe, are always seen as flexible 'tools for the job'.

Stan in action: Text

So now you need to write something for your show. Of course, you could just sit down and write it and that would be great, but maybe you could surprise yourself or stretch yourself or make things easier for yourself by not approaching dramatic writing in such a prosaic manner. Reference was made above to the Inland Revenue/Space Talk from *Ocean of Storms*. Here are three other approaches we've used.

Constricted language: Trying to say what's beyond words

Collect as many tourist phrase books as possible by a mix of publishers. Using just the English phrases from these books, try writing the following scenes (you will have to be inventive and the performers will have to be resourceful to make the script work):

- A stranger arrives and explains they are an alien from another planet and comes in peace to rule Earth.
- Someone goes to the police to confess to a murder.
- A scientist tries to persuade a politician that action is taken against global warning.
- A child tells a parent they suspect they have been adopted.

Notice how it is very difficult to talk about the past – what strategies does this force you into? How do you cope with the multiple options offered by the phrase book style? It is easy for scenes generated in this way to be comic, but these stimuli are designed to encourage you to explore other tones.

Be Proud of Me was made with this as our central approach to text. We built this up in the rehearsal room, writing/compiling the text one moment and trying it out in practice the next, then making adjustments. Ultimately we ended up intercutting this very restricted language with much more relaxed semi-improvised dialogue.

Reading one thing as another

Find a text that contains lots of instructions or advice, such as a car repair manual, a DIY or cookery book, a management guru inspiration book, a new age 'well-being' book or a book on how to perform medical procedures (presumably these exist). Write the following scenes using as many phrases from your source text as possible:

- A couple whose relationship is in crisis
- A CEO whose company faces bankruptcy
- A doctor or psychiatrist treating a patient

As with lots of these exercises, this material could 'just' be funny, but try to make it more than that; wring pathos, frustration or terror from the inadequacy of the language used.

In *Home of the Wriggler*, a car maintenance manual explains how to put a life back together, and in *Made Up*, a make-up artist's tutorial for removing a prosthetic scar spoke of how to heal emotional damage.

Just write dialogue and don't worry too much about who is present in the scene

Just write lines that people say, with a little dash in the margin to say someone new has started speaking. Later, go back and allocate lines to people, or don't bother; let the actors fight it out between them in the rehearsal room.

7

Space and Time

What's in this chapter?

This chapter confronts two of the fundamentals of theatre: space and time. These are inescapable dimensions of performance and Stan's Cafe make particular demands upon them, exploring their elasticity and the limits of their tolerances. The two elements are inextricably linked in theatre, but it is possible to briefly extricate them from one another while acknowledging their symbiosis. The chapter begins with a concise context of theatrical space and time through specific theoretical lenses as a means of framing the company's experimentation with both the material boundaries of spatio-temporality *and* its conceptual potential. These lenses are then applied to specific analyses of spatial and then temporal qualities within the company's work. The chapter concludes with James reuniting space and time in a detailed study of their interrelated significance in *The Cleansing of Constance Brown* (2007).

Setting the scene

Space and time are undoubtedly slippery words and if not examined carefully they will be of little use to us when applied in a performance context. One certainty is that both are ubiquitous elements within theatre, and ever since Aristotle **(TW 1)** proposed the three unities of *action, time and place*, they have always been centralized and even fetishized as its touchstones. It is certainly arguable that while most other elements of theatre could be jettisoned – performers may be absent, design may be forgotten, audiences may come and go – the event itself will always exist in space and time. There are certain theoretical propositions detaching space from time, notably from the French philosopher Henri Bergson who argued that we should 'un-mix' time and space in order to engage with our own consciousness as temporal, but from a theatrical perspective, *our* position is that one is grounded upon the other. This is reinforced by David Wiles in *Theatre and Time* (2014), who proposed: 'Time only exists when we measure and count it, and we can only count something that changes according to a regular measure. That counting is not done in the mind but through a living body, and bodies are only alive when they pulsate' (15). In theatre, time manifests itself through the performers who exist in and function through space; conversely, their performances and the objects and environments they engage with are inscribed with time, chronological and conceptual.

In empirical terms, space can be measured in height, width and depth, while time can be quantified within chronological calculations. However, these rudimentary material descriptions have been frequently deconstructed and augmented by theatre and cultural theorists, both in terms of how they manifest themselves but also how we perceive and think about them. Lars Elleström (2010) **(TW 2)** proposed what is now an influential theory of media deconstruction and intermediality within which he considered the structures and significances of spatio-temporality. Ellestrom identifies that all media, including art forms, consist of a framework of both real and virtual dimensions. In this sense, the actual height, width and depth of space or the chronological sequence and pace of time are intensified and affected by our perception and interpretation of them. How we 'read' a photograph or painting, for example, is affected by our preconceived notions of space, scale or suggestions of motion within what is essentially an immobile fragment of time. Likewise, temporality collapses and expands in theatre every time we are asked to conceive of many years elapsing in the simplest of scene changes. This interpretative process is informed by our cultural context, so our engagements with space and time are always a complex interplay between our initial sensory perceptions and our capacity to interpret them.

At the outset, it is worth remembering the spatial and temporal significances that have already been referred to earlier in the book. In **Stan in Context**, Birmingham was acknowledged as a particular space of creative impetus for Stan's Cafe; therefore, the relationship between the social dynamics of the city and the artistic ethos of the company is inextricably intertwined, as Graeme Rose puts it: 'Birmingham has a reputation as an unpretentious place and that is suspicious of high art, and that had, and still has a grounding effect on what Stan does.' Likewise, Amanda Hadingue reflected that 'there was something about the city that was always present in the shows, sometimes literally with the bus route in *Ocean of Storms*, but the environments we created always seemed to reflect it'. However, a concurrent recurring theme, as was previously noted in **Ideas,** was the suspension of performances in extraspatial and extratemporal situs, resonant of Foucault's heterotopias. There is already, then, an interesting dualism here between the grounding effects of the city and a desire to place the work beyond the realms of distinct physical and temporal boundaries. This creative counterbalance between the reality of the urban and industrial city *and* the conceptual potential of suspended space-time was particularly resonant as the company sought to establish themselves. 'We were trying to capture the mundanity of everyday life in the city' as Rose puts it 'and recontextualize by putting a more grandiose frame around it, so offering new meaning to the mundane. That juxtaposition excited us and the resulting bathos was an important element in the work.'

Space

In terms of the mechanical dimensions of space, Stan's Cafe have frequently experimented with scale, from the claustrophobic intimacy of *It's Your Film* (1998) and *The Black Maze* (2000) through to large-scale work including the industrial workshops of *Of All The People In All The World* (2003) and *Twilightofthefreakingods* (2013), as well as those editions of the *Step Series* which have unfolded across shopping centres, arts campuses, parks and city streets.

Alongside its dimensional attributes, the potency of conceptual space has long been of equal fascination to theorists and theatre practitioners. Tadeuz Kantor, the Polish theatre-maker (**TW 3**), notably stated that

> Space is not a passive receptacle
> In which objects and forms are posited....
> SPACE itself is an OBJECT (of creation).
> And the main one!
>
> (1993: 217)

Henri Lefebvre, the renowned French philosopher, argued in *The Production of Space* (1991) that all space is socially constructed and that theatre is a *representational* space within which complex symbolisms manifest themselves. David Wiles, summarizing Lefebvre's proposition, stated: 'Space is *social*, for each society produces its own space, a space simultaneously mental and physical. Space is always *produced*, in the sense that it is always a set of relationships, never a given, never inert or transparent, never in a state of nature untouched by culture' (2003: 10). Lefebvre set out a typology of spaces, including the idea of 'counter-spaces' which he envisaged as spaces of resistance 'against quantity and homogeneity, against power and the arrogance of power, against the endless expansion of the "private" and of industrial profitability' (1991: 382). This potency of theatre as a 'counter-space' has long been recognized by the company; the possibility to engage audiences with ethical and political questions through narratives that subtly run counter to current trends or received wisdoms.

Robert Wilson has remained an ever-present influence on Stan's Cafe and his view of the stage as what he often referred to as a 'time/space construction' can be seen reflected in how the company visually craft their productions. Events are framed with the 'eye' of a painter, so that space, the relationship between bodies and objects and the interplay of light and darkness are central to the concept. Consideration is always given to the conceptual spatial frames in terms of how the event is to be conceived by an audience. James and the actors often refer to the extensive rehearsal discussions which focus on how to frame the ideas within productions: *In what spatial context are we seeing them? Are the audience acknowledged in this 'shared space'?*

These increasingly sophisticated approaches to thinking about space are also reflected in the greater emphasis on the practice of scenography rather than mise en scène in the work of theatre-makers devising their own original material through process-led methodologies. Where mise en scène carries connotations of interpreting an extant written text, the practice of scenography is more dynamic, as Pamela Howard sets out in *What Is Scenography?* (2002): 'Scenography is the seamless synthesis of space, text, research, art, actors, directors and spectators that contributes to an original creation' (130). Scott Palmer suggests that

> the term is replacing that of 'theatre design' and has come to represent the complex inter-relationships between space, object, material, light and sound that define the space and place of performance ... the term advocates a more active intervention and a holistic approach to design for performance in which the design of space is central – a space created for performing bodies to interact with rather than against. (2011: 52)

Allied to this, theatre continually absorbs the practices of related art forms in how it utilizes and creates meaning through bodies in space. For example, the *static* temporality (to use Elleström's term) of still images and the heightened spatial relationships these emphasize have been adopted for many years within the framing of tableaux by practitioners, notably Robert Wilson, whose performers often move slowly and precisely from one defined pictorial moment to the next. Hans-Thies Lehmann **(TW 5)** notes that

> Wilson's theatre is a primary example for the use of frames. A bit like in baroque art, everything begins and ends here – with framings. Framing effects are produced, for example, by special lighting surrounding the bodies, by geometrical fields of light defining their places on the

floor, by the *sculptural precision* of the gestures and the heightened concentration of the actors that have a 'ceremonial' and thus again framing effect. (2006: 151)

Time

There has been an ongoing obsession with time in theatre in terms of its capacity to embody the uniqueness of the experience. From major figures including Peter Brook to Jerzy Grotowski, and Peggy Phelan to Simon McBurney, the *co-presence* of performer and audience is celebrated as theatre's defining feature. McBurney, the artistic director of Complicite theatre company, unequivocally stated: 'Theatre has a special relationship with time that no other art form has, in that it exists in the present, and human beings have a need to be present in this life … theatre is unique in that everything happens in the present' (McBurney in Giannachi and Luckhurst 1999: 72–3). However, in many regards, this certainty has been destabilized by the developments of postdramatic and technologically infused performance genres. In the last few decades, co-presence has had to be reconsidered, with digital bodies now co-existing in the same intermedial theatrical space with live bodies, as can be seen in the practices of the Builders Association, Imitating the Dog and Station House Opera, among many others. Allied to this, the very premise of *who or what* is co-present has been questioned. As lines are blurred or dismantled between the performance 'event' and the fictional frame, there has been an increasing acknowledgement of the 'shared time' directly between performers and audience. Lehmann suggests that 'The basis of dramatic theatre was the demand that the spectators leave their everyday time to enter a segregated area of "dream time" abandoning their own sphere of time to enter into another … the postdramatic aesthetic of real time signifies, however, that the scenic process cannot be separated from the time of the audience' (2006: 155–6). From this stance, he proposes that theatre has now sought 'to turn time *as such* into an object of the aesthetic experience' (ibid.). Within this repositioning of time, he also notes, citing the work of both Robert Wilson and Pina Bausch, that experimentations with *duration* and *repetition* are now central to contemporary performance practice. For avant-garde theatre-makers, the risks and rewards of 'real time', a subtle recalibration of co-presence, are now fundamental considerations. There are challenges in this temporality as we have to engage in the event rather than drift into 'dream time', and if duration and repetition are integral, then fatigue, frustration and sustained concentration may take their toll. However, we are sustained by the prospect of the intellectual and sensory rewards that such practice may bring in the form of critical, contemplative distance or, conversely, intimacy, frisson and at times exclusivity.

From a temporal perspective, Stan's Cafe have always sought to recognize the real-time relationship between performers and audience before playfully distorting this affiliation. James has perennially been wary of 'the ambition to utterly convince people of something that isn't true or to remain prosaically in the present, I am far more interested in audiences experiencing a "play" or co-presence between the "real" and the "fictional"'. Thus, this initial, shared temporal layer has always been concurrent with a sense of extratemporality, so it is never simply an immediate shared experience (as with stand-up comedy or a music gig, for example) but a multidimensional frame in which the ambiguity of location and time has to be embraced. Sequencing of time is pivotal; for example, some pieces use the power of *static* objects or tableaux while others such as *Bingo In The House of Babel* (1994), *Voodoo City* (1995) or *Tuning Out with Radio Z* (2010) exploited the unpredictable potential of improvisational elements. Notably, in *Framed* (2002), commissioned for the Croydon Film Festival, and in *A Translation of Shadows* (2015), the company also experimented with notions of co-presence. In the latter, inspired by the early history of Japanese films, a live Benshi (narrator) describes the action of a prerecorded film projected on a cinema screen; increasingly this narration appears to disrupt the smooth predetermined unspooling of the cinematic narrative until eventually the film's principle protagonist, in a fit of pique, vacates her 'absent' position on screen to invade the live theatre space. Here, she berates the Benshi in Japanese, assaulting him and taking on his role. In this guise, she first appears to restore the film's original 'happy ending' before using her new-found power to place the now absent Benshi in the film, provoking an ending with a more obviously 'feminist' resolution. Disrupting expectations of how we expect the sequence to unfold (in this case the predictability of film, we think) is always part of the potential to be exploited with time.

Playing with spatial dimensions

Stan's Cafe relish inventing new spatial arrangements to suit the theatrical demands of each project. Their focus on the exploration of ideas rather than on character and linear plot has allowed them to uncouple their practices from traditional modes of audience reception and experiment with a spectrum of *experiences*, from the intimate to the epic. These experiments have also been fuelled by the company's concerted engagement with a range of cultural influences including television, film and radio as well as fairground attractions and art installations. It is important to remember, however, that form is always strongly coupled to the idea, so spaces created for performance have to be integral to the performance's purpose rather than simply aesthetically pleasing.

Scale has been utilized in Stan's Cafe's work to explore ideas as varied as the vulnerability of the individual through to international socio-economics and ethics. Large and small scale have been applied discreetly as techniques, but at times poignancy has been created by the combination of intimate and epic experiences in the same production. As initially mentioned in **The Route to @AE Harris**, there is a recurring exploration of human vulnerability or fragility in terms of how we construct our identities or relationships, how we respond to anxieties and fears and how we cope through the vagaries of history, culture and

Figure 7.1 By placing audiences in a viewing booth, *It's Your Film* (1998) allows for the creation of curious live ghosting effects.

social expectations. These ideas have been explored in, among others, the intimate performances of *It's Your Film* and *The Black Maze*. In *It's Your Film*, an individual audience member sat inside a small viewing booth and watched as two male protagonists, one apparently a detective, the other a jilted lover, search a mythical cityscape (Birmingham in disguise) for a third, apparently absent person – revealed at the show's conclusion, 240 seconds in, to be the viewer. The curious live filmic experience, created in this show in part by means of the Victorian Pepper's Ghost illusion (see **Ideas**), was acted out by performers only a few inches from the spectator, giving the event a particularly intense atmosphere. The intensity was accentuated by an intimate spatial language appropriated from film, with live enactments of close-ups, long shots, cuts and dissolves, despite the fact that the performers and audience were only separated by the wood and glass of the viewing booth. The performance explored the experience of watching and being watched, what it is to be a voyeur and simultaneously the recipient of voyeurism, the subject and passive star of a film you initially believed you would merely be watching.

In *The Black Maze*, audience members were more active, invited one at a time to step into a pitch-black corridor housed, like a forbidding fairground ride, in the back of a lorry.[1] The corridor continued to become a maze, which grew ever more unpredictable and claustrophobic, until the audience arrived at the exit a few minutes later. While there were no performers within the maze, the space, with its twisting, echoing, sometimes inflated or star-pocked walls and unpredictable sensations underfoot, acted as an 'intimate other'. However, it was arguably the unknown personal space in front of you, as you stepped forward into the dark, that induced most anxiety. Leslie Hill and Helen Paris, drawing upon the proxemics theory of Edward T. Hall (**TW 4**), have considered the potency of intimacy *and* potential intimacy in performance, stating that 'it is the possibility rather than the actuality of closeness that defines the close phase of personal space; the frisson of the almost but not quite intimate. The flipside of this frisson is, of course, tension and anxiety, a mutual fear' (2014: 11). These close spatial encounters draw the audience into confronting their own preconceptions or anxieties of personal and intimate space and to what extent we are prepared to be vulnerable and place our body 'at risk' in space.

Epic spaces are only ever utilized when the idea seems to be correspondingly epic. *Twilightofthefreakingods*, for example, required an extensive use of the @AE Harris venue, partly as the piece was a final 'eulogy' to the voluminous factory floor and partly because Wagner's *Götterdämmerung* demanded an epic scenographic context in which the human protagonists were dwarfed by fateful events. From the conception of *Of All The People In All The World*, James had a clear vision of human statistics on a global scale being embodied as piles of rice. The display of 106 tonnes of rice in an evolving sculptural landscape required a large space to accommodate large audience numbers and allow them freedom to explore this landscape from a range of perspectives. In discussion with several of the performers for this piece, the significance

---

[1] The original version was gallery based, the lorry conversion followed two years later to aid touring.

Figure 7.2 Inside *The Black Maze* (2000) – in a non-black moment.

of relational space and its ability to create meaning came to the fore. Rose remarked how 'placing two piles of statistics down creates a phrase, then three is a conversation. The spaces in between are a dramatic pause'. Even within the epic World Version of this production there is evidence of how the company find poignancy in the combination of intimate and epic spatial relationships. Here, huge numbers requiring millions or billions of grains of rice (national populations, millionaires, those displaced by conflict, etc.) are juxtaposed with singular grains or select piles representing presidents or billionaires, thereby exposing and questioning the inequalities of power or wealth. As the piece was in the form of a theatrical installation curated by discreet performers in their ubiquitous brown coats, the audience could find moments alone to observe and reflect on these statistical narratives within what might be considered a contemplative 'counter space'.

There are also occasions when the company change the scale of their theatrical space within a single performance. In *The Cleansing of Constance Brown*, the stage starts 2 metres wide and less than 1 metre deep, before a rapidly retreating back wall extends the stage depth to 14 metres; the back wall advances and retreats twice more before the show's conclusion, changing the viewer's experience of scale on each occasion. In *The Voyage* (2012), a 12-minute long opera made with composer Michael Wolters, it isn't the stage but the audience that moves. Starting with an intimate scene of farewell, the audience of fifty, with main protagonist aboard, are withdrawn on a wheeled seating bank 20 metres from the original action, uncovering a blue fabric sea as they retreat. Once the audience is stationary, the sea, in turn, is withdrawn, revealing a running track. The main protagonist races to the finishing line followed rapidly by the returning seating bank, compressing the stage back to its original dimensions, but not before our hero has fallen and passed under the seats and a new hero takes her place to claim the laurels.

The boundaries of conceptual space are similarly tested and often rearranged or challenged. In *It's Your Film*, for example, the show begins with a clear sense that the performers occupy a separate fictional space, even if it is only a few inches away from the spectator, but as the piece progresses the spatial boundaries are unexpectedly redrawn to enfold

Figure 7.3 Rochi Rampal in *The Voyage* (2012), as the seating bank retreats from the main action to reveal a fabric ocean.

the solo audience member within the narrative as a protagonist. On a larger scale, this enclosure of the audience is exploited in *Lurid and Insane* (2001) as we become embroiled as the crowd in a political rally, fuelled by rock music. The brittle yet often impenetrable divide between fictional space and audience space has been probed in many shows. In an early production, *Canute the King* (1993), the king was not only seen to be impeded by the physical barrier of the water that was encroaching but also the unseen obstacle of the fictional perimeter. The stage version was nominally set in the top tower room of a flooded palace and was staged in a rectangular pool of water bounded by a wooden barrier lined with linoleum. Occasionally, a character would announce their intent to perform an action that required them to go somewhere else (such as the servants' quarters), then stride in determined fashion towards the edge of their reality before suddenly losing enthusiasm for this idea, as if recognizing but failing to address the problem that their reality ceased to exist beyond the edge of the stage. The sense of entrapment is reinforced by the confines of the theatrical heterotopia. This uncertainty of the void beyond the fictional space is also shown in *Good and True* (2000), in which one of the characters was finally given permission to leave the interrogation room but was clearly perplexed as to where to go beyond the limitations of the stage. The interrogation room itself, though a raised 'island set' placed in the middle of the venue's stage, did have an offstage area. Characters occasionally disappeared upstage centre but none of them had a very confident sense of what the offstage world was like and so they often reappeared unnaturally quickly. Likewise, when reference was made to 'the stairs in this place' being 'lethal', the inference was that the stairs were rhetorical rather than actual. The unreality of the 'offstage' world in *Good and True* was highlighted in the show's finale when Hadingue's character happened to be the suspect when the show ended. At this point, she is abruptly told she can go – she is no longer under suspicion. Rather than coming as a relief, this news brings with it the existential terror that she is expected to leave the stage, but she has no idea of her identity. In order to help her on her way, she is given the interrogator's sketchbook in which

Figure 7.4 The offstage space in *Good and True* (2000) is used for costume changes but has an ambiguous status; here, there is some confusion as a waiter has been called to give evidence.

they have been making notes and drawing pictures through the show. Somehow, this sum of all the evidence must be who she is and, armed with this information, she steps tentatively off the front of the stage and exists through the audience into the 'real world'. In this instance, the pretence of the stage space is harnessed to underscore the anxiety of the 'pretenders' themselves.

Scenography

Stan's Cafe's practice undoubtedly reflects Howard and Palmer's conceptions of scenography, a point reinforced by Fragkou, who states: 'Scenography is integral to the conceptual framing of its pieces' (2015: 213). Throughout their history, significance has been placed upon the entire staging as a means of communicating ideas. The framing of the theatrical space has always been carefully constructed so as to tread a careful line between delineating the event while leaving the exact time and place ambiguous for audience interpretation. Even when the company was in its infancy, the attention to scenography was ever present. The earliest shows are perhaps best described as ambitiously low-tech, exemplified by the deliberately wobbly two-dimensional scenery hung from a moving washing line in *Perry Como's Christmas Cracker* (1991), designed by Graeme and James, which was to stage a triumphant return with higher production values twenty years later in *The Cardinals* (2011), designed by Miguel Bravo. In *Memoirs of an Amnesiac* (1992), a Super 8 film shot in Birmingham stands in for Paris and 'treasures' (supposed relics of French composer Eric Satie) are displayed in a medicine cabinet hewn from reclaimed wood.

An early indication of their scenographic ambitions was *Canute the King*, for which they surprisingly got approval to perform in Moseley Road Swimming Baths, a large and ornate Edwardian pool on the south side of Birmingham. With the audience seated in the pool's three-sided balcony, the cast of Hadingue and Rose, accompanied by two opera singers and a blues harmonica player, were to perform around the pool's edge, on a pier floating out on the water and also under the water. Music was to be live and prerecorded and spectacular lighting bouncing off the building's barrelled ceiling and glazed tiles was to be augmented by slide projections on the water and back wall.

> We were a bit ambitious to think we could pull all this off on the miniscule budget we'd managed to raise. The first night was pretty rough as the safety guy wouldn't clear us to use our theatre lights, but we got things sorted for the final two performances and then converted the show to tour theatres with a flooded stage rather than a full swimming pool. The setting for those first shows was amazing and put us on the map locally as a company prepared to go for it – we still meet people who claim to have been at those early shows.
>
> James

Despite some of the artistic and technical difficulties this production encountered, it indicated an aspiration to find or create evocative and

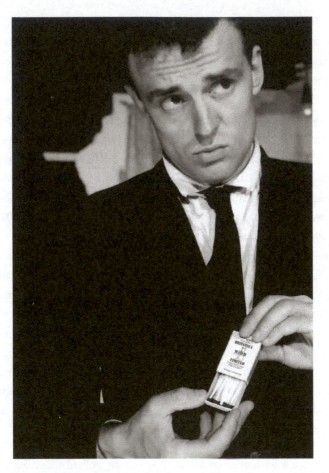

Figure 7.5 Graeme Rose, as Eric Smith in *Memoirs of an Amnesiac* (1992), displays one of his treasures, a collection of Erik Satie's umbrellas.

visually stunning spaces, no matter how demanding this may prove for devisors, designers or performers. Over twenty-five years, the company have located productions across a wide variety of spaces and sites, both within traditional theatres and also industrial spaces including their own venue at @AE Harris. *Lurid and Insane* (2001) visited gig venues and a farmer's barn and *The Steps Series* has changed its content to respond to more than twenty settings indoors and outside across the United Kingdom, Europe and the United States. One of their most challenging site-based commissions was to create a piece for the Midland Metro Line between Birmingham and Wolverhampton. Their solution, *Space Station* (2002), saw the creation of a new station, Earth North Central, just north of Wednesbury Parkway. This new station was marked on all the maps in all the trains as a connecting station for the moon and nearby planets.

For *Space Station* (2002), Stan's Cafe built a new station on the Birmingham–Wolverhampton Metro line. Called Earth North Central, this stop was added to the maps within all the trains and marked as a connecting station for journeys to the moon and local planets. Three performers dressed as astronauts spent two days on the platform with silver boxes, newspapers, knitting, sandwiches and other props, waiting for a Metro Train to stop for them, which finally it did, whereby they climbed aboard and disappeared forever. Before then they were an unusual sight, glimpsed from a passing Metro train, visible from the far end of the neighbouring Wednesbury Parkway Station or across scrubland from local houses.

On this new station three astronauts waited, in space suits, with helmets and boxes, for their connection to take them off the planet, to complete their onward journey to Mars. After waiting on the platform for two days, reading newspapers, knitting, talking to the local youths, growing excited as every fresh train approached, disappointed as it passed by without stopping, the travelers were at last picked up by the space tram and left West Bromwich with a triumphant farewell speech ringing in their ears.

James on Stan's Cafe website

Space Station embraces the juxtaposition between the mundane space and the extraspatial; the specific industrial landscape is acknowledged yet, unlike much site-specific practice, it then seeks to relocate the narrative literally in an 'outer-space' rather than ground it in the

Figure 7.6 Three astronauts wait for their connection to the planets at station Earth North Central in *Space Station* (2002).

history and geography of the actual location. The piece was not reliant on spoken text and was only witnessed fleetingly by either passengers looking through the windows of the trams or waiting 100 metres away at Wednesbury Parkway Station, or by the occasional local walking within sight of the tracks. This emphasizes the importance of scenography in conveying the entirety of the idea and the capacity of precise tableaux or slowly moving images to capture an ambiguous narrative. Their work has always responded to the site, but James is clear that site-specific theatre is not a dominant style for the company:

> Site Specific interests me more for its emphasis on specificity than on site. Every theatre show we make has to justify its location, whether that is in a Studio Theatre or a Metro Line. If we are making a show for a studio theatre, we should be as alive to the specific nature of this venue as any other. What is special about this space (the theatre)

and how does this speciality add to the quality of what we are doing? Clearly once you get to grips with this for one studio theatre space the challenge remains fairly consistent in similar spaces. By taking theatre out and about you challenge yourselves to learn what is special about each new location and apply this knowledge to each new production. We enjoy working in and out of theatre buildings, the variety keeps us fresh and everything we learn in one arena can inform what we do in another.

James on Stan's Cafe website

James attitude to site is echoed by Rose in his approach to establishing *Of All The People In All The World* in different locations: 'I always take my cue from the building, that's the inspiration for how it gets designed and what the focus of interest is. That's the great beauty of the show for me in how it responds to architecture, it responds to history and the function of the site.'

Specificity as a creative impetus is often to be found, counter-intuitively perhaps, in tandem with intentional ambiguity, and both are central to the perceptual and conceptual framing of theatre space for Stan's Cafe. The precise structuring of the images on stage, their *exterior* aesthetic quality, is constantly addressed alongside the more elusive *interior* space; how is the fictional action framing the idea and how are the audience being asked to conceive of these events? While the scenography is attended to in great detail, the audience are still given room to inhabit and interpret the events, suspended as they are in extraspatial and extratemporal frames. The visual framing is always arresting but this is not to be conflated with immediate communication and instant interpretation. From the foreboding corridor (framed by an intense soundtrack by Nina West) in *The Cleansing of Constance Brown* to the deep crimson stage within a stage of *The Cardinals*, a setting is established in the first few moments yet the full potential of this space where these locations and occupants reside in time and space and what this may signify are questions an audience must resolve for themselves.

One of the signature qualities of their framing is hypermediacy, how the mechanics of the stage are often revealed or what Rose refers to as 'an exposure of the means of production' (**TW 6**). In *Of All The People In All The World*, the deliberate processes of measuring and curating the rice are as significant as the piles of statistics themselves, while in *The Just Price of Flowers* (2009), all the performers were present on stage throughout the performance, overtly demonstrating any changes of role or costume. In *The Cleansing of Constance Brown*, this exposure of the physical mechanics was made integral to the piece as at the end of every performance the audience left through the set, witnessing the detritus of the performers practice, and the company even went as far as selling tickets for the backstage area at one festival so that the audience could see the complex choreography from scene to scene and the rapid costume changes. This experiment directly informed the framing choices made for *The Cardinals*, as the backstage area that the cardinals inhabit was explicitly shown around the perimeter of the puppet stage. This stripping away of artifice is an acknowledgement of the co-presence in real, shared time between performers and audience and an embracing of the constructed nature of the fiction. It also exposes the figures on stage as being human, figures who are struggling, menacing, confused, tender.

The postdramatic aesthetic of their work is reflected in the careful editing and selection of what is placed on stage, eschewing any peripheral props or set dressing that 'fixes' the events in a specific space and time. Robert Wilson notably stated that 'The more space around something, the easier it is to hear it or see it', and so it is the case that all elements on a Stan's Cafe stage are refined down to what is essential; thereby the impact of a single object, single figure or lighting change becomes compellingly significant. This quality can be seen in *The Just Price of Flowers* (2009), labelled as an 'austerity production' due to its thematic exploration of the banking crisis and its aftermath. This austerity is reflected in the bare stage and monochrome costumes, black with white paper ruffles fashioned using origami. The flowers, at the centre of the narrative, were fashioned in red paper so that our attention was drawn to their symbolism as objects of avarice and foolish speculation. In discussing the use of origami in the production with Jack Trow, one of the performers, he noted an apt analogy between the Japanese art of paper folding and the company's minimalist aesthetic:

> There are two schools of thought with origami. One is about making something out of paper with as many folds as possible to make it as realistic as possible. How realistic can this rabbit be? The other school of origami advocates the fewer folds the better. So if there is a way to express rabbit in one fold with your piece of paper, then that's better than the very detailed one. I think the Stan thing is the fewer the folds the better.

Editing down to what is essential is not to be necessarily equated with sparsity though, as often what is necessary is rich and textured, what is essential is that all elements need justification and a purpose. Here again, we see the influence of filmic framing in the precision of what is revealed at any moment and how it reveals itself over time as a series of edits, cutting and dissolving across space and time. The cinematic works of Andrei Tarkovsky and Sergei Parajanov are identified by James as major influences upon recent work, the latter of whom particularly informed *The Cardinals*, in which the symbolic potency of images (religious iconography specifically) is given space and time to resonate through the focus of the central puppet frame and the use of recurring images to build layers of significance. Often these images were richly textured, the cardinals in precise positions reflecting the geometry of Renaissance art as well as vibrant backcloths and precisely honed elements of set within the puppet frame, but we are given time to linger over them, to decode and interpret the signifiers into signs.

Time as form

The shows are as long as they need to be. I take myself as a measure – If I'm not engaged then we need to fix something.

James

Throughout the long days working on *Of All The People In All The World*, performers' time was marked out every 100 minutes by a chime, placed in the soundtrack by Jon Ward. In *Twilightofthefreakingods*, every minute of the four-and-a-quarter hours was announced by a relay of actors, voicing a 'speaking clock' for the cast to time their performance by. In *Tuning Out with Radio Z* (2010), the radio hosts gave regular 'real-time' time checks to reinforce the formal adherence to 'on-air' protocols. These inscriptions of time within performances are indicative of how significant time structures have been as formal elements within productions. As seen in the early university pieces *Alice Through The System* (1987)[2] and *Infected* (1988) and other *instructional* texts, James has always been alert to the potential of constructing performance tasks around a temporal frame and using the mechanical dimensions of time – sequence, duration and repetition – as both formal *and* conceptual devices to explore an idea to its fullest.

Experimentation with temporal form (*sequentiality*, to use Elleström's term) has ranged in their productions from *static* images, objects and tableaux in such works as *Of All The People In All The World* and *Twilightofthefreakingods* through to the seemingly fixed sequencing of film throughout *A Translation of Shadows* as well as improvisational work containing unpredictable timescales and progressions, particularly in *Bingo In The House of Babel*, with its live bingo finale and more fully improvised *Tuning Out with Radio Z*. Not only are different modes of time used but they are also combined, as in the case of *Of All The People In All The World*, which blends static piles of rice alongside semi-improvised live performance, and also subverted, as seen in the disruptive conflation of the Benshi's co-presence and filmic presence in the finale of *A Translation of Shadows*. The diversity of temporal sequentiality reflects the breadth of cultural and media influences upon their practice and also the experimentation with spectatorial modes. This goes as far as acknowledging that the audience may 'drift

---

[2] James's first devised show, *Alice Through the System* (1988), pitted a heroic protagonist, Simon Graham, against an implacable multicharactered foe, Kate Buchanan. Simon had to drive a script full of variables through to its conclusion within a time limit voted for by the audience. If successful, he was rewarded; if unsuccessful, Kate was deemed to have won. James acted as a master of ceremonies/referee. Upstage, a clock showed the time left and script kept the audience aware of how many pages were left.

in and out' of the work, both literally and cognitively. *The Anatomy of Melancholy* programme notes suggested to the audience that this may occur and that they should feel relaxed with this experience, and for *Twilightofthefreakingods*, there was even physical evidence of this pragmatic attitude to spectatorship in the form of a bar and a toastie van outside @AE Harris which were open throughout the show. In this sense, the audience are creating their own sequencing of events, editing the content and filtering their interpretation through their own presence or absence (see **Audience**).

Giving status to the filtering of ideas over extended timescales has created a particular emphasis upon stillness and measured pace, evident in many Stan's Cafe productions and resonant of the contemplative time evoked in the theatre of Robert Wilson, who once said in interview: 'I do not consider my theatre as slow. In fact, I work in real time. I have always found that conventional theatre does not have enough time. It is too fast for me' (1997). On some occasions in Stan's Cafe's practice, time is slowed by the measured and detailed delivery of text, as in the case of *The Anatomy of Melancholy*, where Burton and his fellow academics take the time necessary to ruminate on the various melancholies that may befall us. In some instances, time to think is created by the stripping away of an easily read narrative to be replaced by the slow development of an image, as in *Simple Maths*, where the only narrative present was that generated in the audience's imaginations as they interpret the actors slowly shifting seating positions and emotional states. In *Twilightofthefreakingods*, Seigfried's journey across stage to meet Gunther, Gertrude and Hagen takes twenty-two minutes, cycling an exercise bike to power headlights all set on a wheeled, flat truck pushed, centimetre by centimetre, by a Machinist on his hands and knees. Such slow, unfolding images in uncluttered scenographic space, precise and at times repetitive, generate conceptual space for the audience as time is specifically encoded as a means of spatializing ideas. Scenography is sculpted, through temporal control, to create the visual narrative. The Soviet/Russian film-maker Andrei Tarkovsky is a formative influence on James's aesthetic and it is instructive that the book setting out his approach to cinema is called *Sculpting in Time*, in which he wrote: 'Time in a film shot has to flow independently and with dignity, then ideas will find their place in it without fuss, bustle, haste' (1989: 120). This perspective undoubtedly finds resonance within the theatre practice of Stan's Cafe, but any assumption that slow revelations of time are always their modus operandi is erroneous as many shows inject frenetic tempo at key moments, such as in *The Cardinals*, when difficult scene changes have to be hurriedly made, and there are certain shows which employ accelerated time throughout, notably in the case of *Time Critical* (2016).[3] This production drew upon the past twenty-five years of the company's history and world events from across the same era, finding the poignancy in the juxtaposition of the epic and the small scale, the sombre and the trivial. All of the extensive visual and dialogic material was delivered by two performers who were constantly and ever more urgently under the time pressure of a chess clock counting down to zero hour. The company website describes the challenge of this show:

> Two performers each have 25 minutes set on a chess clock – one minute for each of the 25 years of the life of Stan's Cafe. One performer has the job of describing the last 25 years of world history, the other deals with the history of the company. Personal stories, births, marriages and deaths, tales of travel and fragments of past productions are pitted against the major events of the past quarter of a century. Sometimes working together, sometimes against each other the performers compete to bring in all their material within their allotted time.

The twin dials of the chess clock are always visible on stage and their significance heightened by a live camera feed on to a TV screen, giving the audience a close-up on the exact times remaining. In the latter stages of the show, as the minutes and seconds ebb away, we witness (often with great amusement) the performers increasing struggle to communicate the text with a vestige of composure. This frantic distillation of shared, real time between performers and audience, down to a finite point

---

[3] *Time Critical* was initially created for the Stan's Cafe 25th anniversary party at MAC Birmingham on 30 November 2016. It was directed by James, and the two original performers were Rochi Rampal and Craig Stephens.

when time runs out, simultaneously exposes how intense and turbulent time and events are within our lives, yet also how curiously elusive and forgettable they may become.

Duration, as James clarifies in the opening quote to this section, is determined by the needs of the idea or ideas, and so the potential for expanding or contracting the norms of studio theatre timescales has always been on the agenda, if necessary.

> I suppose, because my introduction to theatre was through studio theatre shows that were all approximately an hour and ten minutes long this has always felt like the paradigm length for a theatre show. To help me through this ridiculous conventionality I started to think about the different conventions of music; I noted that symphonies have a conventional structure that defines them as symphonies and this leads them to have a certain average duration. Pop songs have a different conventional structure that means their average duration is shorter, minuets have another structure, classical operas another and so on. *It's Your Film* is for us a single, *Come Together* (2008) was structured around an actual single (Primal Scream's *Come Together*) – both had simple ideas that were worked through and when they were resolved the piece ended. *The Anatomy of Melancholy* was looking at bigger ideas in greater depth so it needed more time, an operatic length of approximately three hours. The 70-minute studio theatre shows I think of as our symphonies, there to be compared with the 70-minute symphonies created by other companies working in this field.

Of course, it must be remembered that these artistic activities take place within a quasi-commercial context. Arts centre venues tend to be reluctant to book shows of three hours, believing their audience will be put off buying tickets by the duration. Larger theatres may be equally reluctant to book shows without an interval as this would represent lost revenues in bar takings. It requires a special setting to promote a theatre show that is merely four-and-a-half minutes long as this doesn't conform to the cultural norm of theatre as 'a good night out'. Conversely, the novelty of a very short duration or the challenge of a very long duration may convert such performances into 'events', whose distinctiveness makes them attractive.

Performances lasting several hours place unusual demands on both actors and audience. *24 Hour Scalextric* (2009) consisted of a 24-hour unbroken webcast sports commentary on a slot-car race. The two performers were the only people who were expected to remain throughout the performance and, in that sense, became the subjects of the experiment in fatigue and resourcefulness. Other, shorter shows have asked audiences to share the commitment, as indicated above; the audience for *Twilightofthefreakingods* was excused from paying full attention for the whole duration, but the running time of *Tuning Out with Radio Z* was reduced to three hours in order to not challenge people's bladders too much and to attempt to keep people fixated for the whole duration without a break. The structuring of *The Anatomy of Melancholy* allowed for an interval, but the density of the performance content made this break necessary. With their physical and mental stamina potentially under strain, audiences and performers experience new risks and rewards. James is keen to exploit this potential:

> If you want a piece to have an epic feel then one of the things you can do is extend its duration. I find it a very attractive notion that people will leave the theatre exhausted, so filled up with something that they have to go and have a lie down afterwards. But of course you have to keep people engaged for that length of time, you want them filled up not fed up.

Performers in such works are exposed to the risks of fatigue and of the loss of concentration this may bring, but the long duration also allows for 'the erosion of artifice', as Hadingue puts it, potentially creating significant moments of shared time between performers and audience. Ward, who worked as a sound designer and computer coder on *Tuning Out with Radio Z*, highlights the fine line trodden by the company in their longer durational practice:

> I think James is very keen on doing shows that feel like a marathon. It requires more time commitment and more emotional commitment to watch work like *Tuning Out with Radio Z*. These long pieces are an

acquired taste, they take some getting used to. If you're not careful, at some point you might just 'break your brain' and feel like you've failed.

Hadingue, who performed alongside Craig Stephens in *Tuning Out with Radio Z*, candidly noted that this show, while it may have explored the intimacy of prolonged shared time, also 'just felt like a bloody long time'. What duration does enable, is to work ideas further and more rigorously than in shorter shows. Rose explains his view on this in relation to *The Cardinals*, which was 105 minutes long with no interval: 'Threads of narrative and motifs such as an object or a picture are revisited. As the piece unfolds there is a repetition, a recycling of those ideas within a different configuration so that the initial meanings resonate differently in the later stories. You are working with a limited vocabulary but you can build complexity as you play with this.' An example of what he refers to here is the image of a walled city, which is first seen in the siege of Jericho, returned to in a sequence depicting the Crusades and detonated as a contemporary phenomenon when representing the Israeli West Bank barrier. In its reframing of the biblical image through reoccurrence and juxtaposition, it elucidates Lehmann's perspective, who suggests that repetition

> is now used for the destructuring and deconstructing of story, meaning and totality of form. ... The very position in time of the repeated is different from that of the original. We always see something different in what we have seen before. Therefore, repetition is also capable of producing a new attention punctuated by the memory of the preceding events, *an attending to the little differences*. (2006: 156–7)[4]

Real time and extra time

Sometimes, time is precise and sometimes it is fluid, fragile and elusive. While specific chronologies of time can, in certain circumstances, create

---

[4]   Patrice Pavis also writes vividly on the potential of repetition in theatre in *Contemporary Mise en Scène: Staging Theatre Today* (2013), pp. 168–9.

the narrative, on other occasions time needs to be treated as a corruptible resource. This mutability of time enables performers to occupy both real and extratemporal spaces, for past, present and future to dissolve into one another and for the past to frame the frailties of the present.

On some level, the co-presence of performer and audience is always acknowledged as James reiterates: 'I am uneasy about simply having a single fictional frame. We need a real time frame to remind us that we are in the theatre.' Real-time co-presence is sometimes very significant on its own, as in the case of installation-based theatre such as *The Black Maze* or *Of All The People In All The World*. In these instances, the presence of the performers as 'gatekeepers', mediating and framing the event, is crucial. Rose notes that, for these productions, 'it demonstrates to an audience how they should behave in the space, it's a mental frame to how the work gets viewed, it frames their response'. However, once the concept of shared real time is established, layers of ambiguity and simultaneity of time may be added, evoking real or imagined pasts, presents and futures; what Hadingue refers to as 'fully-dreamed worlds, with logics of their own'. Echoing Lehmann's conception of the 'postdramatic aesthetic of real time', John Freeman accentuates the changing perceptions of theatrical presence: 'The notion of "presence" is shifted away from something that is ascribed to the performer acting "in the moment" and "in the light". It is in turn relocated in the interplay between the watchers, the watched and their negotiation of the type of space they occupy, and also to the manner of that occupation' (2007: 70). These subtle negotiations can be seen in a production such as *The Cardinals* (2011), which conspicuously grounds the performance in the 'here and now' as the cardinals are clearly setting up and preparing to perform for the theatre audience before them. However, the ambiguity lies in which historical time periods we are also occupying. The puppet show, which sits within its own frame centre stage, seems arcane and out of step with our shared real time; likewise, the cardinals are dressed in what could conceivably be medieval robes but interact with modern technology and the apparently contemporary figure of the female Muslim stage manager. The historical frames create perspective on the events and space to consider our attitudes to faith and morality while the acknowledgement of real time exposes the fragility of the cardinals/actors as human beings, struggling under the toil of their epic puppet show. Paul Arvidson, who designed the lighting, also highlights the importance of scenography in creating this ambiguity of time as 'the lighting always allowed you to see the wider frame of events (the panic of moving backdrops, the arguments between themselves and the stage manager) so that the puppet show was always framed by the reality of what they were doing'. In *Finger Trigger Bullet Gun* (2014), events hover between the action set in the lead-up to the First World War and the constant real-time presence of thousands of dominoes lined up on stage, a metaphor for the unstoppable chain of events that triggered the conflict. While the actors perform in their fictional frame, a stage manager patiently – and with the utmost care – fills in the safety gaps between vast sections of dominoes, an action which is ever more acutely a 'real-time' activity. The frisson of historical time metaphorically framed by the jeopardy of real time is ever present and the two only collapse together in the moment when the dominoes fall.

The elasticity of time, and the audience's capacity to deal with such elasticity, allows Stan's Cafe to create their own imaginings of past, present and future times. *Canute the King* is framed within a fictional, faked past in which Canute/Edward VIII/Prince Charles grapple with duty, identity, fate and personal fallibility, while *Bingo In The House of Babel* operates within an imagined future-past where three librarians struggle with what it is to be human in the 'tea or coffee?' room of Einstein's brain. *Home Of The Wriggler* (2006), meanwhile, is set in some ambiguous, post-apocalyptic future from where performers enact a mosaic of memories telling the story of Birmingham's relationship with the Longbridge car plant. Several shows 'feel' as if they reside in the present, including *Be Proud of Me* and *Good and True*, both presenting a semblance of the here and now (names, locations, colloquial language, etc.), but their claustrophobic, insularity makes it impossible to define their place or time. *Simple Maths*, with six chairs sitting in an empty landscape, travels even further on the temporal scale as it sits 'out of time', stripped of any fictional context, a minimalism that brings our attention on to the shared time between the performers *and* between performers and audience.

The Cleansing of Constance Brown: An experiment in space and time

Many diverse examples have been drawn upon throughout this chapter to explore distinct spatial and temporal qualities and how Stan's Cafe manipulate them in practice. As a means of revisiting and re-emphasizing the symbiotic relationship between space and time, this chapter concludes with James offering a detailed reflection on one specific production – *The Cleansing of Constance Brown*. His description highlights, among many things, the sophisticated and slippery interplay between these two elements, the use of filmic space-time, the significance of precise timing and repetition as well as the complex scenographic choices that are made to harness all this potential.

* * *

The Cleansing of Constance Brown is a theatre show that takes a playful approach to time and space. Built around half a dozen thematically linked narrative strands which each play out in one to three brief scenes, the show leaps backwards and forwards in time across four hundred years, both sides of the Atlantic and to the Middle East. In practically every scene, the setting is a corridor and, operating without recourse to substantive speech, the show relies on a visual code to introduce its audience to evolving conventions and borrows and adapts a number of these codes from the cinema.

The first scene the audience witness is of a corridor in a court complex; they see a military servicewoman arriving for a hearing in the court. Rather than progressing forward in time to discover the outcome of the trial, the show instead jumps back in time to witness her perpetrating the crime, but not before more narrative threads have been set running.

The second scene is brief and works as a teaser. A cleaner, who has arrived to mop a floor, sees a strange mark on a wall and starts cleaning it. We see a few other 'flash frames' of cleaning in various anonymous corridors, and then a cleaner with a vacuum emerges into what we come to realize is a hotel corridor being made ready for the arrival of someone very powerful. After towels, whisky and a large picture in a frame have been delivered, the cleaning takes a more sinister edge as secret service agents arrive to sweep the room for bugs.

Within this scene, time does not run smoothly. While civilian figures operate at a conventional 'frame rate', the secret service agents appear to operate in an otherworldly 'slow motion' time. As the president and his entourage sweep in, secret service time speeds up but the president and his chief of staff hit slow motion upstage to enter the hotel room.

As much as five minutes of stage time have been devoted to demonstrating the secure nature of this corridor, so it is startling when a woman with two large shopping bags appears upstage where there has previously been no door. For a few disorientating seconds, she cohabits the presidential corridor with his security detail, then they step out of sight and the configuration of the corridor's doors changes along with the lighting and music; we realize a slippage of time and space has occurred. A form of theatrical cross-fade has created a complex 'poetic', difficult-to-resolve moment by overlaying two quite straightforward scenes.

From the domestic corridor scene, we move back to an office block in the United States, sometime in the 1980s; the clues are there in costumes, a water cooler, props and a hint of an accent just audible over the all-enveloping soundtrack. Here we watch the crumbling of a corporation caught up in some kind of fraud. A boss we have never seen may have committed suicide in their office at the height of the crisis, a visitor runs screaming from this office smearing blood on the corridor wall as she leaves.

The shredded paper mess of this scene is picked over by two figures in protective suits more suitable for dealing with a chemical spillage than forensic accountancy. Was that firm dealing with 'toxic financial assets' or is this scene more metaphoric? Are we actually somewhere else in time and space?

The new narrative threads continue to spool out: we are flung further back in time to the corridor of a Victorian hospital patrolled by someone who may be Florence Nightingale; she spots a mark on a wall, she enters a ward to investigate and emerges with a bloodied sheet. This is the third indication of blood on a wall; narrative logic suggests it can't be the same wall, but it is on the same piece of set so maybe space and time are layered on top of each other in unusual ways.

As she leaves, the nurse harangues a poor cleaner for her lacklustre sweeping. When the light increases, we see this cleaner is in a contemporary nylon tabard; we have leapt forward in time – maybe cleaners have long been chastised for a lack of enthusiasm in their work.

As this sweeper exits, another enters but, again, we have travelled through time and space. Now we are in a tenement block in central Europe in the late 1930s. We watch a Jewish man leave for work five times and the differences in his and his wife's emotional state, their changing relationship with their neighbour, the husband changing clothes he wears and the props they carry tell a story of increasing persecution, culminating in their fleeing. The hard editing, together of these departures, which we imagine taking place over the course of a year, indicates that time has advanced in a series of jumps through the scene. This time compression has already been used more subtly in the courtroom and office crisis scenes and continues to be used throughout the show. As the show is only able to advance action by showing what is happening in the corridors, the show artificially contracts time whenever the audience is being asked to imagine offstage.

'Intercutting' the second, third and subsequent Jewish Departure scenes are snippets of action from a different but conceptually related scene, as an aggressive militia force loot and eventually set fire to a residential tower block somewhere in the Balkans. This intercutting is initially alarming as it disrupts the comfortable Jewish Departure scene conventions by introducing new characters that don't 'fit' the scene, who appear from an unexpected location upstage and break conventions by crossing the corridor diagonally. Moments later, when this new 'intercutting' convention has been established, it in turn is disrupted to disturbing effect as the militia cohabit the stage space with the Jewish Wife; one appears to enter her flat, but as the two characters appear invisible to each other we must assume they are separated by time, or space, or both.

At this point, the show 'turns for home' and, rather than introducing another new narrative thread, returns to the familiar scene of the 1980s office. On this occasion, the water cooler is upstage right rather than downstage left and the doors have shifted; we are viewing the same corridor but from the other end. Our perspective has been rotated 180 degrees and the last time we were here, the firm was in meltdown, but now there's a party going on. The explanation is simple: we are watching an earlier scene from the same narrative and, eventually, an alert audience member will recognize the moment a Polaroid photograph is taken that we saw being used to tease its subject in the previous office scene.

This photograph is a sign that the party is turning ugly, quite how ugly we never discover as it is 'gatecrashed' by the next scene. In a now familiar device, a spectral military figure from the next scene walks diagonally through the party corridor, but rather than the party scene ending, it is simply co-opted by three military service people – including the woman who we have previously seen facing trial. The indignities heaped on the figures who were once the drunken revellers and now appear to be prisoners are reminiscent of those captured in photographs taken at Abu Ghraib prison in Iraq. We realize this must be the incident which led to the woman being in court at the start of the show. This deduction is encouraged as the strobing flashbulbs that mark her exit from this scene echo those that marked her arrival in the first scene: she exits the prison corridor into the media spotlight.

A symbolic/stylized orange billowing mass of flame engulfs the corridor and, once it has retreated, the corridor drops out of fictional time and space. The corridor is empty – there is no music, and we hear noises from backstage: the actors going about their private backstage business. The lighting, usually bold, is now bland. We get brief glimpses of 'real' backstage place as performers hold mirrors up into the corridor space, angled so they can see the audience in the auditorium and we can see them backstage. We know they can see us. They know we can see them. There is a mutual knowing.

One by one, the doors have been closing on the empty corridor, the mirrors are withdrawn, the final doors close and now, for the only time in the show, all the doors are closed. The corridor is a dead end, with angled razor-thin lights crossing it from the cracks round the door frames; it is perhaps becoming a fictional space again. The razor lights fade and the music of the soundtrack resumes. We are soon back in a familiar narrative time and place, outside the president's room at night: we recognize the corridor layout and the security agent.

Here, the simplest sequential time movement, from 'the President arriving in a hotel' to 'later that same night', gives way to its most audacious leap. The twenty-first-century American secret service agent comes to the end of his shift and is replaced, without so much as a quizzical look, by his English counterpart from 400 years ago. The slow silhouetted walk of the contemporary agent downstage away from the brightly light historic agent can be seen as a moment of time travel. The prisoner, Elizabeth Tudor, is seen entering her chambers and, after a ceremonial wash, is seen returning to the stage gloriously as Queen Elizabeth I. She makes regal progress downstage followed by the back wall, which compresses the stage from 14 metres to little over 1 metre deep, creating a picture frame for the new monarch, who gives the audience a knowing smirk.

Return time travel is accomplished with a simple lighting trick. A strong light shining from behind the back wall directly at the audience creates an illuminated rectangle around the back wall; as the wall slowly retreats upstage, this rectangle of light pulses in width and intensity as it alternately passes sections of wall and open doorways, growing steadily smaller as the rules of perspective come into play.

Back in contemporary time, we see a woman in a black niqab approaching us, much as Elizabeth I has just done. It takes a few seconds to locate this image, but soon we are allowed to recognize it as the contemporary tower-block corridor we have already seen. We are later in the same narrative; again, a neighbour is concerned that he is privy to domestic abuse but this time he does something about it and we recognize the suspect as a man we have previously seen in the court scene. Then, we considered him an incidental figure in the more eye-catching narrative of the service woman on trial, but now he is central to the action as he is taken away by a police officer for questioning.

Now there remain three loose narrative threads. A familiar figure trying to clean blood from a wall initiates a sequence depicting a priest walking purposefully towards what turns out to be an exorcism. It is unclear when this sequence is set, but the flow of striking images suggests a nightmarish labyrinth of contagion, masked figures frantically attempting to sterilize these corridors. Here, theatre is aping cinema, 'cutting together' a sequence of images and moves that work powerfully in a logic of 'montage' rather than a spatially coherent progression of movement. The sequence ends with the back wall downstage forward, this time creating a narrow and shallow box-like room in which the exorcism is attempted.

The final two narrative threads are tied together in the final scene in which the first person we see is the familiar figure of the secret service agent. We are being taken on a final leap through time and space, but this leap is hampered by the fact that the previous scene's exorcism ended in a rainstorm and the front of the stage is now covered in water, water that is impeding our imaginative leap to the White House, except of course there may have been a leak of water *in* the White House. A 'danger slip hazard' sign tells this story and, in a single bound, frees fictional time from real time.

Our trip to the White House is to witness the president preparing to sign a peace treaty with the leader of the Balkan militia we saw rampaging through the tenement block a while back. The commander we saw then, torching the looted apartments with a lighter, is leading negotiations for the militia here; he still has his lighter, which he flicks ruefully while glancing at the dripping ceiling. The security guard looks on disdainfully – after all, didn't we see him a few nights back preventing his boss, the president of the United States of America, from doing exactly the same thing in a hotel corridor?

In real time, *The Cleansing of Constance Brown* is 70 minutes long, more or less.

Stan in action: Space and time

One of the few advantages art has over physics is how much laxer the rules are. You *can* play fast and loose with time and space on the stage, so why *wouldn't* you? Films and novels are happy to deploy flashbacks, dream sequences and hallucinations and use unreliable narrators, so why shouldn't we? Here are some things you could try that focus on space and time.

1. Mark a 2.4 metre × 1.8 metre rectangle on the floor – this is the size of your stage, now get on with it.

    There were three brief moments in *The Cleansing of Constance Brown* when the stage was roughly this size; we enjoyed it so much that we used this restriction for the whole of *The Just Price of Flowers* – our twin excuses being that it saved us having to build a new set and it helped us whip up a Dutch Masters look for the show. You may enjoy how compressed it makes the action.

2. Set up three parallel spaces on stage as 'past', 'present' and 'future', or to represent three different realities or three different physical locations. Experiment with playing your action across the three spaces, then try bringing them together in the same space.

    We used the former arrangement in *Twilightofthefreakingods*, using three parallel, interconnected rooms.

3. Use blackouts to edit your show like a film or splice together key moments or images. The lights may only be up for three seconds at a time in some sequences; build your show like a collage.

    Stan's Cafe inherited this device from Pete Brooks, working with 'glory what glory'; it is present in *Memoirs of an Amnesiac* and *The Cleansing of Constance Brown*. Exercises 2 and 3 were combined when we made *District 12* (2002) with De Montfort University, Leicester, which showed parallel lives across time in a huge block of flats.

4. Interrogate how you get from one scene to the next, abandon the blackout; can you have the actors just change the scene 'unannounced', either subtly or very harshly, possibly with actors playing multiple roles? Think about how DJs mix tracks – can you cross-fade scenes by starting one before the other ends? Can you 'haunt' one scene with another by having actors from two different scenes sharing the same space?

5. If your show has a narrative, write each scene or plot point on a scrap of paper, put these scraps in a chronological sequence and then decide if this is the most dynamic way to approach the narrative. You can move the scraps of paper around; you can also duplicate scraps if you want to show a scene or a moment more than once. If your show has no narrative, you can still use this technique.

8

Performing

What's in this chapter?

It will be no surprise to discover that distinguishing the nature of performing in Stan's Cafe's practice and how it manifests itself in the work is a somewhat difficult enterprise due to the ever-present eclecticism. There is no single style of performance that the actors utilize and therefore no dominant set of skills that they are asked to develop in order to portray a role. Nevertheless, there are certain principles that could be seen as indicative of the Stan's Cafe performance style, particularly in their creation of personae which, through their unselfconscious *presentation* and *representation* of character and narrative, stands in contrast to some of the more autobiographical or overtly presentational practices from recent decades. In order to understand their approach more fully, the chapter begins by initially framing their performance styles within a contemporary context to note how there may be resonance or dissonance with twentieth- and twenty-first-century performance theory and practice. Within this frame, we then consider some of the main challenges faced by the actors when performing, including the simultaneous awareness of the individual and collective scenography, the fluid negotiation between persona and character and the impact of texts on the breadth of performance modes.

Setting the scene

The performances in Stan's Cafe's productions may be viewed in the context of, and sometimes running contrary to, specific shifts in twentieth- and twenty-first-century performance, beginning with Bertolt Brecht's innovations in persona and character and the subsequent establishment and centrality of postdramatic practices within contemporary theatre in the last fifty years. As early as the 1930s, Brecht was advocating a delineation between the performer and the persona they created, as a means of heightening social and political objectivity towards the narrative and thereby avoiding the inertia of sentimentality. 'Brecht distances the performer from the performed and differentiates the presence of the character from that of the performer. With characteristic dialectics,[1] Brecht requires the actor to depict her or his character's reality and yet stand outside it observing as an eye witness' (Kowalke 1994: 254). Significantly though, in terms of resonating with Stan's Cafe, Brecht viewed both the characterization *and* this 'eyewitness' role as dramatic constructions as noted by the influential performance theorist Philip Auslander: 'The persona that the Brechtian actor presents alongside of the character that she portrays is a fictional creation' (2002: 56).

In the latter half of the twentieth century, there was an ever-increasing focus, notably through the writings of Erving Goffman, Victor Turner, Richard Schechner and Michael Kirby, on the significance of *performance* as a more capacious term than theatre and the proposal that performance and everyday behaviour were not binary opposites but part of a continuum to be explored. Richard Schechner, informed by his work with The Performance Group in New York, cast a broad net around the term *performance* to enfold a range of social behaviours and rituals including routine tasks, sport and sex, proposing these as legitimate modes of performative action with their own codified procedures which were not discreet from theatrical performance (see **Text – TW**). This more expansive definition, while reframing our everyday activities, also reflected the trends in

---

[1] **Dialectics** – *Dialectical* theatre is the term Brecht came to prefer to *Epic* theatre in the latter part of his career. In basic terms, *dialectical* in this context refers to reasoned investigation of the truth from among two or more seemingly oppositional points of view. The notion of dialectics predates Brecht and has its roots in classical philosophy.

performing arts, including Happenings, Fluxus, Performance Art and Dance-Theatre, which increasingly embraced and experimented with non-representational and non-narrative forms. Michael Kirby wrote his influential article *On Acting and Non Acting* (1972) that similarly extended existing definitions of acting by proposing a broad continuum of stage acting from *non-matrixed performance* in which the performer 'is merely himself' (4) and the audience invests a performance context upon them, all the way through to the fictional construction of *complex acting* in which 'more and more complex elements are incorporated into the pretense' (9), such as physical characteristics or greater emotional depth.

In this period, the *actual* presence of performers on stage was being foregrounded in avant-garde practice, to the extent that role and character were becoming contestable, and at times rejected, terms **(TW 1)**. Lehmann, writing at the end of the twentieth century and drawing upon the ideas of Kirby, contended that 'the actor of postdramatic theatre is no longer the actor of a role but a performer offering his/her presence on stage for contemplation' (2006: 135). Andy Lavender, in *Performance in the Twenty-First Century: Theatres of Engagement* (2016), builds upon the analysis of Lehmann and Schechner, considering the nature of performing in contemporary postdramatic contexts yet noting that there is not quite the schism with dramatic theatre as might first appear, and in this respect his reflection is particularly pertinent for framing the emotionally articulate performance modes of Stan's Cafe. Citing Auslander, he initially summates this late-twentieth-century shift towards the practice and study of performance, when proposing that its rise

> marks the separation between representational drama (let's say fictionalized storytelling) on the one hand and performance as presentation (rather than the pretence of stage acting) on the other. Auslander describes this turn as 'a progressive redefinition of theatrical mimesis away from "character" toward "performance persona," with consequent redefinitions of the function of the performer's self in relation to performance.' (2016: 105)

The development of personae, as opposed to traditional characterizations, is a practice pursued by many experimental companies, including
Stan's Cafe, who, as James has stressed already, are suspicious of certain
pretences inherent in acting. However, as Lavender goes on to suggest,
the creation of a persona is not quite as distinguishable and removed
from dramatic character-led practice as we may initially believe:

> The term 'persona' suggests something person-like, a figure or
> being. It already conveys a tinge of performance, derived from its
> etymology: it means 'mask' in Latin. One can adopt a persona, or
> present a persona – be something or someone a little different from
> one's usual state. If persona can mean something more actual than
> a character, it also evokes an appearance that is different from one's
> normative self. …
>
> The distinction, then, between character and persona is not
> necessarily straightforward for 'persona' itself is a slippery term.
> It suggests a radical departure from character, but also a means of
> sustaining some of the attributes of character (appearance, difference,
> personality type) within any given presentation. (2016: 108–9)

The correlations between Stan's Cafe's practice with Brechtian
performance are highlighted by Fragkou, who notes that 'Stan's Cafe
tackles character largely through an exploration of Brechtian *Gestus*
which, according to Patrice Pavis, "radically cleaves the performance
in two blocks: the shown (the said) and the showing (the saying) (1982:
45)"' (2015: 211). Lavender's liminal interpretation of both persona
and character and Kirby's broad definition of acting begin to reveal
themselves immediately when in conversation with the actors from
the company. Amanda Hadingue, when reflecting on her performance
roles, said:

> It's not a character, but it is like a persona. It's all acting for me. You
> always want a bit of you in there, a bit of an imagined version of you. I
> never completely lose myself. You have to trace some sort of emotional
> journey for yourself through the piece. We would create fictional
> worlds and not every company was into that.

Likewise, Graeme Rose states that 'I always enjoyed acting. Characterisation is just a tool. I didn't see character acting as something that was mutually exclusive from making devised work.'

Lavender's analysis of persona as a subtler reframing of the performer's function on stage resonates across the practice of Stan's Cafe's which eschews some of the more austere postdramatic styles in which performers are arguably reduced to symbolic objects or manifestations of a concept, as opposed to real bodies of significance on stage. Likewise, the company rarely draw attention to their 'own presence' as outlined by Lehmann as, more akin to Brecht, there is always a clear, if subtle, veil of fiction. Stan's Cafe readily nurture fictional contexts, however brittle or minimal they may be, rather than resisting them. The performers always inhabit an imagined space and time and determinedly embody personae with recognizable traits of character which we may seek to understand and even empathize with, yet crucially are not coerced to do so through a psychologically emotive narrative. Sarah Archdeacon distilled the subtle difference between dramatic and postdramatic presentation of an emotional role when discussing *Ocean of Storms* (1996), which had the sensitive storyline of a lost child at its core, yet as Archdeacon distinguishes: 'I am showing you that I am caring about this person. I am not necessarily in that emotion myself.' The slight but significant distance between what is *shown* and what is *showing*, to use Pavis's words, is crucial.

The release from narrative and character-led text is also abetted by the diminishing influence of the play text and the development of director-led or collaborative theatre-maker approaches, as noted in the **Text** chapter. The agency of the devisor/actors and centrality of the directorial vision create greater opportunity to, in the words of Lavender, 'privilege the present person and her body over the imagined character' (2016: 106). As has already been discussed in the study of Stan's Cafe's own textual forms, the nature of the performing is fundamentally informed by the type of text that the actors are responding to. The degree of spoken word or precise physical action may determine the level to which they are constrained by the text, and the influence of different *source texts* may inform the performance style that is adopted, to perhaps evoke a filmic or radiophonic atmosphere. As the company's production ranges from *pure written texts* such as *The Just Price of Flowers* (2009), written by James, or *Finger Trigger Bullet Gun* (2014) by Nenad Prokić, *organic physical texts* such as *The Cleansing of Constance Brown* (2007), through to *instructional texts*, epitomized by *Twilightofthefreakingods* (2013), there is an almost infinite spectrum of verbal and physical styles that need to be accomplished and an ever-changing level of performer agency to negotiate within different performances. With a *written text*, the actors may be defined by the clear parameters of the dialogue from one moment to the next, while in an *instructional text*, they may have nothing more than guidance notes or a single instruction to direct them through the next fifteen minutes or even several hours.

This experimentation with text and the significance of the visual and the physical is a reminder of the influence of Robert Wilson upon the performances of Stan's Cafe. While there is definitely no attempt to ape Wilson's style, the impact of his aesthetic and his expectations on actors resonates throughout the history of the company. As noted in **Rehearsing and Directing**, both Wilson and James pay great attention to the detail of the visual image (Wilson refers to the creation of the 'visual book') and the precision of the scenography, including the actors. This requires them to have an ever-present attention to detail on stage, particularly the wider composition of which they are a part. Allied to this precision, the use of exact timings is another feature seen in the work of both practitioners. Ellen Halperin-Royer notes how actors recalled the detailed counting of seconds when working with Wilson on a radical interpretation of Büchner's *Danton's Death* in 1992: '[He] had me walk across the floor in 20, then sit down in 15 and put my hand to my neck, then tilt my head up in 12 and everyone would write that down' (2002: 323). This attention to the visual aesthetic has sometimes led to both Wilson and Stan's Cafe being criticized for a perceived absence of an emotional dimension in productions. Halperin-Royer, in an observation that could (perhaps without the bombast of Wilson) be applied to James and Stan's Cafe, highlights this assumption with Wilson's work but also distinguishes his alternative to the effects of psychological realism:

> Perhaps the most harmful preconception actors brought to rehearsal was an assumption that Wilson did not want the actors to connect emotionally with the material. This assumption was reinforced on the first day when Wilson stated that he hates naturalism, that to act naturally onstage is a lie. Wilson explained his preference for a formal, more distant theatre in which the audience can enter at will and actively interpret the images onstage. Far from telling the audience what to think or feel, Wilson wants to ask provocative questions for each audience member to answer individually. (2002: 328)

An important correlation between the two is the pursuit of an idea to its limits and the ensuing demand this places upon the actors. This requires many different kinds of endurance, as will be considered later in the chapter, in the pursuance of *what is necessary*. From a purely durational perspective, this dedication to the concept led Wilson, in his early career, to create a seven-hour 'silent opera' (*Deafman Glance* 1970), which was then superseded by a 168-hour epic entitled *Ka Mountain* (1972), staged on Haft Tan mountain in Iran. For Stan's Cafe, this instinct to see the idea through to its logical duration manifested itself in, among other shows, *24 Hour Scalextric* (2009), *Tuning Out with Radio Z* (2010) and *Twilightofthefreakingods*, all of which challenged the perseverance of actors and audience.

The idea is more important than the individual components.

This quote from Graeme Rose underscores the recurring ambition for Stan's Cafe to perform ideas. Rochi Rampal's response, when reflecting on her own performance intentions, is indicative of all the actors' perspectives on this subject: 'What matters are the ideas on stage. What is the *whole* thing that is happening? For Stan's Cafe I'm not looking for the satisfaction that comes from a traditional character in a play. I get satisfaction out of ideas, being part of a show that is asking questions and presenting ideas to a group of people.' Once again, there are parallels here with a Brechtian approach to performance, as Roland Barthes identifies: 'The *(Brechtian)* actor must present the very knowledge of the play's meaning. ... The actor must prove that he ... guides meaning towards its ideality' (1974: 37). The implication of this approach is that each individual actor is always considering the *wholeness* of the piece while simultaneously responding to their own individual, and often sizeable, performance challenges. This understated commitment to the performance as a collaboration reflects the continuing emphasis on the collective endeavour, ideally achieved without demonstrative displays of acting prowess, as Barthes also notes: 'He must not show that he knows how to act well' (ibid.).

As a final observation for this introduction, it may have already become apparent that there is a degree of fluidity between the terms *acting* and *performance*. Those who have performed for Stan's Cafe use both of these terms, often interchangeably, which first reflect the stylistic hinterlands and media-hybridity through which the productions roam and also the broadening definition of what acting can be conceived of in the light of new theorization and the collapsing of traditional performance boundaries. Both *acting* and *performing* will therefore appear as equivalent terms in the following pages, with the caveat that we accept that not every theatre-maker or theatre-scholar may wish to conflate them in this way.

Bigger pictures: Keeping an understated eye on the *whole*

How does this look, how do I look, how do we look together?

Rochi Rampal

It would be overstating the case to say that the actors in a Stan's Cafe performance always have a clear sense of the overall aesthetic and how the whole event is being perceived by an audience. Amid the intensity of the logistical, physical or dialogical challenges they face during a show, it would be unrealistic to expect them to retain an ever-present sense of the 'bigger picture'. However, there is a recurring impression, which comes across strongly in conversation, that they try to be alert, wherever possible, to how their individual performances may at any given moment be contributing to the scenographic whole. This disposition of self-observation is highlighted in Sarah Archdeacon's assertion: 'There is something about being present in order to show the material. I have to be really certain about how I am showing myself on the stage so I can best execute the material.' This view is echoed by Craig Stephens: 'I'm often thinking about what kind of stage pictures I'm making, particularly with the visual shows.' Rampal, when discussing *Twilightofthefreakingods*, commented that 'You become aware of the image that you're a part of because of the other people on stage, things are falling into place and making sense. There's a relief from the terrifying unknown to the safety of some kind of logic or beautiful image or flicker of a story that you realise is coming together.' Jack Trow, also recalling *Twilightofthefreakingods*, remembers one set of events in the production which epitomizes the need for the actors to be mindful of and embrace the larger image that they are involved in:

> There was one part with me, Jake [Oldershaw] and Chris [Dugrenier] swapping a spear between each of us whilst everyone was on the bouncy castle upstage having what seemed to be a food fight (which we had no instruction for) but we could hear all this, everyone was laughing and getting covered in sandwiches. So you have this realization that I'm part of an image but I can't see it and I can't look around to see it but we just have to trust that this is the image and that it's doing something for the audience. There is an outside eye, a sort of out of body sense that you need because it's so visual, you're thinking about what's the image you're creating and then doing it as simply as possible.

Performing in such circumstances necessitates a particular blend of performance attitudes. Notably, it requires a significant degree of humility as performers have to accept, particularly in the larger scale pieces, that they are part of a greater endeavour, of which they may only be able to control or influence certain elements. Secondly, it demands the ability to adopt a dual perspective simultaneously, as the actors navigate their own embodiment of role while conceptually 'stepping out' of their own position on stage to be alert to how they 'fit' within the larger image. It may be suggested that all performers in any genre have to accommodate this, but the precision of the image composition is so significant with Stan's Cafe, influenced as it so often is by filmic and visual artistic imagery, that their actors must be more adept than most. In *The Cardinals* (2011), for example, which will be looked at more closely later in the chapter, the toil and sweat of the performers is testament to the actors 'in the moment' commitment to their role yet their contortions within the puppet theatre, in order to 'present' the image out to the audience as beatifically as the cardinals would wish, demonstrates this dual responsibility.

Here *and* there: Negotiating persona and character

Real is a special pretend

from *Bingo in the House of Babel* (1994)

Brecht and Lavender's interpretation of persona and character alongside Kirby's reappraisal of acting as a continuum provides germane lenses through which to view the performing modes of Stan's Cafe. For the performers in the company, there is no conflict between the presentation of a role as a persona and the capacity to make that presentation heartfelt and, if necessary, through representations of character, emotional. Inherent in this approach is a fluid interpretation of *presentational* and *representational* acting; an interplay between the *here* of the shared space and time yet simultaneously residing in some degree of fictional *there*, as considered earlier in **Space and Time**. This interplay between *here* and *there* is constantly in negotiation, often suspended ambiguously. The performers may address the audience directly in *presentational* mode, as in the case of the *Lurid and Insane* 'gig', while they are in role. In *The Anatomy of Melancholy* (2013), and more obviously in *Home of The Wriggler* (2006), the stage fiction gains an extra layer as the performers adopt personae who in turn take on roles as part of a performance within the performance. This is explicit in *Home of The Wriggler*, where the first line frames the show as a mere section of a much larger script:

H   *Do you know where we're going from? Section 49. Ok 3, 2, 1.*

C   *Trev worked on security.*

A   Trev his father Stan and his uncle Frank all walked through B Gate together in 1969.

Later, the fictional personae correct each other on factual inaccuracies in the story they are telling or need reminding of who is related to who in the intricate web of relationships connected to the car factory.

C   Jim.
    Jim would have been Frank's son-in-law.
    They would have got on he thought.
    Jim moved to Birmingham when he was 21.
    He liked the fact people made things there.
    He worked as a waiter part time to pay for his writing.
    Jim met Fi after she split with Nick

A   Rick

C   Jim met Fi after she split with Rick, after the rallying crash.

In these cases, the performers are always *representing* complex personae inhabiting extraspatial and extratemporal worlds. Personae, reflecting a Brechtian approach, are always the conduit and the company never look to address the audience literally as themselves, no matter how the roles may seem to adopt the everyday accents and mannerisms of the real performers; it is that slight distance from self that creates the potential. Michael Kirby identified the duality of such a performance mode and, by his judicious use of speech marks, acknowledged that the performer, however 'real' they may seem, is always a staged variant of themselves: 'In almost all performances, we see the "real" person and also that which he is representing or pretending. The actor is visible within the character' (1972: 10). Such personae, as created by Stan's Cafe, liberate the performers to fully commit to the events in which they find themselves and to each other as they struggle to achieve their tasks or attempt to understand who they are and what they are about.

The personae are often fragile entities, unsure of their identities, and the performers' task is to build their reality one moment at a time. *Good and True* (2000) explored such roles, as the description of the show on the company website indicates:

> Four lost interrogators are thrashing around in areas they're hopelessly underqualified to deal with. They try everything they can to discover the truth but when they get close to it, they don't recognise it. Questions are asked and answers are given but nothing ever quite adds up. Facts slide around, become crystal clear for a moment, but then are gone.

Hadingue, who devised and performed the show, reflected on the acting challenge this created:

> *Good and True* was about forming identities as you go along. 'Is this my identity?' I don't mind not knowing who my parents are, where I went to school. I just like convincing the other person on stage who I am. You're sort of responding to it moment by moment, building the fiction as you go along. That is the level of challenge.

This attention to the ephemeral reality that the performers find themselves in and the acting challenge of constructing the fiction they inhabit consequently diminishes the need for psychological character development. Rampal reinforces this point: 'Those complex motivations, causes and effects, whilst they are there, they're not part of the process of the shows that I've been involved in.' This approach does not suit all performers, as Rose notes: 'There are a lot of performers who can't cope without having those things pinned down but I think what's typical of a Stan performer is that implicit understanding that this is their job. You find your own individual route through the material and you don't necessarily have to have the conversation with the other performers.'

Those who have worked with the company for a long time have adapted their rehearsal and performance strategies so as to embrace and exploit the independence and potential for spontaneity such practice brings.

Although psychological complexity may not be central to the performers mindset, there are undoubtedly intricate strata of *presentation* and *representation* to be constructed and the challenge for the actors within *The Cardinals* epitomizes this. When the cardinals are 'offstage' (an area that the audience have full view of), they adopt a hyperrealistic style, shuffling or running about the entire stage in readiness for each scene, whispering anxiously to each other and the Muslim stage manager. By contrast, within their own biblical narrative and framed in the tiny central 'puppet' stage, they adopt an abrupt shift in scale and also in acting style. Here, there are two more subtle acting strata at work, as the Stan's Cafe performers must convincingly portray *both* the integrity of the cardinals' evangelizing conviction but also their characters naïve and flawed theatrical skills when exposed on stage. 'It's a very narrow line that you teeter along in this production' recalled Gerard Bell, 'and sometimes you can act too well. I think it is genuinely touching though.' Kirby (1972) wrote of the commensurate challenges of *simple* and *complex* acting, warning against the assumption that complex psychological acting must be more demanding. In the instance of *The Cardinals*, the actors have to negotiate the difficult enterprise of embodying the complexity of the central characters' faith, yet expressing it so incisively through the limitations of their 'simple' dumb-show acting; any self-awareness of the cardinals own dramatic failings is clouded by the mist of their religious fervency. Stephens, making specific reference to *The Cardinals*, explains his own perspective on the layers within Stan's Cafe personae, reflecting a conscious creation and *presentation* of role yet with (as Gerard Bell also intimated) an emotional, *representational* intent:

> I think what I do is acting but it comes from a more external process rather than thinking about the characterization. We are pretending to be other people but we are not taking on all the mannerisms of those

people. We are visible through this mode of performance. If we were to put an accent on it would be deliberate, 'Here's me putting it on'. But then within that pretense there are moments of emotion. In *The Cardinals* when I'm Judas and Gerard [Bell] is Jesus, I'm pecking him on the cheek and he's being taken away. That's quite an emotional moment and we're aware of that and giving it space. We are clearly not those people as you've just seen us be someone else but within that moment hopefully there is a real emotional charge between us two. It is a moment of *us* acting and it is a moment of *them* [the cardinals] acting.

The potential of the more 'nominal' acting roles is equally attended to, however lightly the personae are worn, as in the case of *The Black Maze* (2000) or *Of All The People In All The World* (2003), which superficially would only appear to demand a degree of supervision over the proceedings, yet this would underestimate the precision required for these undemonstrative portrayals. Such roles, which various performers have referred to as 'curators', 'functionaries' or 'guardians', undoubtedly *present* themselves directly to the audience in the 'here and now', yet the performers imbue their actions and their environment with just enough representation of a fiction (a *side-step*, to use Hadingue's phrase from earlier) so as to reframe the experience for the audience. At the entrance to *The Black Maze* installation, an actor was stationed as a 'gatekeeper' to police the waiting audience and regulate the number of people allowed in at any given time. However, as Rose explains, their function was more nuanced than that 'as that gatekeeper I held a really valuable function that no museum usher could do, it was definitely a performance role. It was so important to drop in enough little indicators to frame the audience's expectations.' So, even in this brief meeting between actor and audience member at the top of the steps into the maze, there is the potential for a persona to build dramatic tension, not through histrionics but a more low-key enactment, more akin to a fairground waltzer attendant, aloof yet radiating a 'Dare you?' demeanour that simultaneously attracts and repels you. 'Is there an acting challenge in this?' was Trow's inceptive question before working on the piece. 'I initially saw it as a front of house role but then I saw Graeme *(Rose)* really embellishing it. Then I thought, you've got those thirty seconds before you open the door to have some kind of engagement, some fun, adding to their experience.' This low-key quality is also evident in the curators in *Of All The People In All The World*, who attend to the creation of the piles of rice throughout each day's performance, present yet unobtrusive. Trow, who has worked on many versions of the show throughout the world, explained that he saw his challenge in terms of 'How low can I go?', working on the maxim that 'less is more'. These unassuming presences are crucial, however, in framing the work as a theatrical piece, as it unfolds and shifts over the course of its duration in a site, as he emphasizes: 'I see it as a piece of visual art done by a theatre company. If it were visual art, it would just be created and left. Because it's us, Stan's Cafe, stories are at the heart of it and so it has a fluid and amorphous quality.' As with *The Black Maze*, the performers in *Of All The People In All The World* have that crucial interaction with the audience, the brief moments of conversation or simply sharing the space in which the personae, through their presence, transform the rice from inanimate objects into bodies to be witnessed and cared for. Stephens has reflected that, integral to his role in this piece, is his presence in the space, 'completing the image' as a custodian of the rice. There is a correlation here with two stages within Kirby's matrix, both *non-matrixed representation* and *received acting*. In the first of these,

> the referential elements are applied to the performer and are not acted *by* him. … The character and place matrices are weak, intermittent or non-existent, we see a person, not an actor. As 'received' references increase, however, it is difficult to say that the performer is not acting even though he is doing nothing that we could define as acting. … When the matrices are strong, persistent and reinforce each other, we see an actor, no matter how ordinary the behavior. (1972: 5)

The performers of Stan's Cafe inherently understand the potential of inhabiting an environment with conviction but also offering subtle prompts; functional but evocative costumes, slight tonal change in voice and deliberation over actions, in the case of *Of All The People In All The World*, as a means for the audience to invest a set of references and significances upon them. Likewise, they are able to finely increase and adjust the 'received references' so that even the most innocuous roles, such as those manning *The Black Maze*, are reframed as acting performances. It is through these modes that such events, which may in other circumstances be bracketed as visual art or installations, become theatrical.

Tasks are a central strategy in how personae manifest themselves within performance. These tasks are presented in more or less overt ways, depending on the production, and reflect the direct, uncluttered style of the company, as identified by Rose:

> A lot of the work is driven by task, not driven by character psychology as the sheer fascination of watching the animal activity on stage is what's often so much more appealing. So knowing these people have got tasks, a sense of purpose, is really crucial. What's true of so many shows is that there's an intention in performance which is very direct. It's not about flannel, it's not about psychology, it's not about wrestling with internal motivations, it's a very real practical solution being delivered in the moment.

Sometimes these tasks are easily observable, as in *Of All The People In All The World*, which outlines very specific activities and advice for the actors in terms of weighing and presenting the rice and the statistics, and these are clearly framed and witnessed *as* tasks being undertaken within the performance. This section, taken from the production's Performer's Book, highlights the attention to detail in how the tasks should be carried out:

Weighing and Displaying the Rice

There are three sets of scales available to use during the performance. The large set will take around 3 kg of rice, the middle set up to 300 g and the scientific scales should be used for measuring small amounts up to about 4 or 5 g. Although it may seem laborious it's a good idea to split up the weighing out of a quantity of rice so that the technical scales are used to measure the small part of an amount, rather than weighing out 2 g for example, on the larger scales. Using all the scales looks good. Small numbers (certainly less than 120) should be counted out grain by grain.

PLEASE KEEP THE WEIGHTS TIDY AND PUT THE VERY SMALL ONES BACK IN THE PLASTIC BOX TO AVOID THEM BEING LOST.

Below is a table showing what quantity of rice will fit onto what size of paper. (Amounts are grains of rice/numbers of people).

There are 60 grains of rice in 1 gram.

  A4 = 15,000 grains
  A3 = 50,000 grains
  A2 = 200,000 grains
  A1 = 600,000 grains
  A0 = 1,000,000

YOU CAN FIT ABOUT 5 MILLION PEOPLE MAXIMUM PER METRE ON THE ROLL OF PAPER.

YOU CAN FIT UP TO 2.5 MILLION PEOPLE ON A 1M X 1M SQUARE SHEET.

The labelled sheet corresponding to the amount should be placed in the centre, front edge of the pile of rice and stuck with Pritt Stick.[2] We'll try to keep piles evenly spaced and neatly lined up.

However, even these tasks within *Of All The People In All The World* are interpreted differently by each performer as they construct the event afresh in different locations, from factory floors to churches, around the world. Trow refers to this production as a 'writing job', in the sense of crafting different narratives in the comparisons and juxtapositions of statistics, and viewing the show in this frame allows for a significant

---

[2] Other small tubes of adhesive are available.

degree of ownership and authorship for the actors. Rose reveals the impact of individual approaches to performing in this production:

> It will always betray our own particular knowledge and perception of that place whatever it may be, which is why it's useful to have local performers to counter-act that. In terms of the Stan cohort, each of us has a different way of approaching it and it's quite free-form in how that's designated. There is a co-operative approach, it isn't necessarily dictated, there's a lot of space 'from above'. For example, Jake's [Oldershaw] own personal interest are the big statistics whilst Jack [Trow] spends a lot of time on detailed statistics. Some spend more time than others neatening things up. Each have their favoured territories. A personal interest of mine is in smaller statistics. I'm interested in the graphic layout and how a series of related statistics work. One I've always enjoyed laying out is comparative CO2 emissions as a spiral form.[3] And I think of the real-time delivery of this as a performance.

In many other instances, the tasks are not overtly enacted to the audience, the rehearsal origins fading into the background as the performers discover how to adapt the presentation of them on stage, as Stephens remarks: 'What actors do is transform those mundane tasks into something else. You might be able to see the task in there somewhere but the acting transforms it into performance.' This shift from task to performance is also reflected upon by James: 'In *The Cardinals* the "off stage" action started as 90% task and 10% performance and as they grew to master the tasks the performance quotient went up so now although they continue to execute the logistical tasks of costume and set changes, prop manipulation and technical operation they think about this less.' Hadingue recalls how Stan's Cafe's tasks were always framed within a fictional context rather than being purely performer orientated: 'Our tasks were not all encompassing as for companies like Impact Theatre Co-operative. We might have had real things to do, such as dance

---

[3] A set of statistics 'The residents of Chad it would take to emit the same CO2 as one citizen of [insert other country]' are often included as part of *Of All The People In All The World*. Note the nominal 'citizen of Chad' is used to convert a 'per capita' statistic into a 'number of people' statistic (the only kind of statistic the piece allows).

around flat out for ten minutes in *Voodoo City*, but I never lost sight of other actors and the audience. You're always feeding from the audience. I never completely lost myself.' In these circumstances, tasks can become a series of signposts to mark the way through a performance, onto which the performers can hang moments of significance, as Stephens notes: 'I try to find moments within a piece, a line through a show, which isn't specifically an emotional or character-driven line. I know I've got these moments I want to hit; a tone I want to find at certain points. It can be an emotional form of journey. It's about relating to the other performers on stage.'

> I was always told that I was very good at enigmatically 'walking around' for Stan's Cafe.
>
> Sarah Archdeacon

Throughout this section, a constant refrain has been an emphasis on transparency, simplicity and understatement that is so typical of Stan's Cafe. It is evident in Archdeacon's comment above, likewise Stephen's reference to consciously 'putting on an accent', Rose's dismissal of 'flannel' and Trow's consideration of 'How low can I go?' The performance palette from which they draw is never embellished with unnecessary trickery, as Trow deftly summarizes: 'It has to be uncomplicated, there's no room for self-indulgence or frills. It's about finding the cleanest and most efficient way of presenting a story.' This measured approach to performance must not be conflated with reticence or effortlessness, however, as when a show requires an injection of anarchy or 'animal activity' to pursue *what is necessary*, then Stan's Cafe will readily oblige.

What is necessary

Rose believes that the company has always been attracted and accustomed to hard, physical work:

> This was instilled in us when studying under Pete Brooks. There was a sense that performance had a brutal quality to it, you could feel the

impact of the physical work, the repetition to the point where meaning changes, your sense of time and space gets manipulated and you have quite an intense emotional reaction to it. For James, the concept needs to be played out to its logical end, it doesn't pander to safe territory.

This last comment reinforces the comparison with Robert Wilson, and *endurance* is a term that many Stan's Cafe actors use, but in this context is perhaps best thought of as *what is necessary*. On occasion, this may involve enduring long spells on stage while at other times this physical commitment manifests itself in more liberated and ludicrous releases of energy expended during the show, but also before and after in physically demanding 'get ins' and 'get outs'. This range is evident from the riotous quality of early shows including *Voodoo City* (1995), where 'slabs of material' were butted against each other, including un-choreographed dancing and improvised psychic possession, to *Lurid and Insane* (2001), with its flamboyant rock and roll tropes. Sheer physical effort is manifest in so many productions, from *Canute the King* (1993) and *The Carrier Frequency* (1999), both performed in water, through to the durational demands of *24 Hour Scalextric*, *Tuning Out with Radio Z* and *Twilightofthefreakingods*, or the stamina required for the four-and-a-half-minute *It's Your Film* (1998), performed sixty times each day for days on end. Trow reflects on how endurance may be interpreted in the context of Stan's Cafe:

> Endurance is at the heart of lots of Stan shows and there are lots of ways that endurance manifests itself. With *Of All The People In All The World* its standing up all day for six hours a day, walking around slowly, deliberately slowly, doing things the long way round in steel toe-capped shoes. Sometimes there is an existential endurance, for example in Copenhagen there was a massive team of us performing twelve hour days but the festival marketing didn't work and literally no-one came. Sometimes the endurance is physical *and* mental as with *Constance* or *Cardinals* as even when you're off you're never 'off'. There's always a bit of set to move or someone else's costume to help with. In Cologne, for *Constance*, it was so hot that I got

simultaneous cramp attacks in my legs and couldn't walk for hours after a show.

Stan's Cafe's actors are clear that performing in many of the productions is physically gruelling. Bell sums up this view:

> They are physically arduous to perform. For *The Cleansing of Constance Brown*, it's also the physical weight of the set and so the *get-in* is heavy and likewise for *The Cardinals* you have an enormous re-set before you can do the show again, which also adds to the arduousness of it. So you have an arduous performance, an arduous preparation and re-preparation for each and quite arduous *get-ins* and *get-outs* so there is a lot of … arduousness.

Bell's liberal use of the word arduous underlines the physical effort that the actors expel in performance, but this is often matched by the mental effort of remembering extensive bodies of text in shows such as *The Anatomy of Melancholy* or *Finger Trigger Bullet Gun* (2014). One show which embodies this spirit of endurance is *Home of The Wriggler* (2006), in which the actors had the task of powering the show themselves, for the whole eighty minutes, through a series of hand-cranked dynamos and exercise bikes. The scenographic effect of this was to create a flickering, early cinematic world, evoking an ethereal, post-apocalyptic time and place as envisaged by James in the early ideas phase of the project. This task was often done simultaneously with performing complex dialogue in a scene. The physical effort can be seen by the audience as, with each down-stroke of a pedal, the car headlight flares, the performers own faces shine more brightly and their breath comes more falteringly as the job of performing the show about work takes its toll. In an interview with *Time Out, Beijing* in 2010, James commented that 'it is best for the show when they get out of breath, I don't like it when they are too fit, it makes it seem easier than it should'. The importance of this strategy, therefore, was not to simply make the actors work physically hard for the sake of it but to witness the effort of 'manufacturing' both as a metaphor for its decline and our own fragility *and* as a means of creating a specific stage atmosphere. Fragkou, citing *Home of The Wriggler*, identifies the results of such 'arduous' practice: 'In a number of the company's productions, the distinction between character and actor is rendered visible through devices that draw attention to the performers physical effort as a commentary about the story being told' (2015: 211). Her observation reflects the company's intention that, however eccentric it may appear, the form and content must justify their relationship.

Inherent in this phrase *what is necessary* is an emphasis, therefore, on *not* enduring for the sake of it, with any intimation of narcissism such excess brings with it. It could certainly be argued, as noted earlier in the book, that Stan's Cafe are keen to position themselves as 'manufacturers' of theatre, grounded as they are in the Jewellery Quarter of Birmingham and consciously demonstrating their physical means of production. This ethos within the company guards against any degree of self-absorption on the part of performers, as Bell advocates: 'Performing in itself is hard work but there doesn't need to be excess of hard work. The performance should be as easy as it needs to be.' However, he then goes on to say 'I wonder if there is something of a puritanical element in Stan's Cafe. The feeling that what we are doing is frivolous and so to justify itself there has to be hard work.' While there is never any hint of self-indulgence, such a comment raises the question of whether the company can sometimes push themselves too hard in pursuit of an idea. This question is reflected upon by a number of performers who wonder if the company may, on occasion, severely test the tolerances of actors and audience by going 'the long way round'. For example, both Hadingue and Jon Ward speculated on whether *Tuning Out with Radio Z* could have accomplished the same result in two hours rather than its initial four hours.[4] However, it can be equally argued that such duration and the associated technique of repetition begin to reveal new levels of

---

[4]   *Tuning Out with Radio Z* (2010) was originally performed at MAC Birmingham, with two hours of radio webcast followed by four hours of stage performance (with simultaneous webcast). The staged section was cut to three hours in later versions.

performance and meaning as the layers of artifice peel away over time, as noted in **Space and Time**.

Such exposure, created by duration, complexity of task, physical effort and sheer brinkmanship, heightens the element of risk and the importance of trust which often feature in discussion with the actors. Rampal emphasizes the level of jeopardy and the need for mutual reassurance that is sometimes experienced:

> In terms of my time with the company, I've sometimes felt that my job could not work on stage. In *The Cardinals* for example, the stage manager is frantically running around the stage, the cardinals are flying up and down behind the puppet theatre, things have to happen at precise moments. So much could be missed and not work. There's so much that could go wrong. Logistical risk, physical risk, risk in how the audience perceive it. For *Twilightofthefreakingods* that first show came down to a terrifying leap. That first night was like the first time in a rehearsal room where we've had an idea and we've got to put it up on it's feet. Here is your task, this is what we want from this moment, show me what it looks like. It's a mix of thrill, fear and safety. That fear is the thing that all that liveness relies on, if there isn't that then how is it going to work. But you *really* need to know it's going to be OK!

All of the actors who worked on both of these shows refer to a sense of brinkmanship, in *Twilightofthefreakingods* because it only ever had two untested performances and, with *The Cardinals*, because the early shows, particularly at its premiere in Montpellier, France, were shown before the whole production had had the chance to be run in its entirety, hence Bell simply referring to this as the 'Montpellier panic'. Rose ruefully recalls this first performance in France:

> Performing *The Cardinals* for the first time was abject terror because we'd never strung the whole thing together before, so it was literally an endurance; the mental and physical ordeal of trying to get from start to finish intact. There was something very real and visceral about that experience that could never be repeated and as a performer

you'd never want to repeat it because it was fear and terror driving it. However, this gave the audience a visceral appreciation of the show's mechanics.

The actors also wryly note that James always viewed this first show as the best ever as it captured an unrepeatable sense of tension and endeavour against the odds; the cardinals' intensity manifesting itself through the actors' real experience. Unrepeatability and unpredictability in a performance, either because it is only scheduled as a 'one-off' or because its structure permits endless permutations, unrepeatable from one show to another, are regular features of their experimentation. *Tuning Out with Radio Z*, performed by Hadingue and Stephens,[5] was a notable case in point in its durational improvisational structure, loosely based upon and a subversion of hospital radio tropes.

Tuning Out with Radio Z was an attempt to share with audiences the seductive long-form improvisations of the Stan's Cafe rehearsal room. Each performance responded to a different theme, decided shortly before 'curtain up', and was set in the studios of Radio Z during the broadcast of their late-night show *Tuning Out*. Each performance had two audiences: a live theatre audience watched the performers on and off air as they broadcast *Tuning Out*, which was listened to by a radio audience listening remotely. Both audiences were encouraged to contribute to the improvisation via the show's online message board, which was moderated by an offstage 'producer'.

Hadingue recalls that 'this epic, incredibly challenging piece (from a performer's perspective, at least), really showed the extent to which James trusted Craig and I to improvise a Stan show from scratch'. This

---

[5] Graeme Rose and Bernadette Russell replaced Amanda Hadingue for later performances of *Tuning Out with Radio Z* (2010).

Figure 8.1 Broadcasting to the auditorium and audiences across the web in *Tuning Out with Radio Z* (2010).

level of trust creates a certain level of performance jeopardy, as Stephens remembers:

> This was a scary performance to do. We would do a little bit of preparation before once we had been given the theme by James a couple of hours before the show – getting together a list of possible features, chatting about ideas that the theme suggested but beyond that we didn't know what would happen and of course didn't know what the audience might offer up. The show relied on trusting your fellow performer and having a sense of their performance style, their interests, quirks and so forth, being able to spot when some fruitful material was developing and being able to develop that between you. Being able to take a risk hoping that your partner would be able to come along on the ride. Knowing when material wasn't working as well and being able to get out of it.

Whatever generates the risk, this sense of continuous exploration is a fundamental feature of Stan's Cafe, as Jon Ward identifies: 'You're not there to make something finished, it's experimental. If you've finished, then you've experimented inadequately.'

Performance and text

One of the most striking features about Stan's Cafe's performances is the breadth of styles on show and the range of skills and aptitudes required to articulate these styles successfully. This breadth stems from the ideas-driven artistic policy and the subsequent range of texts that are created to realize those ideas, from dialogue-led performances such as *The Just Price of Flowers* or *The Anatomy of Melancholy* through to non-verbal, physically dexterous work including *The Cleansing of Constance Brown* and beyond to the low-key 'facilitation' of shows like *The Black Maze* or *Of All The People In All The World*. Text is a key factor in establishing the type of performing/acting required in each circumstance. This statement is reinforced when we consider how the text types of Stan's Cafe noticeably correlate with Raymond Williams analysis of text and action, written in 1954 yet still pertinent in the twenty-first century, as a means of seeing the impact of text on performance (see **Text**). These types of stage action, as interpretations of a written text, illuminate the scope of the performance challenges faced by the company's actors as they highlight the levels of autonomy or constraint that different text types facilitate.

Scripted, dialogic text has played a significant part in Stan's Cafe's practice, generated either through improvisation, in the case of many of the early shows, and written up into a *notational text* or authored by an individual writer as a *pure, written text*. Williams refers to the performance of these as 'acted speech', for which he writes: 'Speech and movement are determined by the arrangement of the words, according to the known conventions. ... Performance, here, is a physical communication of a work that is, in its text, dramatically complete' (1991: 162). Williams' observation indicates that such a text requires the performers to draw upon a more conventional set of performing strategies, as was the case for *Finger Trigger Bullet Gun* or, a few years earlier, with *The Just Price of Flowers*. Trow recalls how this latter show 'felt like a much more natural habitat for me, to which I could bring my actor training. It felt less like a Stan show as there was a preexisting script. We weren't devisors. It was more a case of – Turn up, learn your lines and don't bump into the furniture.' While the performance tasks for this show may have been a trifle more loquacious and specific, in reality, Trow's summary of the acting parameters and the confidence with which he was able to approach the show with his conventional actor training skills reflect some of the implicit demands of Kirby's notion of *complex acting*, encompassing a greater degree of characterization and script-led decision making. However, as Kirby is eager to point out, this does not equate to a higher level of skill as 'the acting/non-acting continuum is independent of value judgments' (1972: 9). Likewise, for Stan's Cafe, there is no hierarchy of performing styles as the value or success of any performance mode is always judged against its capacity to communicate the specific ideas of a production. Some actors from the company identify different levels of acting required (phrases such as 'low-key' or 'full-on' are used), and sometimes they signify a preference for one type rather than another, but this is never with a sense of one being more difficult than any other or one production having greater kudos than the next due to the acting required.

The *instructional texts* may potentially be seen as antithetical to the dialogue-based work yet it is immediately evident how equally challenging such texts are for performers, although for differing reasons. The detailed frame of time codes and instructions in a work such as *Twilightofthefreakingods* creates a tension for performers to work to a schedule, yet simultaneously leaves them with voids of space and time to fill. Rampal remembers her own reactions when faced with the time-coded tasks of that production: 'I had an instruction to make an image of some blackbirds flying using some black umbrellas. How am I supposed to make blackbirds fly for twenty minutes? Are they supposed to flap or glide, what are they supposed to do?' Trow, echoing the earlier reactions to risk, was even more agitated about his experience: 'I was terrified. I had the instruction, for forty-five minutes, to solve a Rubik's cube until someone climbs through the window. That was my only instruction!' These experiences of Rampal and Trow resonate with Williams' description of what he referred to as 'visual enactment', for which, in some cases, 'the text does no more than prescribe an *effect*, of which the means must be worked out in performance' (1991: 162). Performances with such a degree of freedom for interpretation, yet bounded within a precise frame, are a common thread throughout Stan's Cafe's practice and can be seen, for example, in *Of All The People In All The World* which, although lasting up to several hours per day, only requires a few pages of instructions for the actors to base their routines around.

The range of *source* texts has created a plethora of genre- or media-specific challenges for the company, requiring actors to inhabit performance modes that appropriate from film, radio or carnival sideshow as much as from theatre. Film, as has been suggested in other chapters, plays a major part in the aesthetic of certain shows and reflects the diaspora of inspirations that James and the company draw upon.

Figure 8.2 Rochi Rampal improvises according to a memorized timetable in *Twilightofthefreakingods* (2013).

Stephens highlights its interplay alongside other acting tropes: 'How can we make that moment work best? Maybe it needs a bit of naturalistic acting to work best, maybe it needs a bit of film acting. I wonder in fact whether it's a bit like film acting as you've often got to literally hit a mark.' *It's Your Film* was a live four-and-a-half-minute performance in a small booth for one audience member, but was heavily influenced by noir film as well as carnival sideshow trickery in the form of Pepper's Ghost. Among the plethora of skills required by the actors was the need, as Stephens's comment highlights, to 'hit a mark' over and over again. In such a short, intense performance, the acting challenge was to sustain precision and intensity time after time, particularly as familiarity (up to ninety shows a day) could engender a loss of focus. Rose recalled how they would reinvigorate their performances for this show by 'writing places and dates on slips of paper, *Paris 1950, London 1898* and so on, and then deliver the same lines but with an intention inspired by the suggested time and place. Just finding little tiny glimmers of purpose like this, to help motivate you, can add a lot of colour.'

The skills of a film actor are demanded in many of the productions, including *The Cleansing of Constance Brown,* which relies on short, intense bursts of action, often out of sequence so there is no emotional arc to hold on to. However, as Stephens points out, there is still a need to develop character for those brief moments on stage: '*The Cleansing of Constance Brown* is very filmic, but even though it's so fragmented and you're playing seven different roles, there's a lot more characterization in that than in many other shows.' *The Cardinals,* as well as taking influence from Renaissance art, was inspired by the films of Parajanov, which therefore necessitated the actors, when inside the puppet frame, to articulate their bodies so as to evoke a filmic or painterly point of view directly from head on. Two recent productions, *A Translation of Shadows* (2015) and *Made Up* (2016), have overtly taken their form and content from film, the former exploring the world of Japanese silent films and the role of the Benshi narrator while the latter centring on the relationship between a young film actress and her make-up artist, using a range of screens to blur the lines between the actress's real and fictional worlds. For *A Translation of Shadows*, Stephens played the Benshi role and had to balance the competing demands of the film behind him and the need to engage the live audience whose attention was potentially drawn solely towards the screen. Stephens recalls how he approached the performance of this role:

> It felt that the key in performing the Benshi was to know the film inside out in order to interact with it with confidence. As the Benshi I wanted to have most of my performance played out to the audience, to be able to engage with them as a live presence in front of the screen. So I was keen not to be constantly turning my head back to glance at the film. I tried to make my looks at the screen be deliberate and part of the action rather than checking to see where we had got to. As the run of performances developed inevitably my skill at this grew as I became more familiar with the rhythm and detail of the film. It was great to be able to anticipate moments in the film, land parts of my text at just the right place, gesture to the screen to highlight an image or place myself within the filmic frame.

Figure 8.3 Marie Kitagawa is trapped in a cinematic loop by the controlling Benshi in *A Translation of Shadows* (2015).

Conclusion

It is self-evident from this chapter that to perform for Stan's Cafe across a number of productions require a plethora of strategies and an awareness that your role is always woven in to the wider vision on stage and the pursuit of the idea. The creation of personae is central to their methodology but these are presented with care, curated by the actors, and no matter what the apparent values or emotions they present, from pious pomposity to emotional vulnerability, these characters are presented without self-conscious irony or self-deprecation. Even when the roles seem to be minimal, removed from the intricate *matrix* of complex acting, they are never underestimated as there is an understanding of how their presence is fundamental in making theatre manifest. There is always an integrity to their performances, which sometimes demands feats of endurance from duration to heavy lifting, and often the yielding to significant creative risk with leaps into the unknown. Simply put, performing for Stan's Cafe is hard work but it is never ostentatious or full of 'flannel', only what is necessary.

Stan in action: Performing

Actors should talk to actors about acting, not directors. Actors are the experts on acting. As a director, I'm sure I spend more time creating problems for actors than solving them. So here are some problems for you!

1. Play with doing real things while you are acting.
   a. Do simple tasks that mesh with what's going on: knitting, cooking, painting; if it's a kitchen-sink drama, do the washing up!
   b. Do something tangential and possibly initially inexplicable while you're acting and tie it into the show at the end. So make a custard pie and throw it in someone's face at the end of the show.

In *Finger Trigger Bullet Gun,* we set up dominoes through the show.

c. Do something complicated and real that also helps the show do its thing.

d. Applying different make-up looks on stage did this job for us in *Made Up.*

2. Add inverted commas around your acting. Try adding – 'she said' before you say what she said. Try adding 'then he said' as a cue for another actor to say what their character then said. Read out stage directions as prompts for actions you then perform ('he puts his arm round her waist'). Play around with holding the performance at arm's length like this, then see if you can pull the performance close and get a dividend from this contrast. This was something we enjoyed playing with in *Home of the Wriggler.*

9

Audience

What's in this chapter?

There is a mercurial relationship between Stan's Cafe and their audiences and in this chapter we aim to illuminate how this unpredictable affiliation manifests itself in both distinct yet interconnected forms across the range of production aesthetics, from the one-to-one intimacy of *It's Your Film* (1998) to experiential work such as *The Black Maze* (2000) and the *Step Series* (2008 onwards), the visual minimalism as exemplified by *Simple Maths* (1997), the occasional sensorial onslaught epitomized by *Lurid and Insane* (2001) through to the physical and attentional demands of durational shows like *Tuning Out with Radio Z* (2010) or textually complex work, notably *The Anatomy of Melancholy* (2013). All of these instances are ubiquitously underpinned by an invitation to engage in an intellectual or contemplative discourse with the practice. The chapter begins with a consideration of how performance/audience dynamics are being reconceived in the late twentieth and early twenty-first century, particularly the collaborative role of the audience in creating connections between ideas and the potential of their direct engagement with, and at times within, the performance. This then frames the investigation of Stan's Cafe and how their own practice is reinterpreting the performance/audience relationship. In particular, we look at the company's eclectic range of spectatorial modes, their attentiveness to co-authorship, the manipulation of space-time, notably the potential of contemplative space and, finally, the role of the audience as performer.

Setting the scene

Theatre is not the providing of lunch.

Howard Barker, *Honouring the Audience* (1988: 46)

'The desire to reconfigure the relationship between theatre and its audiences was a recurring theme in experimental theatre practice during the twentieth century and continues to preoccupy many practitioners' (Freshwater 2009: 2). Helen Freshwater's observation in *Theatre and Audience* alerts us to the significant shifts created by the destabilizing of traditional spectatorial modes within theatre, fuelled through experimentation with new forms of presentation and representation as well as the adoption of unconventional spaces that challenged the passive model of performance and reception epitomized by proscenium arch productions. Contemporary audiences now experience performance in multitudinous frames, making it ever more labyrinthine to discover what constitutes an audience, what its function may be and what forms it takes, as Freshwater then highlights: 'Do spectators simply watch? Or are they gazing, or gawking? Are they impartial observers, innocent bystanders, or voyeurs? The terms employed to describe audiences and their relationship to performance are laden with value judgements. Are they just viewers, or accomplices, witnesses, participants? Are they a crowd, a mass, a mob, or critics and connoisseurs?' (2009: 2–3). Back in 1974, Erving Goffman, in *Frame Analysis: An Essay on the Organization of Experience*, delineated a range of theatrical frames navigated by actors and also audiences, distinguishing between the coexistent modes of 'theatre-goer' and 'onlooker' (1986: 130); the former is engaged with the real-time events of the theatrical experience while the 'onlooker' engages in the fictional time-space of the performance. Both these modes of spectatorship arguably coexist when watching a Stan's Cafe production and certainly mirror the performers disposition of *here* and *there*, as outlined in **Performing**. Goffman also goes on to highlight the specific spectatorial demands of different dramatic media, including how film and radio differ from stage drama. He notes how the stage frame enables an audience to comprehend when one actor is demanding our full attention while simultaneously accepting that others 'will act as though they themselves are disattending one another' (144). In other words, we self-edit the image on stage and select our points of attention, guided by the actors and scenography, whereas on film 'the spatial boundaries are much more flexible' (ibid.) so that a director or editor can manipulate where our attention should be placed. With radio, meanwhile, a listener 'cannot carve out his own area of attention' (145); all auditory material has equal significance, so sounds have to be faded in and out to signal the start and end of their importance. For theatre companies experimenting with a range of dramatic and postdramatic forms and across many media and multiple locations, the variety of spectatorial perspectives described by Freshwater and Goffman creates unique challenges for how to frame the audience experience, and likewise for the audiences themselves to respond to the new performance experiences.

Accepting, indeed embracing, the unpredictability and significance of the audience as co-authors of artworks has been of central significance to many writers in recent decades, with the dominance of the authorial voice brought directly into question. In 1967, the French philosopher Roland Barthes boldly referred to the *Death of the Author* in an essay of the same name, arguing that the interpretation of a text should be disconnected from any influence (cultural background, political persuasion and so on) of the original 'Author-God' and any attempt to deduce the authorial intention must therefore be abandoned. Referring to the greater importance of the reader's interpretation, he wrote that 'a text's unity lies not in its origin but in its destination' (1967: 148). Barthes' perspective finds resonance with the playwright Howard Barker (**TW 1**), who twenty years later wrote his own essay entitled *Honouring the Audience* in which he bemoaned what he saw then as the fatuous state of theatre-making and so implored writers and practitioners to constantly challenge audiences and resist easily interpreted narratives. He wrote:

> It is always the case that the audience is willing to know more, and to endure more, than the dramatist or producer trusts it with. The audience has been treated as a child even by the best theatres. It has

been led to the meaning, as if truth were a lunch. The theatre is not
a disseminator of truth but a provider of versions. Its statements are
provisional. In a time when nothing is clear, the inflicting of clarity is a
stale arrogance. (1988: 45)

The growing vigilance to a multiperspectival reception of theatre has been
reflected in the increasing influence of *relational aesthetics* as an analyti-
cal lens to understand performance/audience dynamics. 'Art is a state of
encounter', wrote Nicolas Bourriaud in his influential work *Relational
Aesthetics* (2002: 17), and this statement, resonant of Barthes, indicates
a new emphasis on the creation of interpretative relationships and the
agency of the audience rather than the pre-eminence of a single authorial
voice. Radosavljević notes that Bourriaud's writing was a response to 'an
apparent increase towards the end of the 20th century of artistic works
that placed an emphasis on "relating" to the viewer rather than on representation itself' (2013: 159). She goes on to write that 'the most interesting feature of this new relational genre – which has appeared in various
forms in galleries, theatres and artistically non-designated sites – is that
it has, at least temporarily, entered the mainstream' (161). The increasing
influence of contemporary postdramatic theatre suggests that the term
'mainstream' in this instance can justifiably refer to such new practices as
much as to more traditional forms of representational theatre.

As the exploration of audience as co-authors has increased, specific
theatrical concepts have also arisen to explicate this phenomenon.
Gareth White creates his own premise of 'horizons of participation'
(building on Susan Bennett's interpretation of Hans-Robert Jauss's
notion of 'horizons of expectation') to describe the manner 'in which
audience members perceive the range of behaviours through which
they are invited to participate in a performance' (2013: 57). White is
specifically writing about immersive forms of theatre but equally the
term *participation* can be applied to a broader range of contemporary
practices which ask the audience to rigorously engage in the event on
intellectual and/or physical levels that are often unconventional. Such
participation requires agile responses from the audience as they may

arrive with a 'horizon of expectation' set by their preconceptions of what theatre spectatorship is but immediately, and perhaps continually throughout the event, have to recalibrate what a specific performance is asking of them and then decide and enact their response. This may be as overt as Punchdrunk inviting you to have autonomy over the narratives you witness in *The Drowned Man* (2013) by having a free rein to roam across all floors of the venue, or more subtly in the case of Stan's Cafe when you may be encouraged, via the programme notes, to 'drift off' from shows such as *The Anatomy of Melancholy* or *Twilightofthefreakingods* (2013) for which you are physically shifting your perspective of three parallel performance spaces or absenting yourself briefly in pursuit of a beer or a gourmet toastie while the four-and-a-quarter-hour performance continues.

Such experimentation with unconventional sites is not a new phenomenon as can be seen, for example, in the practice of the Austrian-born theatre and film director Max Reinhardt who, in the early twentieth century, constantly sought radical new 'stages' to suit the specific demands of his productions, from small cabaret venues to the vast scale of the 'Faust City' built outdoors at the Felsenreitschule (Summer Riding School) in Salzburg to stage his version of Goethe's *Faust* in 1933. However, in the latter part of the last century, there was an exponential rise in the use of non-conventional spaces as postdramatic practices often sought to uncouple themselves from the strictures of dramatic theatre buildings and the cultural conventions that may encumber them. As noted previously in the book, Robert Wilson, early in his career, utilized rugged outdoor sites such as for *Ka Mountain* (1972), staged on a summit in Iran, while other practitioners began to exploit the potential of alternative interiors, including museum spaces. In 1969, the composer and conceptual artist Meredith Monk created *Juice: A Theatre Cantata in Three Installments*, staged on the spiral ramps within the Guggenheim Museum in New York. Nat Trotman, writing in 2014, noted that 'even after forty-five years, *Juice* feels remarkable not just for its ethereal beauty but for how profoundly it reconfigured the audience-performer relationship within a specific architectural setting'.

As more artists have practised across formal boundaries, performance work created by theatre companies is now regularly situated within industrial and natural landscapes, public spaces and in other artistic situs, including galleries and museums. Alison Oddey identifies the potential shift in performance/audience dynamic that the influence of galleries may induce: 'The contemplative space, once found in the gallery space, is being absorbed into notions of performance. The gallery experience is becoming a "performative act." This experience demands concentration from the spectator, a quality of contemplation that becomes silent, reverential and with sensual awareness' (2007: 196). The blurring of the distinction between theatre and non-theatre spaces has been accompanied by a correspondent muddying of the waters between notions of performer and spectator. Allan Kaprow famously stated that the sixth quality of a Happening was that 'Audiences should be eliminated entirely – everyone at a happening participates in it' (1966: 88–98). Practitioners have continued to experiment with the audience as partial or fully immersed performer, from one-to-one events to groups co-opted into collective roles. A notable example of the latter is Zecora Una's production of *Hotel Medea* (2009 onwards), which was performed from midnight until 8.00 am and placed the audience at the centre of the action, 'playing' various roles including guests at Jason and Medea's wedding, members of a media focus group and Medea's children. Andy Lavender, who experienced the production first hand, writes:

> The dramatic action is thereby differently *figured*. It is played out for us, but also populated by our own bodies. The separation between actor (specialist to be watched) and spectator (amateur and observer) remains valid but is nonetheless blurred. We are in the midst of what Boenisch describes as 'a complex interference of representation and presence' (2010: 171).
>
> The production is thereby structured by way of *multiple perspectives*, more overtly than might be the case in a theatrical arrangement

that places the performance in one place and the spectator in another. (2016: 96)

In the past few decades, there have been fundamental reconfigurations of theatrical spectatorship, creating new opportunities for theatre-makers to engage with their audiences and new risks as audience responses become potentially unpredictable and tolerances are tested through duration, location, intimacy, immersion or the provocative nature of the content. Experimental practice in the twenty-first century undoubtedly challenges the audience to co-create the work, often uncompromising in its presentation of unresolved, eclectic or contradictory elements. Yet, as Howard Barker asserts, contending with these challenges is incumbent upon theatre-makers and audiences: 'A new theatre will concede nothing to its audience, and the new audience will demand that nothing is conceded to it. It will demand the fullest expression of complexity, it will command the problem is exposed (but not solved)' (1988: 47).

Stan's Cafe and audience

Let's assume the audience is really clever.

James

While there is an undeniable fidelity between the company and certain audiences around the world who are familiar with a range of their practices, this attachment is always tested by the next production, which often confounds any expectations. The range of performance styles and audience modes makes it problematic for the company to predict or retain audiences beyond a certain number, and James admits that 'it's difficult to get a regular audience'. For audiences new to Stan's Cafe, their first encounter, even their first two or three, may give meagre clues as to the full gamut of spectatorial experiences that the company are capable of creating. Indeed, due to the ideas-led methodology, there is no theoretical limit[1] on their performance/audience dynamics. This brings its own creative challenges for the company, as James explains:

> Its remarkable to what extent people think that what they have seen is all that you do. For example, having watched *It's Your Film*, some people asked what other things we did in that format, 270 seconds long in a booth! It's tricky because often people want more of the same and or another version of what has already been successful.

Repetition or rehashing of previous achievements has no interest for James and so the unpredictability of future productions continues unabated. The root of this becomes clearer when discussing directorial approaches with him and he is predictably reticent to foresee what strategies may be deployed in the future:

> I'm often asked if I think about the audience when directing and the answer is always 'No, not at all and yes, all the time'. I always try and watch a show as an audience member not the director. I walk in, the show starts, what do I know about it now, two seconds in? Or now that the lights have changed? Or this music has started? Or now the first actor has walked on? What am I thinking now when I don't know what's going to happen? But this audience member is always me, I am directing for myself, not in a selfish way but setting myself really exacting standards and not trying to second guess what other people will think or like – who knows, who can anticipate, we sometimes surprise even ourselves, how can we make judgements for other people? Graeme and I started the company in order to make theatre we wanted to see on stage that no-one else was making and it feels important to stay true to that vision.

As has been discovered throughout the book, what may seem initially too eclectic to decipher is actually underpinned by a clear theatrical

---

[1] Of course, it is worth pointing out that there are often practical limits on performance/ audience dynamics due to the restrictions or parameters of a specific theatrical space or timescales imposed by a venue or festival schedule.

rationale, as James goes on to explain how he envisages the relationship between the practice and the audience:

> It's always about them being co-authors, it's just that their level of participation is on a continuum and grows more physically obvious at one end of the continuum but conceptually remains consistent. So you can sit in the dark without moving a muscle in one of the studio shows, but your brain is having to whirr away making the connections and keeping up and working out what's going on, and that's participating and authoring and at the other end there's *The Black Maze*, you go in on your own, there's no performer there and you are performing for yourself, physically working your way through the set. It's all the same.

In James's explanation, it is interesting to note the use of the term *participation* as a spectrum encompassing intellectual reflection as well as somatic experience, encountered through the body. Fragkou emphasizes the importance of this approach for Stan's Cafe: 'Experimentation with ways to engage audiences is a chief concern, and viewing is regarded as a "participatory and creative act"' (2015: 213). As it is the ideas that drive the spectatorial experience, no particular mode of audience reception is relied upon and there is always a wariness of creating relationships between the stage and the spectator which are shortcuts to emotional or sensorial 'highs', as James emphasizes: 'I really want them to laugh or cry, be shocked and amazed but I want them to cry because something makes a deep connection with them, not because we've cranked the sad music up to 11, trying to pursue some sad mechanistic thing. I want to give people the opportunity to make an emotional connection.'

There is a fine balance at play here between an acute attentiveness to the audience but without subservience to a desire to please. The company are willing to make it complex and difficult, building layers of meaning into the work, but they also wish it to be accessible, with a strong emotional core. 'We want to make shows where people can come with their kids' says James. 'The kids may not get 90 percent, but there's enough for them and then there are layers and layers above that.' There is an aspiration, rather than an assertion, that the work is thought-provoking as Stan's Cafe are too prudent to predict momentous political change or catharsis. When asked about the impact of their shows on the audience, Amanda Hadingue reflected that 'We hoped it would be profound, but we didn't really go looking for audience feedback or check what it was. The political is in the unexpected nature of the work, the breaking of form.' This is epitomized in *Of All The People In All The World* (2003), which functions on the boundary between theatre and installation, in order, as Simon Parry notes, to 'enable … spectators to make cosmopolitan ethical judgements and to learn more about the world and their place in it' (2010: 335). Dan Rebellato similarly commented that the show 'feeds the cosmopolitan imagination, giving us new ways of grasping the enormity of the world' (2009: 74). The political ideas in the performance are understated, presented with a simplicity (piles of rice and signs denoting what the piles represent) that invites the audience to participate in a conversation about the statistics. James emphasizes the directness of the approach: 'We might use a sign that simply says "the number of children going blind today who will be dead within a year." It's left as coolly as that.' Graeme Rose underlines James's point when he remarked how 'it throws up lots of questions because it's so pure in its form. It doesn't say where facts are from and there are no citations.' Theatrical devices are as minimal as possible, magnifying the impact of the form and text that are present. Jon Ward reinforces this when commenting that the pared-back aesthetic of *Of All The People In All The World* 'heightened the emotional relationship to the things which are depicted, it seems very humanising. It's the opposite of what you think it is, like many of Stan's shows.' This is also apparent in the design elements; Nina West's compositions, for example, are often a blend of abstract, suspended chords and mechanized, industrial tones, but as she said in relation to *The Cleansing of Constance Brown* (2007), 'all the pain of human life is in the music'. As mentioned earlier in the book, the emotional intensity crafted by Stan's Cafe is generated precisely because of the rigorous distillation of ideas and form, a stripping back of sentimentality as opposed to an excess of emotional triggers.

Co-authorship

Don't colour everything in for me, create the sketch that trails off. Hint at the monster, don't show me the monster.

James

Co-authorship is of central importance to the company and informs the crafting of the work wherein the personas and narratives created are precise yet intentionally ambiguous; Pinteresque in their navigation between recognizable traits and unworldly mannerisms and preoccupations. Trust is placed in the audience to connect ideas and construct connotations as they perceive them. Craig Stephens succinctly describes the relationship between the work and the reception of it: 'The audience is part of making the final piece.' The narratives in *The Cleansing of Constance Brown* are a clear manifestation of this intention as each one is fragmented across the duration of the piece and often with their chronology inverted. The absence of dialogue and transitory appearances of the characters for each storyline invites the audience to reconstruct each set of events, but more significantly, construct their own meaning from the juxtaposition and conflation of historical scenes. Each narrative is 'sketched' and none are fully resolved, so that space is created for the observer to 'assemble' the ideas and provocations as they wish to. The role of the audience to 'think for themselves' is paramount for James:

A writer can flatter themselves and think they know what the audience is going to think at this point but the writer has no idea, audiences make different connections and think in different ways so you must acknowledge that. Resign yourself to it and that you're in dialogue with the audience's experiences. Leave them to do some of the work. Underpinning all this is our ambition to make theatre that we would like to see ourselves. I find nothing more boring or offensive than being told what to think, the authorship job leaving you with nothing to do, just sit there like a sap and get it!

In his approach to co-authorship, there is a striking resonance with Tim Etchells' view on the construction of meaning in theatre:

> I get excited by theatre and performance work that is brave enough to surrender control – trusting its audience to think, trusting that they will go useful places, when they're let off the leash of dramaturgical control, or even trusting that a trip through the ostensibly not so useful places (boredom, drifting, free-association) can be more than useful or constructive in the longer run. (Cited in Brine and Keidan 2007: 28–9)

Such an approach to theatre-making is not without risks in terms of how far you may challenge an audience, and also to what degree you trust that they will make coherent interpretations of the work. James has a salutary tale about *The Cardinals* (2011) in this regard:

> There is a moment, with hi-energy dance music playing over Penderecki's *Threnody for the Victims of Hiroshima*, in which Craig plays a border guard, not permitting a Palestinian through the wall to work. His costume was a camouflage military hat and vest. We'd all been perfectly happy with this until an audience member mentioned to us: 'The bit where the Palestinians is turned away from the gay nightclub.' So we immediately found Craig a camouflage jacket to wear! You can give the audience narrative work to do but ultimately there are some readings that aren't very helpful!

Howard Barker's *Honouring the Audience* (1988), a particular influence for James, is apposite at such a moment, as he writes: 'A theatre which honours its audience will not therefore make an icon of clarity. If a scene might mean two things it should not be reduced to one' (1988: 46).

At times, co-authorship is a more overt process and the development of new digital media has allowed the company to experiment with digital interactions. Stephens highlights its use in reference to *Tuning Out with Radio Z* (2010), which was based around a late-night radio broadcast but with both a live and remote audience. Listeners and viewers could send requests and suggestions into the show via an online bulletin board:

> It was important to be able to utilise the audience input as this was always at the heart of the show. We wanted them in a sense to be co-authors, to help us develop and shape the progress of the performance. Sometimes this was a simple matter of reading out dedications but it was better when we were able to turn audience contributions into performed moments or have them as recurring features or themes during the show.

However, as James highlights, this instant connectivity between performer and audience, albeit through the filter of James, editing material on a screen offstage, brought its own challenges:

> Craig and Amanda were on stage. I'm off stage working as producer and vision-mixer. I would regularly make the online bulletin board visible to the theatre audience on stage in an attempt to encourage the audience to author the show in a more fundamental way. But it was difficult to get the audience to suggest things that would shift the performance in new and interesting directions.

In this instance, the agility of the audience and performers to manipulate and respond to new media was undoubtedly tested and only partially successful. The challenge was magnified by the demands of radio to fill the air with content, whereas in theatre the audience can recognize, as Goffman (1974) noted, where on stage to be attentive to or to register when performers are not to be focused on. 'There was a need to be aware of both the theatre audience and the radio audience' Stephens recalls. 'There was an imperative to keep the radio broadcast going so that there wouldn't be "dead air". The theatre audience were aware of this and so it was fun to sometimes play with that dynamic.' Attempting to balance the demands of a radio *and* live theatre audience with different spectatorial expectations, as well as responding to live digital feedback over several hours, certainly falls into the category of 'risky experiment'.

The term 'conversation' is often used by the collaborators within the company to describe the interaction between performers and audience. Rose underlines this quality when discussing *Of All The People In All The World*: 'Conversation is vital in this show. They become part of it, they impact on the conversation, you can see them taking it with them and coming back for more of it because they are in control of the narrative.' Inherent in this conversation is a sense of attentive care for one another, as Sarah Archdeacon commented: 'It feels like there is some camaraderie, an empathy with the audience.' Subtly developing this empathy over the course of their history as a company, whereby audiences trust the integrity of the company's practice, and more precisely over the course of a show, means that the performers can elicit connections to characters and events which might normally seem beyond a sympathetic or empathic response. Stephens, for example, notes how audiences 'really cared for the cardinals despite their failings'. Again, it is the ethos of the company which frames and encourages a collaborative, participatory response, prompting audiences to make connections and, in that regard, Stan's Cafe can only ask for their commitment to engage. Bourriaud writes that 'each particular artwork is a proposal to live in a shared world' (2002: 22), a reminder that it is an invitation to the audience to co-author, and the artist must therefore seek to be compelling rather than to compel.

Audience, space and time

Stan's Cafe audiences are subject to a multitude of spatial and temporal experiences that frame their interpretation of the performances. These interactions range from a fleeting glimpse of an event as it briefly appears alongside a tram through to sustained periods of shared attention in the @AE Harris factory itself. The intimacy of small spaces is exploited but, likewise, the grandeur of epic space is utilized, particularly when a show like *Of All The People In All The World* goes out to a location such as a cathedral, gymnasium or, in the case of Perth, the imposing General Post Office. There are many shows, of course, which are designed

Figure 9.1 Alexis Tuttle and Emily Holyoake's touching relationship in *Made Up* (2016) drew on input from women's groups in the north-east of England.

for, and function within, the 'standard' studio theatre space and time frame and this very 'conformity' is often exactly what is required for the intended audiences. For example, *Made Up* (2016) was inspired by the relationship between women and their make-up and how this reflected or shaped their identities. Leading up to rehearsal, research was undertaken in the north-east of England with a range of women's groups, including senior citizens, and the subsequent tour focused on that area of the country. The final show was designed for arts centres and with a narrative form that might be accessible for, and appeal to, the types of audiences that might not usually watch theatre, including many of the contributors to the research.

Location and duration have opened up new and unexpected audiences for the company outside of mainstream theatre. The staging of certain shows within the public domain has created what may be described as ephemeral audiences, experiencing transitory moments of theatre as part of their everyday lives. *Space Station* (2002), established as a fictional tram stop (see **Space and Time**), was only witnessed by those passing on the trams, waiting down the line at the next station or the occasional local on adjacent paths. It was both an intensely visible event to those who caught a glimpse but potentially invisible to fellow travellers if they happened to be looking in the opposite direction or simply daydreaming at the required moment. The unpredictability of such an experience presents a limitless set of frames through which it is seen and interpreted depending on the time of day, the weather, speed of the tram, atmosphere within the carriage and so on and so on. The incalculable reception of this event is exemplified by the range of approaches taken by the tram drivers when they passed the space station platform, as James notes: 'Some drivers accelerated past, some slowed down and announced it – "On your left ... " etc. It was best when they ignored the station entirely and audience were left thinking: Did I just see that?' With such work, the company are undoubtedly trusting the audience to make instinctive, personal choices whether to engage or disconnect, even to witness or not. This has also been the case with *Of All The People In All The World*[2], which James has always sought to have programmed into public spaces that people may be passing near to, or directly through, as part of their daily lives rather than consciously visiting for an artistic event. In this instance, the audience may only have time to engage with a small part of the performance, one statistic or juxtaposition of two statistics, before they depart. These fragmentary spectacles test our 'horizon of expectation' as theatre appears to us in unexpected spaces and times, outside the matrices (to borrow Kirby's term) of conventional theatre reception. Such practice risks the inattentiveness of the audience but, when successful, it is the very mundanity of everyday life that it finds impetus from, the 'boredom, drifting, free-association' that those in transit, or in brief suspension from their normal routines, experience.

Specific sites have been chosen to evoke different atmospheres. *Lurid and Insane* was framed as an intense gig, outside of the normal strictures of theatrical convention, in which the performers loomed above the

---

[2] *Of All The People In All The World* was first performed in the foyer of Warwick Arts Centre, UK, which is on the campus of the University of Warwick, so many of the original statistics were designed to be of interest to an academic audience.

audience; hence it was staged in various clubs as well as in a barn, with audience members being transported to the venue from a meeting point. The location framed the participation required of the audience, although James is quick to indicate that his notion of participation is a more measured activity than other theatre companies may demand: 'I don't like requests to put my hands in the air but I'm happy to stand there.' @AE Harris has been a major venue for the company, as well as its base for devising. The space itself, as described in **The Route to @AE Harris** and **Stan in Context,** is an unapologetically industrial environment to which the company has made minimal changes during their time there. This atmosphere brings with it a certain cache, as James indicates: 'People like seeing things at @AE Harris as they feel it's a bit niche, avant-garde. It doesn't have the restrictive cultural values that a theatre may have.' The length of the factory floors has been exploited in a number of shows for spectatorial impact, including *The Voyage* (2012), which transported the audience physically across the floor (see **Space and Time**), and *The Cleansing of Constance Brown,* for which the long corridor set and the elongated auditoria could be constructed in one space. *Twilightofthefreakingods* (2013) made use of the three main floor areas adjacent to each other which housed distinct spatial and temporal zones that the audience could watch as discreet stages or step back and see the interconnections between. Such epic use of space arguably reflects the influence of Pina Bausch's large-scale dance-theatre work and Robert Wilson's expansive staging, but the scale is guided by the idea rather than any need to evoke respected practitioners. When working beyond the bounds of both conventional theatre and @AE Harris, the impact of the site can be unexpected, as James highlights:

There's an interesting relationship between found space and the show. Sometimes they work very beautifully together but sometimes the venue overpowers the show. The show may not live up to the space or sometimes with *Of All The People In All The World* we perform in spectacular spaces such as Salisbury Cathedral and people are so busy looking at the amazing ceiling that they accidently kick through our piles of rice!

In contrast to such epic spaces, the potency of intimate, claustrophobic encounters has been experimented with in certain productions, notably *It's Your Film* (1998) and *The Black Maze* (2000), as outlined in **Space and Time**. Stan's Cafe's approach to such work is predictably pragmatic as performing one-to-one is not significant in its own right for James:

> We're not very interested in individual experiences. It's very easy to make something powerful by having it one on one or two on one. Of course it's going to be more powerful because you've got no-where to hide but it doesn't mean it's better. So those individual experiences have only come about to deliver a particular idea. *It's Your Film* ended up as one person at a time because that allowed the optics and sight lines of the Peppers ghost to work.

This 'distancing' of intimacy, specifically as a short-cut to a sensorial 'fix', is actually shared as a view by advocates for one-to-one performance. Helen Paris writes that 'Ultimately it is by maintaining a level of separation that a more tangible closeness can form. … Too close for comfort is when the gap between performer and audience is closed to such an extent that there is no longer any space left for possibility, for communication, for silence, for the unknown' (2006: 191). So while one-to-one practice may not be a central strategy for the company, their work has, in the slim partition of *It's Your Film* or the dark isolation of *The Black Maze*, sparingly exploited its spatial potential to ask questions of the audience and to invite co-authorship rather than impose sensory and emotional reactions.

The contemplative space evoked by Oddey resonates throughout the practice of Stan's Cafe, not only in the non-conventionally sited work, notably *Of All The People In All The World*, but across all their productions, as there is always an attentiveness to leaving temporal 'space' for reflection. Citing Walter Benjamin, Oddey refers to the simultaneity of being 'absent minded and absorbed' (2007: 197), and this is a duality which James and the company are happy to embrace. 'Its okay to zone in and zone out, because it means you're doing some work on the show' says James. Referring specifically to *The Anatomy of Melancholy*, he adds that

> it takes time to think about stuff so if there's something in this show that raises questions you're bound to zone out. In some ways it would be worrying if you only ever watched the show in the present, that would be a sign you've not really thought about the stuff because to do that you'd have to tune out of the present, mull it over then catch up with the show when you'd finished.

It is for this reason that some programme notes reassure the audience that their attention may wander. James clarifies the thinking behind this approach:

> I don't believe in programme notes generally as show should speak for themselves, but just subtly, at times, they're useful to help people think in the right direction. In the early days people would often say about our shows: 'I enjoyed it but didn't understand it.' So we'd ask – 'What are you thinking about when you were watching it?' and they would always describe exactly what we had been discussing in the rehearsal room, they'd have understood the show perfectly but not recognized their own success. It seems useful for the programme to help people with their viewing strategy. In the programme for *The Anatomy of Melancholy* it reads: 'This show is long and full of content. Don't worry if you find yourself drifting off and thinking of something else.'

This state of contemplation is certainly induced by textually rich productions but also within more minimalist work built upon physical narratives and repetition such as *Simple Maths*, in which five performers, in an unspecified domain, slowly sought to construct fragile relationships through patterns of movement, gesture and precise facial expression. The audience watched as tentative friendships, romances and animosities rose and fell but none were resolved and the space was only ever populated by the five performers and six chairs. Rose, akin to James, draws upon a cricketing metaphor to contextualize such spectatorial experiences. 'Some of our work might be called "test match theatre", it's okay to drift off, process it in a different way, but what's important, to use Tim Etchell's words, is the "space you drift off to".

Space and time are endlessly malleable commodities of theatre, but in the hands of Stan's Cafe they are never applied with reckless abandon to sensationalize their work and elicit easily prompted reactions from the audience. They are accepted as sometimes unpredictable factors that may overpower or even misdirect the audience. They are never used to impose a narrative or credo; they are 'tools' to invite participation.

Audience as performer

As James alluded to earlier in the chapter, co-authorship spans the 'whirring' of a brain all the way through to participatory practices in which the audience are physically placed within the performance environment. The Stan's Cafe logic (see **Ideas**) is brought to bear when selecting the appropriate spectatorial mode, and physical participation, in the form of audience as performer, has, like all other elements, to be justified within a theatrical context. James outlines how the 'actor' within such productions is identified:

> Because we're a theatre company, having made a piece like *The Black Maze*, there's a question if that is a theatre piece and if it is then who is the actor? It could be the person on the door but that doesn't seem quite right, so either it's the set itself or the audience member and seeing as they are the human being in there it's more likely the audience is also the actor. In *It's Your Film* they were revealed as a protagonist, in *The Black Maze* they are a solo performer.

The Black Maze begins to frame the audience member as the performer, even before they set foot within the maze itself. As they stand in the queue and witness others disappear into the darkness, they begin to build their anticipation, as if waiting to get onto the fairground ride.

Their construction of 'role' (the attitude they hope they will adopt in the maze) is additionally framed by the gatekeepers on the door (see **Performing**), as Rose identifies: 'It demonstrates to an audience how they should behave in the space, we as guardians offer a mental frame to how the work gets viewed.' As noted earlier in the chapter, the experience within the maze is not a sensory 'overload' but a play on intense darkness, with a restrained series of aural, visual and tactile provocations, in which you are invited to construct your performance from your own memories, senses and anxieties. The adoption of well-trodden immersive theatre practices is not, however, of specific interest to James, and when such a description may initially seem apt in regard to a performance, he is quick to highlight the distinctiveness of the Stan's Cafe experience:

> *The Steps Series* is the opposite of immersive, it's very exposing, as it's in a street or a foyer, almost exclusively in a public place. Even actors worry about performing anywhere but on a theatre stage. This is also audience as performer but this time they're given a script, so we're more prescriptive than in *The Black Maze*. The steps can mostly be read without performing them, as you might read a play-script but by placing yourself in the steps you inhabit the piece in a much more dramatic and more readily readable way. For example, it may only be when you place your hands and feet on the symbols that you realise that you're supposed to be a dead body.

The Steps Series

Inspired by teach-yourself-to-dance floor mats, *The Steps Series* is an installation that, using adhesive vinyl or temporary paint, writes diagrammatic instructions for a theatrical performance across an interior or exterior landscape. While the piece's grammar of brightly coloured footprints, handprints, speech bubbles and object prints remains constant, the narrative is new for each fresh 'edition' of the series and is inspired by its context. The first edition, *Dance Steps* (2008), commissioned by MAC Birmingham, was an episodic piece tracing visitors' lives through the Arts Centre; by contrast, *Revolutionary Steps* (2010), commissioned by the National Theatre for its foyer spaces, was a vinyl version of Brüchner's *Danton's Death. Golden Steps* (2012) was a documentary version on the street of Camden, North London, celebrating great Olympic performances, and *Exodus Steps* (2013) combined indoor and outdoor vinyl across the Skirball Cultural Centre in Los Angeles.

Figure 9.2 Audiences step into the acting roles of *The Steps Series*; here they perform *Spy Steps* (2009) at Warwick Arts Centre.

It's Your Film enacts a subtle recalibration of the audience member as protagonist. Initially, the solo spectator believes themselves to be a select and secluded voyeur on events beyond the screen, but as the piece progresses the performers 're-draw' the boundary between stage space and auditoria so that the audience member becomes a key element in the narrative; the voyeur is now exposed and observed. These subtle liminal divides between performer and audience have been at the heart of James's and the company's practice, all the way from the improvisatory tasks elicited from the audience as far back as *Alice Through the System* (1988), the manipulation of the crowd in *Lurid and Insane* (2001 and 2003) to the spectators contemplative journeys through the sites of *Of All The People In All The World*, their witnessing and discourse with performers and fellow audience members becoming the performance backdrop for all those around them. Crucially, for Stan's Cafe, the performance mode of the audience is always restrained, in the authorial control of the spectator rather than an inundation of instructional and sensorial prompts (music, ritual, discreet location and so on) that urge participation.

Conclusion

At the beginning of this chapter, Helen Freshwater was cited in her speculation over what the functions may be of a contemporary audience – are they merely watchers, gawkers, impartial observers, innocents or voyeurs? Are they accomplices, participants, a mass or a mob, critics or connoisseurs? In the case of Stan's Cafe, they may be all of the above, sometimes several within one show, but the thread that winds between them is the invitation to engage with the ideas. Although different spectatorial modes are utilized, their purpose is always to encourage a personal interrogation of the ideas, to *affect* a thoughtful response and not a specific *effect* preordained by the company. In this ambition, the mediating processes of Stan's Cafe's theatre are used to enable co-authorship of the work, not educe an appreciative but disconnected relationship between performance and audience or extort a singular narrative. The principle of *what is necessary* rather than inexplicably seductive or spectacular informs the choice of how to frame the audience. Agility is required on the spectators' part to adjust to the new relationship that the next show invites them into, and some degree of trust (even if it's the first time they've seen the company) to allow themselves to 'participate' in the wider sense of that word. This trust and an acceptance of the shared risk and effort is perfectly distilled in a story that James's wife relays of a moment just before the beginning of *Twilightofthefreakingods*, in which one member of the audience turned to their neighbour and said: 'I wonder what this is going to be?', to which their neighbour replied: 'I have absolutely no idea but its Stan's Cafe so it's going to be good.' In such safe hands, the experiments may continue for a while yet.

Stan in action: Audience

It's tough to get your audience to turn up to rehearsals, but this doesn't mean you can't work on the part they play. Here are some things you could try to get the audience working for you.

1. If you had to collectively cast the audience in your performance, who (or what) would they be: God, a jury, a conscience, aliens, ancestors, idiots, followers, critics, invisible witnesses, confidants? Ask yourselves this question; occasionally just talking about it may help.
2. Make a show to be watched from an upstairs window.
3. While rehearsing your show, ask yourselves the question 'If I were in the audience, would I think this was good?' If the answer is 'no', then for heaven's sake make it better!
4. Read Howard Barker's 'Honouring the audience' in his book *Arguments for a Theatre* (1988), then have an argument.
5. Try this, it's the game that forms the basis of our show *Simple Maths*:

- You need five performers, six chairs side-by-side in a line and an audience.
- One audience member (the director) lists the performers by name in a sequence left to right.
- Randomly, the actors are called out to be informed in confidence who they are aiming to have seated on their left- and right-hand side (two will be told 'no one' is on one side, as they are on the ends).
- Performers enter the performance space in a random order and choose to sit on a chair at random.
- The arrival sequence is then replicated for each round of moves.
- On each move, the performer must choose to either move to the vacant chair or decline their move, which they do by standing up and sitting down again.
- The objective of the game is to achieve a seating arrangement which everyone is happy with.
- The performers must not talk to each other.
- When a performer has the correct person seated on their correct side, they should hold hands.
- The game is over when everyone is holding hands.

Tips:

- Performers may think of a fictional, everyday setting for this action, for example, a bus station.
- Experiment with the levels of acting; our preference is for minimal acting.
- You may accompany the action with music.
- The holding of hands is a good starting rule; for simple maths, we substituted this with raising your hand when you are happy with people on both sides.
- After each game, ask the audience what their favourite moments were; you will find that they have read narrative into the game that you know wasn't written into it – it's all just simple maths.

6. Benshi fun.

   Watch a movie with the sound off. Write a script for a Benshi to narrate the film to an audience you assume knows nothing about films or how movies work. Switch your attention from explaining plot to the character's thoughts and emotions, symbolism, small details of the film, stories of the making of the film, etc. You can also throw in some personal opinions.

   We did this with two old Japanese silent films before making our own film for *A Translation of Shadows*. For Flatpack in Birmingham, we also had a go with a scene from *Back to the Future*; it was fun and helped us think about how audiences read what they see.

10

Finale

After attending our restaging of *The Carrier Frequency*, our collaboration with Impact Theatre Cooperative in 1999, the author Russell Hoban wrote us a touching message which ran something like this: 'People who make theatre are often dismissed as "luvvies", but you make work with love and that is a special thing.' This observation unlocked something for me. Theatre is about the love of doing it at whatever level it is done. It shouldn't be more fun to do than watch, but it should be done with love and if you do it right with love, all that care and attention poured into the making of that show and that show being at that place at that time, performed for those people, should make those people feel very special.

We resist theatre being our 'commodity'. Theatre has become our business because that's how we make better theatre, as professionals. We are not a theatre corporation, we are a gathering of people who make theatre, a host, a company. We're not anarchic or hippy enough to attempt to make theatre 'outside the system', and to suggest we are 'subverting from within' sounds absurd, but it is our aspiration to conjure a fleeting alternative possibility for theatre, for art, for values, for ethics, for thinking, for how we see or imagine this world. Our primary tool is theatre because its inherent requirements of collective, collaborative working and communal sharing are how we wish to live our lives.

What of the future? Theatre is a shape-shifting monster. When other creatures threaten to devour it, colonize its territory and suffocate it, theatre can twist and slide, absorb and assimilate, travel and regenerate. Theatre is a cockroach, so basic and so durable, so well designed it survives through the epochs and when the bad thing comes, whatever it will be, theatre will still endure. When the sun sends its electromagnetic pulse to wipe all our digital memories clean, theatre will be with us in the cellars, with the singing and dancing and storytelling. I hope not to be alive when that time comes, but if I am then what the hell, fantastic, what an amazing time in which to be making theatre! Let's get on with it.

11

Things in the Wings

Things in the wings: Introduction

1. **People Show**: The longest running British experimental theatre company, established fifty years ago in London. They have been cited as having a major influence on many more recent UK and international experimental artists. On their own website, they write: 'Formed in 1966, People Show has been creating devised performances in theatres, in telephone boxes, on streets, even on water, for five decades, and its radically disruptive influence has made a major contribution to the current theatre landscape.' Many Stan's Cafe collaborators have also worked for People Show, including Amanda Hadingue, Bernadette Russell and Jack Trow.

2. **Panto:** short for **pantomime**. This is a very British form of theatrical family entertainment, often staged around Christmas and New Year. The genre, which has its roots in commedia dell'arte, uses well-known stories, notably Cinderella or Aladdin, and combines slapstick humour, dance, songs and stock characters such as a 'Dame' played by a male actor. Often the audience will know the jokes as they appear and there is an acceptance that the level of humour is 'corny'. Here is an example of a 'panto' joke, so that you get a sense of the calibre:

> **Comic**   I'd like to buy a goldfish.
>
> **Pet shop owner**   Would you like an aquarium?
>
> **Comic**   I don't care what its star sign is.

Things in the wings: The route to @AE Harris

1. **Educational practice**: A significant proportion of Stan's Cafe's work
    is focused on innovative educational practice across the UK. Since
    the beginning of the company, James and Graeme Rose led projects
    in schools and universities, and Jack Trow and Rochi Rampal first
    encountered James when he directed the youth theatre they were
    part of at MAC Birmingham back in 1997. Recently, the company
    have started developing long-term relationships with schools and
    always seek to apply the same experimental and collaborative
    ethos to their education work as to their own theatre-making
    practice, as can be seen in the 2014 production *Any Fool Can Start
    A War*, created with Year 6 students from Billesley Primary School
    and premiered at MAC Birmingham. Unlike the usual school
    productions, this show 'tells the story of how Fidel Castro's revolution
    in Cuba resulted in John F. Kennedy and Nikita Khrushchev leading
    the world to the brink of nuclear disaster'. The depth and breadth
    of this practice mean that a conscious decision has been made to
    omit any analysis of the educational branch of their work, so that
    it may be looked at in its full detail in a future volume.
2. **MAC Birmingham** (originally called the Midlands Arts Centre)
    is an arts centre situated in Cannon Hill Park in Edgbaston,
    Birmingham. It was established in 1962 and, following a major
    redevelopment between 2008 and 2010, continues to be a
    significant regional centre for contemporary arts practice, with a
    particular focus on community and educational work. Stan's Cafe
    were based in an office there between 1997 and 2001.

Things in the wings: Stan in context

1. **Pete Brooks:** British director, born in Northern Ireland, who was
    one of the founding members of Impact Theatre Co-operative and
    then Insomniac Productions. In Amanda Hadingue's words,

> Pete Brooks is the missing link in British theatre, and I don't just
> mean biologically. Fiercely intelligent, roots totally in theatre,
> literature and philosophy, a founding member of Impact Theatre
> Co-op and director of Insomniac Productions, he made beautiful,
> funny, sometimes terrifying shows that broke boundaries while
> still defining their terms as theatrical. Unfortunately, where
> money was concerned he was a total mentalist (admittedly usually
> due to trying to stage shows with budgets way below requirement
> – we know for a fact he wasn't spending the money on clothes
> and haircuts), and Insomniac collapsed in the late 1990s. Pete's
> now a senior lecturer in scenography at Central Saint Martins in
> London, but his work thrilled a wide spectrum of audiences and
> it should have been the way in to The National for all of us. (2007)

Several members of Stan's Cafe, including Graeme Rose, Craig
Stephens and Amanda Hadingue, made work with him in the
early 1990s including *L'Ascensore* (1992) and *Clair de Luz* (1993),
which were strongly influenced by a filmic aesthetic. Pete is
now also a director for Imitating the Dog theatre company,
based in Lancaster. In 1999 Stan's Cafe restaged Impact Theatre
Co-operative's most famous show *The Carrier Frequency* (1984).

2. **Forced Entertainment:** One of the most influential UK theatre
   companies over the past three decades, led since its inception by
   their artistic director Tim Etchells. They are based in Sheffield, UK,
   and are renowned for their experimental postdramatic practice
   combining live performance, installation and durational work.
   Some of their notable performances include *200% and Bloody
   Thirsty* (1987), *Club of No Regrets* (1993), *Dirty Work* (1998), *The
   World in Pictures* (2006) and *The Last Adventures* (2013). In 2016,
   the company won the prestigious International Ibsen Award for
   their contribution to theatre.

3. **Birmingham Arts Lab:** An experimental theatre co-operative
   active in the city between 1968 and 1982. Thirza Wakefield, in
   her article for the British Film Institute, entitled *Beau Brum:
   remembering the Birmingham Arts Lab*, writes that

The genesis of the Lab can be traced to a meeting between five men (Tony Jones, Mark Williams, Dave Cassidy, Fred Smith and Bob Sheldon) who had all worked at the Midlands Arts Centre in Birmingham and grown fed up with its too-sensible agenda. They decided to create their own exhibition space that would permit them to display and explore experimental cinema, music, theatre and dance.

The group established avant-garde, interdisciplinary events and set up The Triangle Cinema, based at Aston University. Wakefield cites one of the key members, Terry Grimley, who recalled how the Lab was 'a kind of Noah's Ark which swept up a lot of talented, creative and/or odd people to help them survive a really drab low-point in Birmingham's history – sandwiched between the demolition derby of the 1960s and the 1980s renaissance' (2015).

4. **The Custard Factory:** The name of this complex of buildings, in the Digbeth area of the city, derives from its original purpose as the Bird's Custard factory. It was re-developed in the early 1990s, at which point the nascent Custard Factory Theatre Company (graduates from Birmingham University) set themselves up in the complex. The Custard Factory is now well established as a hub for the creative industries and independent retailers.

5. **Graeme's Rose's initial departure from Stan's Cafe:** Rose attributes this initial break from the company to his own need for a more physical and instinctive development of material which felt at odds with the 'intellectual enquiry that seemed to be the focus of James's attention around the time of *Bingo In The House of Babel*' (1994). Hadingue reflects on this moment in the company's history:

> Of course, Stan was started by James and Graeme, and *Memoirs of an Amnesiac* couldn't have been made by anyone else. I think it was a critical moment when Graeme chose to opt out of making Bingo in order to accept a foreign tour with another company (I probably would have done the same in his position), because Bingo

was the first show to secure proper funding, the first show to fully establish what became (for a while) the Stan rehearsal process, and it possibly cemented a working relationship between me and James. I suspect it was hard for Graeme to re-enter the company when he joined the cast of *Voodoo City* the following year.

Rose stepped back from performing with the company after *Voodoo City* (1995) but has returned to work as a devisor and performer on a regular basis from 1999 onwards with productions including *Lurid and Insane* (2001), *Of All The People In All The World* (2003), *The Cleansing of Constance Brown* (2007), *The Cardinals* (2011), *The Anatomy of Melancholy* (2013), *Twilightofthefreakingods* (2013) and *Finger Trigger Bullet Gun* (2014).

6. **Station House Opera:** A British performance company formed in 1980 by Julian Maynard Smith, who remains the artistic director. It is particularly renowned for its physical and visual style, incorporating cutting-edge digital media. They have worked all over the UK as well as Europe and the rest of the world. Notable performances include *Roadmetal, Sweetbread* (1998, revived 2012), *The Bastille Dances* (1989), which used and collapsed over 8,000 breeze blocks to symbolize the storming of the Bastille, and *Dominoes* (2009 onwards), which again used large-scale breeze-block 'dominoes', lined up and toppled in site-specific locations across the globe.

7. **Pina Bausch:** German-born Pina Bausch (1940–2009) was one of the most influential choreographers of the late twentieth and early twenty-first centuries. In her role as artistic director of the Wuppertal Theatre, she developed the concept of dance-theatre (*Tanztheater*), which amalgamated dance with dramatic performance, including spoken text. In several of her shows, the performers were required to subject themselves to complex physical challenges, including being blindfolded and then stumbling and falling through a stage set littered with chairs in *Café Müller* (1978). The sets often focused on a single, elemental

metaphor such as a stage covered in soil in *Frühlingsopfer* (*The Rite of Spring*) in 1975 and *Nelken* (*Carnations*) in 1982, in which the performers moved amid a vast field of fake carnations. The emphasis on arduous physical tasks and elemental metaphors can be seen in a variety of Stan's Cafe shows (see **Ideas** and **Performing**).

8. **Robert Wilson:** Wilson (born 1941) is an American theatre director and visual artist, often described as one of the most influential avant-garde practitioners in theatre. He has created works across a multitude of art forms including sculpture, theatre and video art, among many others. He has worked with many important artists including Lou Reed, Laurie Anderson and Maria Abramovic. However, he is perhaps best known for his collaborations with the composer Philip Glass, with whom he created *Einstein on the Beach* (1975) – an opera in four acts that was inspired by sketches and spaces envisaged by Wilson. Glass composed the music using these ideas instead of a storyline.

9. **Theatres of Kindness:** It is worth noting that, although a certain proportion of postdramatic practice presents itself in rather austere and ironic forms, there are many practitioners who embrace and articulate what may be described as an aesthetic of kindness. Practitioners including Hugh Hughes and Hoipolloi as well as Lone Twin foreground their intention to explore acts of kindness and emotional connectivity rather than disconnection. Gregg Whelan, the co-artistic director alongside Gary Winters of Lone Twin, stated in an interview with Lyn Gardner that 'the world is full of acts of kindness, and we experience them all the time'. Gary Winters, in a text written as a companion to a performance piece in 2001 in which he crossed the Chelmer river in his tracksuit, wrote: 'We will walk towards happiness, friendship, community, clean air and money. We will walk towards knowledge, understanding and patience. We will walk towards hard work and blood and sweat and tears. We will walk towards being good people and changing things for the better'

(2011: 141). Bernadette Russell, a regular Stan's Cafe collaborator, gained significant media coverage for her performance project *366 Days of Kindness* (2013) in which she undertook an act of kindness with a stranger every day for a year. This ethos resonates in the practice of Stan's Cafe, an attitude of kindness, tolerance and humanity.

10. **Sergei Parajanov:** Parajanov (1924–90) was a critically acclaimed Armenian film director known for his strong visual aesthetic. His most renowned film is arguably *The Colour of Pomegranates* (1969), inspired by the life of the eighteenth-century troubadour Sayat Nova, which Elif Batuman describes as

> a life story told in brilliantly coloured and animated Persian miniatures. The actors, dressed in outlandishly detailed handmade costumes, move as if by some strange clockwork, performing repetitive stylised gestures, tossing a golden ball in the air or gesturing enigmatically with some symbolic-looking object: a seashell, a candle, a rifle. Paradjanov himself compared *Pomegranates* to a 'Persian jewellery case': 'On the outside, its beauty fills the eyes; you see the fine miniatures. Then you open it, and inside you see still more Persian accessories.' An accurate description: every last article and action in the film seems precisely placed, exquisitely detailed and designed to serve a particular purpose in some unknown ritual. (2010)

This attention to visual detail and stylization can readily be seen in Stan's Cafe's *The Cardinals* (2011).

Things in the wings: Ideas

1. **Drama versus theatre:** It's important to note here that anything we say about definitions of drama versus theatre will always be contentious, but with that health warning out of the way, there is some consensus that theatre is a broader term than drama

and therein encompasses many media, of which drama is but one. Alison Croggon, for *The Guardian*, once wrote that 'I think of theatre as a general noun, and of drama, like comedy, as a subset of theatre' (2008). On a more theoretical level, theatre has been referred to as a 'hypermedium' in terms of its capacity to enfold other media within its bounds. Freda Chapple and Chiel Kattenbelt stated that 'theatre has become a hypermedium and home to all' (2006: 24) within which all media can be sited and remediated to create 'profusions of texts, inter-texts, inter-media and space in between' (ibid.). This capacious, accommodating aspect of theatre is part of the reason why Stan's Cafe have been so eclectic in their scope while always happily sailing under the banner of a theatre company.

2. **Idea constellations: Lone Twin**: This attraction to a multitude of seemingly disparate ideas that slowly coalesce into a constellation can be found throughout the practices of contemporary performance companies. For instance, look how Gregg Whelan and Gary Winters from Lone Twin (a UK-based theatre company) describe their first piece, *On Everest*, which they made in 1997. The resonances with Stan's Cafe are clear as they draw upon history and the frailty of human figures in a threatening landscape, and situate this within a bold physical concept.

> **Gregg**   It was an attempt to merge two places very simply: the studio in which the piece was going to be performed, and Mount Everest. I had become very interested in various bits of writing and thinking about place – how as humans we establish and maintain meaningful relationships with the places we find ourselves in. I was drawn to the idea of Mount Everest because it's such a dynamic place … sacred ground, a religious site for some people; for others it's a kind of leisure playground. … While I was undertaking this period of research, I discovered a little piece of information that the piece then hinged on – that the early symptoms of altitude sickness enact a kind of biological

nostalgia … you start to become very mindful of things that have happened in your past.

Gary There is a line in the studio space that is 1/400th the height of Everest in length, a line of white gaffer tape on the floor. The performance lasts an hour … . Throughout that hour, there is a journey up and down that line.

(Williams and Lavery 2011: 28)

This creative strategy of utilizing mathematical patterns and shapes reoccurs in a variety of their pieces including *Spiral* (2007), in which they attempted to follow a centripetal route through the streets of London towards the Barbican as its centre point.

3. **Tension and Constraints:** These may be seen as fundamental counterweights underpinning the vast majority of Western dramatic practice.[1] Dramatic tension is often described as synonymous with *suspense*, a realization that something is *at stake* for the characters involved, primarily their relationships, their physical or mental health or potential financial losses and gains. To prevent characters merely fulfilling their aspirations and avoiding suspense or consequence, constraints are placed in their path to force them into situations that are not easily dissipated and hence towards more climactic resolutions, which may be tragic, comic or both. An elegant example from a dramatist who understood the balance between tension and constraint is in Anton Chekhov's *Three Sisters*, written in 1901. Masha (the middle sister) is married to the uninspiring schoolteacher Kulygin. Tension is introduced with the arrival of Vershinin, the army colonel, as the couple embark on a clandestine romance. The relationship is tragically flawed, of course, held in check by a variety of constraints: the conservatism of Russian rural society,

---

[1] It is important to note, however, that with the rise of postdramatic practices, which eschew conventional linear narratives and plot construction, the reliance on tension and constraint working in parallel is waning in certain forms of contemporary theatre.

Masha's reluctance to leave her sisters and Vershinin's loyalty to his suicidal wife. Hence the play ends with their poignant separation as the army battalion moves on.

4. **Site as metaphor – Robert Lepage:** Many theatre-makers utilize sites and locations as metaphors for the human condition, exploiting the geological, meteorological or industrial changes they are subject to as commentary upon the vulnerability and ephemerality of our existence. Canadian-born Robert Lepage (1957–) is one of the most influential directors of the late twentieth and early twenty-first centuries. *Dragons Trilogy* (1987–2003) focused on the experiences of the marginalized Chinese and Japanese communities in Canada. Drawing on historical documentation and testimony, Lepage 'grounded' this epic piece in the site of a sandy parking lot, conceived as covering the remains of the old Chinese quarter of Quebec City from which characters from the past first emerge from the parking-lot cabin. 'In *Trilogy*, the space, the sandy parking lot, became a unifying resource, a symbol of digging to discover your past in order to understand your future' (Dundjerović 2007: 82).

5. **Heterotopias:** The French philosopher Michel Foucault (1926–84) proposed the notion of *heterotopic* spaces, which exist within the real world but outside the normal rules of space and time. In *Of Other Spaces, Utopias and Heterotopias* (1967), he proposed that cultures around the world had created these spaces in order for events or practices that were taboo or socially challenging to still occur. He proposed that these heterotopias were real spaces all around us, yet inhabited by those in *crisis* or *deviation* from the everyday norms of society. As an example, he used the *crisis* of the elderly, whom we subtly remove from everyday life (and our reminder of mortality) into discreet accommodation, or prisoners, in *deviation* from society, who create new measures of behaviour, time and space when incarcerated in jails. The *theatrical space* can also be conceived of as a *heterotopic* space. It is an actual environment but also exists in its own space-time, within which

the censured moments of everyday life can be exposed and scrutinized. Stan's Cafe arguably take this one step further by establishing their own fictional heterotopias on stage in which locations, events, actions and speech are several frames removed from our everyday experience in their own extratemporality and extraspatiality (see **Space and Time**). Yet through this distortion and dislocation, we perhaps see our own humanity with greater clarity.

6. **Brian Eno** (born 1948): British composer, musician, record producer and recording artist who has worked across a broad spectrum of styles from ambient electronica to pop music, at one time being the keyboard player with Roxy Music. In recent years, he has produced bands including U2 and Coldplay. *Oblique Strategies* (subtitled *Over One Hundred Worthwhile Dilemmas*) were created by Eno and Peter Schmidt in the mid-1970s to break creative blocks for artists. They consist of a set of cards on which are printed various constraints to work within.

Things in the wings: Rehearsing and directing

1. **Frame:** Patrice Pavis outlines theatrical *frames* in detail in *Dictionary of the Theatre: Terms, Concepts, and Analysis* (1998). He writes:

> The frame or framework of the theatre performance is not only the type of stage or space in which the play is performed. More broadly, it also refers to the set of the spectators' experiences and expectations, the contextualization of the fiction represented. *Frame* is to be taken both literally (as a 'boxing in' of the performance) and abstractly (as a contextualization and foregrounding of the action). (155)

He delineates different types of frame including the distinct conventions denoted by the variety of physical *Stage Frames*, such a proscenium arch, and the *Framing* of the audience through degrees of critical distance. He reflects upon the *Fiction and Function of the Frame* as he notes 'The modern work of art is often characterized by imprecise boundaries … some productions (influenced by Pirandello) sow confusion and tend to erase boundaries between stage and the real world', to the extent that many artists experiment with *Breaking the Frame* by giving 'the impression that there is no division between art and life, contemporary art has often endeavoured to invent forms in which the frame is eliminated' (155–6). Stan's Cafe, along with many contemporary postdramatic practitioners, experiment with all of these elements of framing, selecting different physical locations from traditional theatres to site-specific spaces alongside exploring the frames through which the audience may experience the work from fully immersive practice through to voyeurism or critical objectivity, remote from the physical action – perhaps through the use of telematics or virtual technology. The blurring of boundaries between the theatrical time-space and the audience time-space has been exploited by many companies, notably Forced Entertainment in the UK and the Wooster Group in America. The influence of different media manifests itself in framing as theatre-makers may draw upon transmediative inspirations such as filmic or televisual lenses to manipulate or contextualize the viewers' perspective, as seen in *It's Your Film* (1998). What is seen and what is obscured are also central framing questions for practitioners to consider and exploit, as deployed in *The Cleansing of Constance Brown* (2007) in which the corridor reveals moments of action but also conceals what is behind the doors. In **Audience**, there is further analysis of theatrical frames in relation to Erving Goffman's *frame analysis.*

2. **Task-based improvisation:** In American avant-garde practices of the 1960s, there was a growing emphasis on articulating the activities of everyday behaviour within performance, reflected in the Happenings, created by Allan Kaprow, and the task-based

dance improvisation of artists such as Trisha Brown, working with the Judson Church Dance Theater in New York, and Anna Halprin, who established the San Francisco Dancer's Workshop. The intention was to strip away the artifice of performance by undertaking and concentrating on an activity that had purpose in itself rather than a fictional motivation. Performance in this context grounded itself in the *performativity* of everyday life. Many practitioners since this period have utilized the technique to generate devised material or create the frame for improvised performance, particularly when characterization and fictional narrative are of less significance (see **Performing**).

3. **Performer backgrounds:** While there is a strong 'family' dynamic to Stan's Cafe, the company is enriched by the range of other practitioners and projects that the collaborators have worked with either before their time with the company or interwoven with their Stan's Cafe commitments. Graeme Rose formed 'glory what glory' before establishing Stan's Cafe with James and then went on to set up The Resurrectionists with Richard Chew. He has worked with a variety of companies including Bodies In Flight, Red Shift, Talking Birds, Black Country Touring and Kindle. By the time Amanda came to work with Stan's Cafe she had already been making work with Pete Brooks, People Show and IOU theatre. Her reflections on IOU are indicative of how other practices have informed Stan's Cafe's development:

> IOU was an interesting influence for me, as the company comprised musicians, poets and visual artists and took a broadly non-narrative approach to assembling shows. I have a musical background too and I think this sometimes informed how I approached the performance, editing, placing of text and the structuring of shows. Throughout my time with Stan I continued to work with other artists, all of which was useful fodder for our process.

Craig Stephens has performed with a number of companies including Insomniac Productions, Plane Performance, Talking

Birds and The Playhouse and has also written for BBC Radio
4. Gerard Bell still often finds himself described as an 'actor',
where that is an element in his work, yet works diversely in live
performance, video, film and installation, dance and Live Art as
well as in more traditional theatre practices and venues. He makes
work by himself and in collaboration, most recently, with Karen
Christopher, Ira Brand and Adam Roberts, and has worked with
an extensive number of contemporary practitioners from Chris
Goode and David Gale to companies nearer to the mainstream
such as Punchdrunk and Improbable. Rochi Rampal has devised
and performed with Black Country Touring, Women & Theatre,
Sonia Sabri Company and Oxfordshire Touring Company and
she has written theatre projects for the Birmingham Literature
Festival and Birmingham REP, while Jack Trow has collaborated
with People Show and worked for the Belgrade Theatre, Coventry
and the Custard Factory in Birmingham. These additional
commitments have at times re-aligned the orbits around Stan's
Cafe with some members of the 'family' shifting into more distant
and infrequent trajectories around the company, as in the case
of Amanda Hadingue, who started working with several major
companies including the RSC, the National Theatre, Complicite
and Station House Opera after *Home of the Wriggler* (2006), and
also Sarah Archdeacon, who focused more specifically on her
role as director for Corali Dance Company in London from the
late 1990s onwards. A more comprehensive outline of all the
performers' credits (including many not listed here) can be found
on the Stan's Cafe website/About Us.

4. **Yasujiro Ozu:** The work of Japanese film-maker Yasujiro Ozu
   is cited as a significant influence on *A Translation of Shadows*
   (2015). His films, notably the Noriko trilogy of *Late Spring*
   (1949), *Early Summer* (1951) and *Tokyo Story* (1953), are
   recognized as some of the most outstanding cinematic works of
   the twentieth century, with the British Film Institute Directors
   Poll voting *Tokyo Story* the greatest film of all time in 2015. He

is acknowledged for his unconventional style, with innovative use of the camera including low angles and direct, intimate focus on the actors' faces, which was unusual for the time. The narratives are often very minimal in Ozu's work, with plot and emotional undercurrents inferred through the symbolism of objects or cutaways rather than shown in detail. Thom Andersen (2015) refers to them as 'empty space' shots, 'still lifes, unpeopled interiors, building facades and landscapes' which have been suggested to represent or evoke the mundanity yet significance of 'lived time'.

5. **Realistic/Non-realistic:** Realism on stage is epitomized by believable and recognizable characters responding to the problems of everyday life, and such productions are staged with scenographic elements that seek to evoke the real world. Often the style is identified with the early productions of The Moscow Art Theatre and the staging of Anton Chekhov's plays, as directed by Stanislavski. In the UK, the genre was brought into prominence with 'kitchen sink' dramas such as *Look Back in Anger* (1966) by John Osborne, which took an uncompromising view of domestic British life. Realism can be delineated from *naturalism*, which seeks an even greater replication of the real world through staging work in real time with fastidious attention to historical accuracy in costume and setting. Non-realistic forms began to develop significantly after the First World War, partly as a response to its inhumanity and futility. Movements including Dada, surrealism and absurdism sought more abstract and expressive forms of representing life that were consciously *not* replications of everyday behaviour. Many contemporary companies working today draw upon a hybrid of styles, often utilizing aspects of dramatic realism but, in the case of Stan's Cafe, framing them within non-realistic settings.

6. **Dramaturgy:** Patrice Pavis, in *Dictionary of the Theatre: Terms, Concepts, and Analysis* (1998), outlines dramaturgy as the 'the principles of play construction', and citing J. Scherer's *Dramaturgie Classique en France* (1956) refers to dramaturgy's focus on the

internal structure of the play as envisaged by the playwright as opposed to the external structure which is performance-related. In this sense, dramaturgy attends to the understanding and explication of the play text as a means of informing the directorial, acting and scenographic choices. For Stan's Cafe, as a devising company, the role of a dramaturg is therefore of less significance as the texts created have their origins with James and the devisor/ performers, wherein the dramaturgical process is more organic and collaborative. A notable exception to this is *The Anatomy of Melancholy* (2013), as outlined in the chapter.

Things in the wings: Text

1. **Meyerhold:** Vsevolod Meyerhold (1874–1940) spoke passionately, in the early twentieth century, of the 'theatre of the straight line'. Robert Leach writes of this model:

    > First, the text created by the 'author' is assimilated by the director. His assimilation is then passed on to the actor, who assimilates this. Finally, the actor reveals his assimilation of what the director had given him to the spectator in performance. The playwright's ideas are the parameters within which the director conceives the production; the director's ideas are the parameters within which the actor creates his character, the character is what is presented to the audience. It is, as it were, a straight line from playwright, through director and actor, to spectator. (Leach 2008: 135)

    This model has arguably predominated throughout the last few hundred years of Western theatre, but its status has been challenged by postdramatic and collaborative devising practices that often focus on organic, ensemble processes.

2. **Happenings and Kaprow:** Allan Kaprow (1927–2006) was an American artist and a pioneer of *performance art*, which

abandoned many of the traditional practices of theatre and focused on improvisation, spontaneity, visceral experience and an emphasis on events rather than narrative. Particular attention was placed on the performer's body as a 'stage' for the work. For example, Yoko Ono famously created a performance entitled *Cut Piece* in 1964, which required the audience to approach her and, using scissors, cut pieces of her clothing away. Kaprow developed the concept of 'Happenings' that were semi-structured events based around a series of seven 'qualities'. These included the guidance that 'The line between art and life is fluid, even distinct', 'Happenings should be performed only once' and 'Audiences should be eliminated entirely' (1968: 88–98). His own definition of a Happening reads:

> A Happening is an assemblage of events performed or perceived in more than one time and place. Its material environments may be constructed, taken over directly from what is available, or altered slightly; just as its activities may be invented or commonplace. A Happening, unlike a stage play, may occur at a supermarket, driving along a highway, under a pile of rags, and in a friend's kitchen, either at once or sequentially. If sequentially, time may extend to more than a year. The Happening is performed according to plan but without rehearsal, audience, or repetition. It is art but seems closer to life. (1966)

3. **Richard Schechner:** American-born Schechner (born 1934) has been one of the leading pioneers of contemporary performance since the 1960s. He founded The Performance Group of New York in 1967 which, after his departure, then became the Wooster Group in 1975. Schechner was central to the development of the academic field of *Performance Studies,* broadening the definition of performance to include the everyday behaviours and activities of all cultures around the world, including rituals, social interactions, sports and ceremonies.

4. **Mise en scène:** In French, this literally means 'put in the scene' and is commonly used in theatre and film to refer to the visual construction of the staging or image. This composition can include set, props, actors, costume, lighting and design elements including colour, textures and so on. Mise en scène has the capacity to communicate *meaning* (significance beyond the literal) in its own right. In **Space and Time**, we propose the contemporary term *scenography* as a more comprehensive alternative to encapsulate Stan's Cafe's approach to staging.

5. **Andrei Tarkovsky** (1932–86) was a Russian film-maker, but with an international reputation. Philip French of *The Guardian* referred to him, in 2011, as

    > the supreme poet, philosopher and visionary of Russian cinema who was persecuted, humiliated and finally driven into exile by the vindictive Soviet authorities. His first feature, *Ivan's Childhood* (1962), is one of the great movies about the horrors of the second world war. His second, *Andrei Rublev* (1966), a portrait of the medieval icon painter, may be his masterpiece. *Solaris* (1972), his first colour movie, is a metaphysical sci-fi film that's a match for Kubrick's *2001: A Space Odyssey*.

    He is renowned for rich scenographic design, with sustained single shots rather than rapid editing.

6. **Nenad Prokić:** Former resident playwright for both the Yugoslavian and Slovenian national theatres, Nenad Prokić was director of the Belgrade International Theatre Festival when he met Stan's Cafe in 2002. Less than a year later, the assassination of his friend, Prime Minister Zoran Dindic, prompted Prokić to form the Serbian Liberal Democratic party. He spent seven years in parliament as an MP, representing an area of Belgrade, and had just left politics when Stan's Cafe made contact, inviting him to the premiere of *The Anatomy of Melancholy*. He is now a professor of contemporary theatre at the University of Art in Belgrade and has resumed writing plays.

Things in the wings: Space and time

1. **Aristotle**: The Greek philosopher Aristotle wrote *The Poetics* (circa 335 BC) as a theoretical analysis of poetry. However, it is important to note that the term poetry, in this context of ancient Greece, also encompassed drama. Within the text, he considered a range of dramatic styles including tragedy, comedy and satyr plays as well as poetry itself. For tragedy, for example, he identified key elements including plot, character and catharsis. He also outlined the importance of dramatic unities, tying the action, place and time together. The classical unities or three unities in drama are:

   - The unity of action: a play should have one main action that it follows, with no or few subplots.
   - The unity of place: a play should cover a single physical space and should not attempt to compress geography, nor should the stage represent more than one place.
   - The unity of time: the action in a play should take place over no more than twenty-four hours.

2. **Lars Elleström** (Professor of Comparative Literature at Linnaeus University, Sweden) wrote an influential analysis of media and intermedia in a chapter entitled 'The modalities of media: A model for understanding intermedial relations' in the book *Media Borders, Multimodality and Intermediality* (2010) which he also edited. In the chapter, he outlines a deconstruction of media into their modalities (what they are constituted of), and spatio-temporal is one of these modalities along with material, sensorial and semiotic. From a temporal perspective, Elleström delineates a range of modes within which time manifests itself. He refers to forms which are fixed in time, such as still images or sculptures, as *static* and then he sets out levels of *sequentiality* which vary depending on how temporally rigid or elastic the medium is, running from *fixed sequentiality* (film, for example, has a fixed running time) through *partially fixed sequentiality* (stand-up

comedy, for example, which adapts its timescales to some extent) to the *non-fixed sequentiality* of improvised forms (jazz may take as long it takes!). He also points out that our perception of any medium (drama, music, film, etc.) is affected by our perception of it and the context that surrounds this experience, which may include our expectations of that medium, the society of which we are a part and so on. He calls these elements the *qualifying aspects*. Art forms are *qualified media* because they are a blend of their material elements but also require our interpretation of them through the lens of the *qualifying aspects* which include our cultural expectations and established conventions. This deconstruction of media then facilitates a more robust analysis of how media interrelate and interact in intermedial configurations.

3. **Tadeuz Kantor** (1915–90) was an influential Polish artist who worked across many media including theatre but also art and assemblage. He was influenced by many of the avant-garde movements of the early twentieth century including Dada and surrealism. Throughout the war, he worked in independent theatre in Poland and in 1955 set up Cricot 2, his own experimental theatre group. He explored many new forms including 'embellage', which involved actors being covered in materials so as to disguise their 'humaneness', and later on 'Theatre of Death', which focused on using base materials that are 'deprived of dignity and prestige'. His influence on Polish and European art has been compared to Andy Warhol's influence on American art. Many of his production texts have been published, including *Journey Through Other Spaces: Essays and Manifestos, 1944–90* (ed. and tr. by M. Kobialka) in 1993.

4. **Proxemics** is the study of human space and was coined as a term by the American anthropologist Edward T. Hall. He referred to proxemics as 'the interrelated observations and theories of man's use of space as a specialized elaboration of culture'. He elaborated his ideas in *The Hidden Dimension* (1966) and part of his analysis focused on interpersonal distances and the behaviours exhibited in

each zone. For example, in the personal distance between 1.5 and 4 feet we perceive this as psychologically belonging to us, within which we have some jurisdiction to permit friends and family rather than the social (4–12 feet) or public distance (12 feet +) within which zones we have less control and less emotional attachment. The impact of proxemics theory on theatre can be seen in many texts including *Performing Proximity: Curious Intimacies* by Hill and Paris (2014).

5. **Hans-Thies Lehmann** wrote the landmark text *Postdramatic Theatre* (2006), in which he considers the new forms of theatre practice, from the 1960s onwards, that have moved away from dramatic texts and mimetic acting and towards a broader definition of performance that embraces, among other things, everyday behaviours, absence of narrative or character and the crossing of boundaries between art forms.

6. **Hypermediacy:** Correlating with debates on framing, perspectives on what we are 'shown' in theatre have been reconsidered by many practitioners, particularly in the twentieth and twenty-first centuries. The mechanics of theatre are now often revealed as a means of making the audience aware of the illusory, mediating process within performance and to blur the lines between reality and fiction. This technique can notably be seen in the performances of the Wooster Group (*Route 1 and 9*, 1981) and The Builders Association (*Jetlag*, 1998). A specific British example can be seen in the work of the director Katie Mitchell, who in 2008 created a piece entitled *some trace of her...* at the National Theatre, London, in which the actors functioned as both performers in a fictional setting and technicians, preparing and filming live camera feeds of themselves, so as to heighten the sense of narcissism and the characters' faltering grip on reality. This pliability of theatre as a 'hypermedium' and its implications has been referred to by Chapple and Kattenbelt (2006) (as already noted in **Stan in Context** and **Ideas TW 1**), building upon the work of Bolter and Grusin (1999). Bolter and Grusin's analysis

identifies the 'double logic' or 'two logics' of *remediation* (the refashioning of older media within new media) which they refer to as 'transparent immediacy and hypermediacy' (1999: 70) Kattenbelt summates their 'double logic' perspective as follows: 'The first logic aims at making the user forget the medium, whereas the second logic aims at making the user aware of the medium' (Kattenbelt 2008: 25 citing Bolter and Grusin 1999: 53). Hypermediacy, as defined here, can be observed in much of Stan's Cafe's practice, as exposing the artificial theatrical frame (while remaining committed to the internal logic of the fiction) is a recurring trait in their productions.

Things in the wings: Performing

1. **Representational and presentational acting:** *Representational* acting is a term which refers to performances that, strictly speaking, represent fictional characters in a fictional scenario without acknowledgement of the shared time-space of the performers and audience. The Brechtian notion of a 'fourth wall' is envisaged as a separation between the two time-spaces. *Representational* acting is synonymous with dramatic theatre in which narrative and character, sealed within a fiction, are central. *Presentational* acting, often associated with postdramatic performance, acknowledges the shared time-space to a greater or lesser extent, thereby 'breaking the fourth wall'. This may manifest itself in a variety of ways from direct address to the audience (asides, jokes, etc.) to a self-conscious performance style (Forced Entertainment often utilize a form of naïve stage-fright) and it can also be heightened through how the artificiality of performance is revealed (the conscious 'revealing' of backstage areas, the overt use of scripts, etc.). Representational acting tends to function within a more predictable time-space with known

durations and boundaries between actors and audience whereas presentational acting creates fissures in which boundaries can be disrupted and timescales expanded or contracted. The two acting modes need not be exclusive, however, as can be seen in Shakespearian monologue or aside that acknowledges the artificiality of the stage set amid dramatic dialogue between characters. In many contemporary cases, including Stan's Cafe, practitioners experiment in the hinterlands between the modes, often disrupting the expectations of one with the application of the other.

Things in the wings: Audience

1. **Howard Barker** (born 1946) is a British playwright who has worked outside the mainstream of theatre practice throughout his career, writing work that is provocative in its form and content, often exploring themes of power, violence and sexuality. To describe his own theatre, he coined the term 'theatre of catastrophe', which took as its first principle 'the idea that art is not digestible. Rather, it is an irritant to consciousness'. Barker resisted the notion that an audience should respond collectively to a performance. In 1988, he formed his own theatre company, the Wrestling School, to stage his own work. He wrote *Arguments for a Theatre*, also in 1988, as a provocation to theatre-makers and audiences, within which is the essay entitled 'Honouring the Audience'. It has been a particular influence on many practitioners including James from Stan's Cafe.

Bibliography

Andersen, T. (2015). 'Ozu Yasujirô: The Master of Time'. *Sight and Sound*, 2 December. Available at: http://www.bfi.org.uk/news-opinion/sight-sound-magazine/features/greatest-films-all-time/ozu-yasujir-master-time (Accessed 4 May 2016).

Auslander, P. (2002). '"Just Be Your Self": Logocentrism and Difference in Performance Theory'. In P. Zarilli (ed.), *Acting (Re) Considered: A Theoretical and Practical Guide*. London and Routledge, pp. 53–61.

Barker, H. (1988), *Arguments for a Theatre*. Manchester: Manchester University Press.

Barthes, R. (1967). *Death of the Author*. Available at: http://www.tbook. constantvzw.org/wp-content/death_authorbarthes.pdf (Accessed 9 October 2016).

Barthes, R. (1974), 'Diderot, Brecht, Eisenstein'. *Screen*, 15(2), pp. 33–40.

Batuman, E. (2010). 'Sergie Paradjanov: Film-Maker of Outrageous Imagination'. *Guardian*, 13 March. Available at: https://www.theguardian. com/film/2010/mar/13/sergei-paradjanov-films-gulag (Accessed 10 November 2016).

Beckett, S. (2006). *Waiting for Godot; a Tragicomedy in Two Acts*. 2nd edn. London: Faber & Faber.

Bolter, J. D. and Grusin, R. (1999). *Remediation: Understanding New Media*. Cambridge, MA and London: The MIT Press.

Bourriaud, N., (trans.) Pleasance, S., Woods, F. and Copeland, M. (1998). *Relational Aesthetics*. Dijon: Les Presses du réel.

Bremser, M. and Sanders, L., eds (2005). *Fifty Contemporary Choreographers: Routledge Key Guides*. London: Routledge.

Brine, D. and Keidan, L., eds (2007). *Programme Notes: Case Studies for Locating Experimental Theatre*. London: Live Art Development Agency.

Chapple, F. and Kattenbelt, C. (2006). 'Key Issues in Intermediality'. In F. Chapple and C. Kattenbelt (eds), *Intermediality in Theatre and Performance*. Amsterdam: Rodopi, pp. 11–25.

Croggon, A. (2008). 'What's the Difference between Drama and Theatre?' *Guardian*, 9 January. Available at: https://www.theguardian.com/stage/theatreblog/2008/jan/09/whatsthedifferencebetweend (Accessed 9 October 2016).

Dundjerovic, A. S. (2007). *The Theatricality of Robert Lepage*. Montreal: McGill-Queen's University Press.

Elleström, L. and Bruhn, J. (2010). *Media Borders, Multimodality and Intermediality*. Edited by Lars Ellestrom. Basingstoke: Palgrave Macmillan.

Foucault, M. (1984). 'Of Other Spaces, Utopias and Heterotopias'. *Architecture, Mouvement, Continuité*, No. 5 (October), pp. 46–9.

Fragkou, M. (2015). 'Stan's Cafe'. In L. Tomlin (ed.), *British Theatre Companies 1995-2014*. London: Bloomsbury, pp. 207–30.

Freeman, J. (2007). *New Performance/New Writing*. Basingstoke: Palgrave Macmillan.

French, P. (2011). 'The Andrei Tarkovsky Collection'. *Guardian*, 24 July. Available at: https://www.theguardian.com/film/2011/jul/24/andrei-tarkovsky-collection-dvd-review (Accessed 9 October 2016).

Freshwater, H. (2009). *Theatre and Audience*. Basingstoke: Palgrave MacMillan.

Goffman, E. (1974). *Frame Analysis: An Essay on the Organization of Experience*. 2nd edn. Cambridge, MA: Harvard University Press.

Hadingue, A. (2007). 'Experimental Theatre and the Legacy of the 1990s – Amanda Hadingue'. Available at: http://www.stanscafe.co.uk/helpfulthings/experimantaltheatreessay.html (Accessed 21 April 2016).

Hall, E. T. (1966). *The Hidden Dimension*. New York: Anchor Books.

Halperin-Royer, E. (2002). 'Robert Wilson and the Actor: Performing in Danton's Death'. In P. Zarilli (ed.), *Acting (Re) Considered: A Theoretical and Practical Guide*. London: Routledge, pp. 319–33.

Heddon, D. and Milling, J. (2015). *Devising Performance: A Critical History*. Basingstoke: Palgrave Macmillan.

Hill, L. and Paris, H., eds (2004). *Guerrilla Guide to Performance Art: How to Make a Living as an Artist*. London: A&C Black.

Hill, L. and Paris, H. (2014). *Performing Proximity: Curious Intimacies*. Basingstoke: Palgrave Macmillan.

Howard, P. (2009). *What is Scenography?* New York: Taylor & Francis.

Jackson, S. and Weems, M. (2015). *The Builders Association: Performance and Media in Contemporary Theater*. Cambridge, MA and London: The MIT Press.

Johnson, S. (2010). 'Where Good Ideas Come from'. Available at: http://www.ted.com/talks/steven_johnson_where_good_ideas_come_from?language=en#t-285955 (Accessed 1 October 2015).

Kantor, T. (1993). *A Journey Through other Spaces: Essays and Manifestos, 1944-1990*. Berkeley: University of California Press.

Kaprow, A. (1966). *Some Recent Happenings*. New York: A Great Bear Pamphlet.

Kaprow, A. (1968). *Assemblage, Environments and Happenings*. New York: Harry N. Abrams.

Kattenbelt, C. (2008). 'Intermediality in Theatre and Performance: Definitions, Perceptions and Medial Relationships'. *Culture, Language and Representation, Cultural Studies Journal of Universitat Jaume*, 6(1), pp. 19–29.

Kirby, M. (1972). 'On Acting and not-acting'. *The Drama Review: TDR*, 16(1), p. 3.

Kowalke, K. H. (1994). 'Brecht and Music: Theory and Practice'. In P. Thomson and G. Sacks (eds), *The Cambridge Companion to Brecht*. 2nd edn. New York, NY: Cambridge University Press.

Lavender, A. (2016). *Performance in the Twenty-First century: Theatres of Engagement*. London: Routledge.

Leach, R. (2008). *Vsevolod Meyerhold: Directors in Perspective*. Cambridge: Cambridge University Press.

Ledger, A. J. (2013). 'Stan's Cafe: The Vision of the Ensemble'. In J. Britton (ed.), *Encountering Ensemble*. London: Bloomsbury Academic, pp. 152–66.

Lefebvre, H. (1991). *The Production of Space*. Translated by D. Nicholson-Smith. Oxford, UK: Blackwell Publishers.

Lehmann, H.-T. (2006). *Postdramatic Theatre*. Translated by K. Jürs-Munby. New York: Routledge.

McBurney, S., Giannachi, G. and Luckhurst, M. (1999). *On Directing: Interviews with Directors*. London: Faber and Faber.

Oddey, A. (2007). *Re-framing the Theatrical: Interdisciplinary Landscapes for Performance*. Basingstoke: Palgrave Macmillan.

O'Toole, J. (1992). *The Process of Drama: Negotiating Arts and Meaning.* London: Routledge.

Palmer, S. (2011). 'Space'. In J. Pitches and S. Popat (eds), *Performance Perspectives: A Critical Introduction.* Basingstoke: Palgrave Macmillan, pp. 52–87.

Paris, H. (2006). 'Too Close for Comfort: One to One Performance'. In L. Hill and H. Paris (eds), *Performance and Place.* Basingstoke: Palgrave Macmillan, pp. 179–91.

Parry, S. (2010). 'Imagining Cosmopolitan Space: Spectacle, Rice and Global Citizenship'. *RiDE: The Journal of Applied Theatre and Performance*, 15(3), p. 317.

Pavis, P. (1998). *Dictionary of the Theatre: Terms Concepts and Analysis.* Toronto and London: University of Toronto Press Limited.

Pavis, P. (2012). *Contemporary Mise en Scène: Staging Theatre Today.* Translated by J. Anderson. New York: Routledge.

Pearson, M. (2010). *Site-Specific Performance.* Basingstoke: Palgrave Macmillan.

Ploebst, H. (2007). Review of *The Cleansing of Constance Brown. Der Standard* (Vienna), 31 May.

Radosavljević, D. (2013). *Theatre-Making: Interplay between Text and Performance in the 21st Century.* Basingstoke: Palgrave Macmillan.

Rebellato, D. (2009). *Theatre and Globalization.* Basingstoke: Palgrave MacMillan.

Schechner, R. (2003). *Performance Studies: An Introduction.* London: Routledge.

Shaughnessy, N. (2012). *Applying Performance Live Art, Socially Engaged Theatre and Affective Practice.* Basingstoke: Palgrave Macmillan.

Steinbeck, J. and Fensch, T., eds (1988). *Conversations with John Steinbeck.* Jackson: University Press of Mississippi.

Tarkovsky, A. (1989). *Sculpting in Time: Reflections on the Cinema.* London: Faber & Faber.

Trotman, N. (2014). 'The Idea of Compression: Meredith Monk's Juice (1969)'. Available at: https://www.guggenheim.org/blogs/checklist/the-idea-of-compression-meredith-monks-juice-1969 (Accessed 6 June 2016).

Wakefield, T. (2015). 'Beau Brum: Remembering the Birmingham Arts Lab'. *Sight & Sound*, 7 August. Available at: http://www.bfi.org.uk/news-opinion/sight-sound-magazine/features/beau-brum-remembering-birmingham-s-arts-lab (Accessed 10 August 2016).

White, G. (2013). *Audience Participation in Theatre: Aesthetics of the Invitation*. Basingstoke: Palgrave Macmillan.

Wiles, D. (2003). *A Short History of Western Performance Space*. Cambridge, UK: Cambridge University Press.

Wiles, D. (2014). *Theatre and Time*. Basingstoke: Palgrave Macmillan.

Williams, D. and Lavery, C., eds (2011). *Good Luck Everybody: Lone Twin – Journeys, Performances, Conversations*. London: UK: Centre For Performance.

Williams, R. (1991). *Drama in Performance*. Philadelphia: Open University Press.

Wilson, R. (2007). 'Interview with Jonathan Vickery'. Available at: http://www.haringwoods.com/robert-wilson-interview/4562830013 (Accessed 12 November 2015).

Yarker, J. (2001). *Future Art Symposia*. Birmingham: Stan's Cafe.

Yarker, J. (2004). 'Technology and Perception'. Available at: http://www.stanscafe.co.uk/helpfulthings/essays-technology-and-perception.html (Accessed 22 August 2015).

Yarker, J. (2007). 'MAC: An Arts Centre'. Available at: http://www.stanscafe.co.uk/helpfulthings/essays-mac.html (Accessed 10 September 2015).

About the Authors

Dr Mark Crossley is a senior lecturer in performing arts at De Montfort University, Leicester, UK. He specializes in contemporary intermedial practice, devised performance practices and performing arts pedagogy, with work published in journals in the UK and worldwide including *Research in Drama Education* (RiDE) and *International Journal of Performance Arts and Digital Media* (IJPADM). For many years, he worked as a drama teacher in secondary and further education in the UK and also as a performing arts advisor to national teaching and learning organizations and examination boards. Having followed the work of Stan's Cafe since the early 1990s, he is now very honoured to collaborate with James Yarker on this first major text about the company.

James Yarker is Artistic Director of Stan's Cafe, which he co-founded in 1991. After a few years washing up, mopping floors and waiting at tables, he started to gain short-term lecturing contracts and in 1997 received an MPhil for his dissertation *Presence and Absence: Electronic Mediation in Performance*. He hasn't done anything but work for Stan's Cafe since then, directing all the company's major productions and writing text for them when required. James is regularly asked to speak at universities and run workshops. He lives in Birmingham with his wife and daughter, who made her debut for the company in 2013 aged eight.

Index